House of Cards

House of Cards

WHY ARMS CONTROL MUST FAIL

COLIN S. GRAY

Cornell University Press

ITHACA AND LONDON

First published 1992 by Cornell University Press.

A volume in the series Cornell Studies in Security Affairs edited by Robert J. Art and Robert Jervis.

Library of Congress Cataloging-in-Publication Data
Gray, Colin S.
House of cards : why arms control must fail / Colin S. Gray.
    p.   cm. — (Cornell studies in security affairs)
Includes bibliographical references and index.
ISBN 0-8014-2703-7
1. Arms control.   I. Title.   II. Series.
JX1974.G58   1992   92-52754
327.1′ 74—dc20
                        Printed in the United States of America

To Valerie, with love

It is the greatest possible mistake to mix up
disarmament with peace. When you have
peace you will have disarmament.
—Winston S. Churchill, 1934.

Contents

Preface

The world is no longer bipolar, but the appeal of arms control is not confined to one condition of the distribution of power. The errors in arms control theory, and hence the futility in attempts at arms control practice, transcend any particular strategic context. The issue of the hour will shift from superpower nuclear arsenals to the proliferation of ballistic missiles in the Third World—there is always an emerging new agenda—but the fallacies of arms control persist, albeit in new clothes.

An atheist invited to participate in a conference on church doctrine would have difficulty making a constructive contribution to the discussion, though he would probably enliven the proceedings. A couple of years ago I was invited to provide a skeptical view of START on a panel in a public forum. My difficulty, dilemma even, was analogous to that of the hypothetical atheist. The organizers of the distinguished panel expected me to be skeptical of some of the terms of the START treaty; they did not expect me to be fundamentally disbelieving in the arms control process.

At the church conference, the atheist may make arguments with which either the more liberal or the more conservative theologians could register considerable agreement, but really, his whole argument is incompatible with all shades of theological opinion. This book contains many items with which middle-of-the-road and particularly conservative, defense-oriented opinion on arms control should agree. But my central thesis is that arms control must fail *by its own leading criteria for judging success* because it attempts to achieve, in George Will's words, either the impossible or the unimportant.

Even though some sections of this book may appear at first glance to be a familiar conservative critique of arms control, in this case, appearances are deceptive. My argument is with people who believe that the processes of interstate arms control can accomplish truly useful things. In principle, I am as critical of a conservative who believes that he can negotiate a more security-friendly START regime as I am of a liberal who has yet to find an arms control idea that he or she does not like.

The argument advanced here will be too fundamental for the taste of many people. After all, the real issues of the day are the terms of START, the safety of what was the Soviet nuclear arsenal, the design of a START II, the compliance problems of the treaty on Conventional Forces in Europe (CFE), nuclear and ballistic missile proliferation, and so forth. To argue that the deity of arms control is a fiction is not a message that many audiences deem useful. People listen to this thesis with some mix of shock, incomprehension, and irritation; they proceed to debate their fine theological points, or pressing policy issues, as if the analogical atheist had not attempted to explode an intellectual warhead underneath their proceedings.

Before a critical reviewer rushes to note that this book by and large is focused upon arms *limitation*, or structural arms control, rather than arms *control* writ large (including what is called *operational* arms control), let me concede the point preemptively though without apology. The same logical and practical weaknesses attend both thrusts of arms control. Operational arms control seeks to place constraints on the behavior of armed forces and embraces such possibilities as regulations on deployment and generally the inhibition of military actions which supposedly increase the risks of war. Structural arms control, or arms limitation, by contrast addresses the quantity and quality of arms rather than their behavior. Disillusionment with the achievements of arms limitation has generated a sizable constituency friendly toward operational arms control. It has even become somewhat chic to praise the latter at the expense of the former. The argument in this book is not specific to efforts at arms limitation. The house of cards that is arms control contains rooms that may be identified as devoted to the limitation of forces or to the shaping of operational matters; those rooms are all part of the same unsound edifice.

I do not claim that the argument in this book is by any means wholly original, though if I owe a major and principal intellectual debt to any persons I cannot identify them. I am certainly not the only person currently advancing so thoroughly skeptical a view of arms control per se. For example, Kenneth Adelman and George F. Will have both leveled critical arguments close in content to the ones presented here. Those trenchant writers, however, provided intellectual support for an enterprise long planned and well under way—in no sense did their work trigger the attitudes and opinions expressed in this book. This is not to deny that my debts are many and varied. Specific contributions are recognized appropriately and in the traditional manner in the notes.

I am obliged to the U.S. Institute for Peace for its financial backing for the research that led to Chapter 2, "Weapons and War."

Two of my colleagues at the National Institute for Public Policy, Keith B. Payne and Roger W. Barnett, have both made important contributions over the years to my thinking on arms control, though neither is responsible for the use to which I have put those contributions. Similarly diffuse but important is my long-standing intellectual debt to two late Hudson Institute colleagues, Donald G. Brennan and Herman Kahn. Much more specifically, I am indebted to my friend Williamson Murray of Ohio State University for his critical review of my analysis of the interwar years. One can learn as much from professional (not personal) adversaries as from allies. With that thought in mind I acknowledge the value that I have found over the years in the writings of Albert Carnesale, Robert Jervis, Lawrence Freedman, and Scott D. Sagan. In my judgment these distinguished scholars are often wrong, indeed, are often very wrong, but they tend to be wrong for the right reasons. In other words, I may disagree with their conclusions, but more often than not, I find that they asked the right questions and recognized the most appropriate candidate answers. Special thanks are due Robert Jervis as editor of this series for his invaluable suggestions for the sharpening of my argument, an argument with which he has some strong disagreement.

It may be important for readers to know that, although I have been critical of Western (particularly American) arms control policy for more than twenty years, full realization that the god of arms control was the fanciful creation of both the well-intentioned and the cynically exploitative dawned rather late. The empirical base for the logical argument in this book comprises: (1) careful study of the interwar experience with negotiated arms limitation; (2) more than two decades of experience as an observer of the superpower strategic arms control process, including five years of service (1982–87) on the President's General Advisory Committee on Arms Control and Disarmament; and (3) more than twenty years of professional experience as a contributing student of the theory and practice of statecraft and strategy. Of course, argument-by-résumé says nothing about the validity of the thesis advanced. Experienced people can write foolish books. My point, simply, is to underline the claim that the radical nature of this book's indictment of arms control is the product of many years of gradual enlightenment.

Statesmen who attempt the impossible fail. Secretary of State James Baker appears to believe sincerely that in CFE and START the United States has critically important opportunities to "lock in stabilizing arms control agreements." The reasons why he is wrong are the subjects of this book.

It is an inconvenient fact that as of this time of writing the new name for what used to be the USSR, the Commonwealth of Independent States, is as novel and unfamiliar as its longevity is uncertain and improbable. I will refer to *Soviet* when the subject is prior to December 1991, and as a general rule to *Russian* for topics subsequent to that date.

An abridgment of Chapter 5 appeared as "Destination Unknown: From SALT to START," in *Strategic Review*, 19 (Spring 1991). Chapter 6 is a revised version of "Does Verification Really Matter? Facing Political Facts about Arms Control Non-Compliance," *Strategic Review*, 18 (Spring 1990). I thank *Strategic Review* and its publisher, the United States Strategic Institute, for permission to use this material.

Colin S. Gray

Vienna, Virginia

House of Cards

[1]

The Magic Kingdom
of Arms Control

The permanent paradox of arms control is that it is either impossible or unimportant.

—George F. Will, 1990

Forlorn Hope

Can it be that arms control is a wonderful idea whose time has come? As peace breaks out in the 1990s, so arms control agreements, from mere glints in the eyes of the faithful, assume the status of truly serious business. But if arms control *follows* the demise of the Cold War, indeed, is possible on an unprecedented scale only because peace is breaking out, just how important can it be? Unless one believes that arms control treaties can "lock in" fleeting opportunities for mutually beneficial cooperative behavior which otherwise might evaporate, the suspicion grows that perhaps arms control itself is a peace dividend, the tail of the dog.

My thesis is that arms control fairly may be described as a house of cards. The theory behind it is not merely flawed but wrong. As a consequence, the ideas that compose arms control theory-as-advice for policy are fundamentally unsound.

The picture is not wholly black. Some actual agreements and treaties, as well as possible ones, are not without merit. That merit, however, is not of the kind postulated and promised in the halls of arms control theory. Not surprisingly, plausible rationales can be advanced in favor of particular arms control agreements; truly, it would be amazing were that not the case. The issues,

[1]

rather, are whether arms control can do what its promoters claim and whether the benefits of the exercise outweigh the costs.

To criticize arms control is not exactly a novel enterprise, even if it is unfashionable in the superpower-peaceable 1990s. The transformation of superpower relations, however, has helped promote a marked absence of peace in areas previously disciplined by the security architecture of the Cold War. What is new about the argument here is that arms control theory and the behavior of governments that theory has spurred are challenged as being hopelessly impractical, indeed, wrongly conceived. Moreover, that theory and behavior are judged not to measure up positively even on their own terms. My argument is that the theory and practice of arms control is to security what the flat-earth postulate was to cosmology: sincerely believed, responsive to some empirical evidence (the world can look fairly flat), attractive to common sense, but alas, invalid.

The central argument of the book is both logically and deductively derived. The historical basis for the argument presented here comprises the better part of a century of frequently renewed arms control negotiations. The enduring character of the states' system and the nature of state behavior toward security ensure the persistence of the conditions which guarantee that arms control must fail. The historical evidence lends itself to simple distillation into what might be termed strategic philosophy. Three points express the heart of the argument.

- Above all else, arms control is about helping to prevent the outbreak of war.
- Therefore, arms control nominally is relevant only between states that might fight each other (e.g., in different periods, France and Germany, Austria-Hungary and Serbia, the United States and the Soviet Union; not the United States and Britain or Paraguay and New Zealand).
- The more likely it is that states will fight each other, the less likely are the prospects for the negotiation and maintenance of substantive, strategically significant arms control regimes. By definition, there can be no strategically significant arms control regimes for state pairs or groups that lack political incentives to fight each other (this partially excepts the special case of states colluding to deprive a third party of

capabilities it might desire to obtain, as with respect to nuclear proliferation, for example).

Considered together, these propositions make up *the arms control paradox*. This and related paradoxes are developed in Chapters 1 and 2 in direct relation to arguments about the causes of war.

Lest there be any misunderstanding, the argument here does not constitute a distinctively conservative critique of arms control. Many conservatives will warm to the thesis that arms control is a house of cards, but my reasoning owes little if anything to traditional conservative complaints. Those complaints include such familiar items as the claims that authoritarian countries cheat on treaties—which is true;[1] that Americans negotiate poorly—which also tends to be true;[2] and that the very existence of an arms control regime has a lulling effect on a democracy—which is sometimes true.[3] The problem with arms control postulated here, the claim that the theory and, hence, the practice rest on *false premises*, could not be solved or alleviated even were the standard litany of conservative complaints to be answered to their authors' satisfaction. Arms control would remain a house of cards even were the new Russia to desist from cheating on treaties, were

[1] In a democracy, extra-official verification of national compliance tends to be reliable. It is not postulated here as a law of arms control that authoritarian countries cheat, but since the Italians, Japanese, and Germans cheated fairly systematically in the interwar years and since the Soviet Union established a pattern of arms control violations in the postwar period, the claim is not a particularly controversial one. See Robin Ranger, *The Naval Arms Control Record, 1919–1939: Axis Violations versus Democratic Policy Failures* (Fairfax, Va.: National Security Research, 1987), and "Learning from the Naval Arms Control Experience," *Washington Quarterly*, 10 (Summer 1987), 47–58; Joseph D. Douglass, Jr., *Why the Soviets Violate Arms Control Treaties* (Washington, D.C.: Pergamon-Brassey's, 1988); and Arnold Beichman, *The Long Pretense: Soviet Treaty Diplomacy from Lenin to Gorbachev* (New Brunswick, N.J.: Transaction, 1991).

[2] Senator Malcolm Wallop and Angelo Codevilla, *The Arms Control Delusion* (San Francisco: Institute for Contemporary Studies Press, 1987), argue that arms control treaties have failed to control the Soviet arms that matter, even within the bounds of agreement, let alone those produced by cheating.

[3] For example, see Charles H. Fairbanks, Jr., "The Washington Naval Treaty, 1922–1936," in Robert J. Art and Kenneth N. Waltz, eds., *The Use of Force: International Politics and Foreign Policy*, 2d ed. (Lanham, Md.: University Press of America, 1983), p. 475.

American negotiators to avoid errors in the negotiation and drafting of treaties, and were Western states not to be lulled, or falsely reassured, by arms control into a persisting underperformance in defense preparation. Recall that arms control is ultimately supposed to be about the prevention of war.

The pursuit of peace with security through arms control, or at the least, with a strong arms control component, may be likened to the toil of a medieval alchemist seeking to transmute base metal into gold. It is Mission Impossible. No ingenuity of theory, sincerity of purpose, or energy in pursuit can achieve the objective set by the route selected. Such vigorous criticism of arms control to date, from conservatives and liberals alike, typically has succeeded in missing the right target by a wide margin. Conservatives are wont to find villainy in the purposes and behavior of adversary-partners and are uncomfortable with the idea of limited cooperation with evil empires and the like. Those few liberals unfriendly to arms control find that negotiations have a way of legitimizing military competition. There is something to be said in favor of both of these positions. There has been a clearly traceable pattern of deception and noncompliance on the part of authoritarian parties to arms control regimes (Italy, Germany, and Japan in the interwar years, and the USSR and Iraq more recently). Also, it cannot be denied that demands for additional negotiating leverage have been deployed many times in order to assist weapon programs in domestic political difficulty.[4]

Faulty diagnosis can hardly help but attract useless prescription. Conservatives sought to correct what they saw as *the* arms control problem—Soviet fell intent and villainous misbehavior—either by prescribing a different Soviet political and strategic culture or by insisting upon more muscle and more courage on the part of the U.S. government. The former solution was beyond U.S. control and would render arms control irrelevant, the condi-

---

[4] In the early 1970s the asserted need of the SALT negotiations provided critical, if tenuous, life-support for the Nixon administration's Safeguard ABM system. In the late 1970s the MX ICBM was endorsed by a Carter administration in need of leverage for SALT II over skeptical minds in the U.S. Senate as well as in Moscow. The mid-1980s witnessed blatant assertions of arms control negotiating necessity on behalf, again, of the MX missile.

tion that now holds. The advice to have muscle behind negotiation is prudent but beside the point. That keen military competitive performance which should ensure that one's country does not lose in a negotiation is not likely to generate an arms control outcome that will starve political hostility of fuel. It should arm one comfortably for deterrence and defense, but that is not the issue here.

Liberals unhappy because an arms control process appears to stimulate military competition, with both sides in quest of the negotiating leverage that should flow from tangible weapon programs, frequently prescribe an allegedly judicious self-restraint by the United States. Notwithstanding their different, even contrasting, diagnoses of what can be wrong with an arms control process and how its consequences can be unwelcome, most conservative and liberal critics would seem to agree that arms control *worthy of the name* is both possible and important. For example, root-and-branch criticism of arms control used to lean overwhelmingly upon claims either for Soviet untrustworthiness (the conservative critique) or for the duplicity of what used to be called the military-industrial complex (the liberal critique).

People running for high public office are very much in the business of retailing hope, in this case, the triumph of hope over experience that is the record of arms control. I am not running for office, however, and I believe that although magic kingdoms are wonderful inventions to enchant an idle hour, they should not seriously detain adult minds on important subjects. I will show the aspirations for arms control achievement to be a forlorn hope. History, logic, and common sense all point to the futility of arms control. But so great is the political momentum behind arms control, or at least what passes for arms control activity, that another forlorn hope appears to be that either this book or a dozen like it will free people of the illusion that arms control in some specific or vague manner is beneficial for peace. Nonetheless, as a long-time commentator upon, and participant-observer of,[5] the super-

---

[5] I was a member of President Reagan's General Advisory Committee on Arms Control and Disarmament from 1982 until 1987.

power arms control process, I elect to attempt even a forlorn wager and let the bargaining chips fall where they may.

ARMS CONTROL: WHAT IS IT?

The founding fathers of modern arms control theory were nothing if not ambitious in their vision. In 1961, Thomas C. Schelling and Morton H. Halperin wrote, "We use the term 'arms control' rather than 'disarmament.' Our intention is simply to broaden the term. We mean to include all the forms of military *cooperation between political enemies* in the interest of reducing the likelihood of war, its scope and violence if it occurs, and the political and economic costs of being prepared for it."[6]

Writing nearly thirty years later, the authors inform us that the three objectives for arms control which they specified were drafted somewhat casually, were not debated between them, and—with only minor reservations—in their opinion, had stood the test of three decades remarkably well.[7] Schelling and Halperin had a breadth of vision that a host of arms control disciples down the road were to honor more in the breach than in the observance. As Schelling has made abundantly clear in his subsequent writings, by arms control he and some of his fellow theorists had in mind far more an ethos and a central organizing idea than an institution or regime of interstate relations.[8] This distinction, between a more or less formal diplomatic process of arms control and the idea of tacit or explicit "cooperation between political enemies," is important for clarity in discussion. In common with other concepts key to this book (e.g., stability and arms race), the idea of arms control can prove extraordinarily elusive. Arms control can be employed to refer to: (1) formal processes of negotiation between states; (2) the outcome of interstate negotiation; (3) the theory of

[6] Thomas C. Schelling and Morton H. Halperin, *Strategy and Arms Control* (New York: Twentieth Century Fund, 1961), p. 2, emphasis added.

[7] Thomas C. Schelling, "From an Airport Bench," and Morton H. Halperin, "From Primer to Policy," *Bulletin of the Atomic Scientists*, 45 (May 1989), 29–31, 31–32.

[8] An idea developed also in Jeremy J. Stone, *Strategic Persuasion: Arms Limitations through Dialogue* (New York: Columbia University Press, 1967).

interstate military cooperation between potential enemies; (4) any activity intended to promote or express interstate military cooperation between potential enemies; and finally, (5) the consequences of behavior (tacit or formal, unilateral or reciprocal) for the objectives of arms control.

The importance of these distinctions becomes painfully apparent when some would-be opinion leader proclaims that "arms control has failed" (or succeeded) or when a strategic theorist postulates that "arms control is a house of cards." What is meant by arms control? Other theorists must answer for themselves, but when I set out to explain why arms control is a house of cards I refer first and foremost, though not exclusively, to the theory of arms control. The occasional practice of tacit cooperation between potential enemies is as old as the history of organized violence, but its formal adoption is a desirable thread to national security policy was controversial in the United States of thirty years ago.[9] Schelling and Halperin advise that "sophistication comes slowly. Military collaboration with potential enemies is not a concept that comes naturally. Tradition is against it."[10] They conclude:

> It is the conservatism of military policy that has caused "arms control" to appear as an alternative, even antithetical, field of action. Perhaps arms control will eventually be viewed as a step in the assimilation of military policy in the over-all national strategy—as a recognition that military postures, being to a large extent a response to the military forces that oppose them, can be subject to mutual accommodation. Adjustments in military postures and doctrines that induce reciprocal adjustments by a potential opponent can be of mutual benefit *if they reduce the danger of a war that neither side wants, or contain its violence, or otherwise serve the security of the nation.*
>
> This is what we mean by arms control.[11]

[9] In an excellent book, Jennifer E. Sims has shown that much of the apparently new thinking on arms control of the late 1950s and early 1960s (what she calls "the Cambridge Approach") had identifiable precursors in the early postwar years: *Icarus Restrained: An Intellectual History of Nuclear Arms Control, 1945–60* (Boulder, Colo.: Westview, 1990). Sims's fascinating book yet again illustrates that the history of ideas is very much a continuum and also demonstrates that the determined scholar is likely to find what he or she is looking for.

[10] Schelling and Halperin, *Strategy and Arms Control*, p. 142.

[11] Ibid., p. 143.

Underpinning Schelling and Halperin's persuasive, reasonable, and imaginative tome is the working premise that weapons, perhaps through an "unstable arms race,"[12] could cause unwanted wars to break out. That premise is examined in detail in the next chapter.

If I am correct in my thesis that although wars are fought with weapons, weapons do not cause wars in any important sense, it follows that the problem lies with the concept of arms control and its core propositions, rather than with this or that particular approach to the subject. A strong body of opinion holds that the United States is overly committed to the formal institutions of an interstate arms control process, at the expense of applying key arms control ideas in a unilateral manner for the achievement of classic arms control objectives. After all, so the argument proceeds, who cares whether or not a Strategic Arms Reductions Talks (START) or a Conventional Forces in Europe (CFE) treaty is signed. What matters is that the United States should so manage its defense activity that the risks of war are minimized.

Anyone who jettisons the narrow interpretation of what constitutes arms control, activity in or closely relating to a negotiating process, soon discovers that the subject has no readily discernible practicable boundary. To quote Schelling and Halperin again: "What is striking is not how novel the methods and purposes of arms control are, and how different from the methods and purposes of national military policy; what is striking is how much overlap there is. There is hardly an objective of arms control to be described in this study that is not equally a continuing urgent objective of national military strategy—of our unilateral military plans and policies."[13] If one thinks of arms control not as "joint understandings with potential enemies," but as effective consequences in support of the objectives of the enterprise (to reduce the risks of war, and so forth), it is obvious that many different roads can lead to the destination. Indeed, one may even find oneself exploring "nuclear strategy, force procurement, and deploy-

---

[12] Ibid., chap. 3, emphasis added.
[13] Ibid., p. 4.

ment *as arms control*."[14] Unless one is careful, deemphasis of a particular instrument of policy (diplomacy), in favor of a focus upon results ("stability" or whatever), leads inexorably to an unbounded consideration of statecraft and strategy. Arms control is supposed to be about reducing the risks of war, but so too are national defense policy and national security policy conceived at its most inclusive.

In order to rescue arms control as a reasonably discrete subject for consideration, we must simply recognize that its three classic objectives can be secured or advanced by several different methods. Arms control, the pursuit of formal or tacit limited military cooperation with potential enemies, might help prevent wars, but then so might distinctly unilateral defense activity, not to mention programs of cultural enlightenment across frontiers, and so forth.

The very concept of arms control logically suggests its obverse of arms *un*control. In popular debate at least, arms control frequently is contrasted with that obverse. It can be difficult to argue for arms *un*control. Similarly, if a debater can lay claim to the vestment of "stability," few people are willing to stand beneath the banner of "instability." Self-appointed guardians of a somewhat vague idea of arms control, an idea associated no less vaguely with "peace," in effect can win a public debate virtually by initial assertion. If I stand for arms control, which *means* peace, what can you stand for?

Whatever may or may not be said in praise of arms control (the diplomatic institution *and* the idea of cooperation with potential enemies), its absence does not equate strictly to a lack of control over arms. Moreover, Chapter 2 explains, it is not self-evident that the control of arms necessarily is very important. Very often indeed, arms control in general, as well as specific recommended arms control regimes, is endorsed as superior to the alleged anarchic and supposedly dangerous alternative of an unbridled arms race. For the record, let it be understood that the idea and diplomatic practice of arms control have been historically trivial in their impact upon the control of competitive armament. In practice,

---

[14] The title of a 1989 study that I wrote for a project on arms control "beyond negotiation," organized by Bennett Ramberg of UCLA.

arms have been controlled by budgets, doctrine, strategy, domestic politics, and often somewhat generalized perceptions of the threat or lack of threat. In fact, so strong is the political determination of defense programs that in any true causal sense arms control is not capable of controlling arms.[15] For example, the Washington treaty of 1922 on the limitation of naval arms controlled the construction of capital ships (battleships and battlecruisers) that Britain and the United States did not intend to build,[16] while the ABM treaty of 1972 controlled the construction of ballistic missile defenses that neither of the high contracting parties were motivated to procure.

The reality of the practical control of arms is demonstrated all the time by the politics of the defense budgetary process. Arms control can help shape a military posture, but its influence relative to such factors as the general political judgment of foreign threat, public mood, economic climate and policy, bureaucratic politics, and doctrinal and strategy preferences tends to be very modest.

Judgment Is Possible

In their generally balanced, positive-leaning assessment of the record of achievement of superpower arms control, Albert Carnesale and Richard N. Haass, claim with good reason that "the public debate about arms control discloses more about the debate participants than about arms control. Individuals and organizations tend to bring to the debate strongly held beliefs about the pros and cons of arms control processes and agreements."[17] An omniscient observer from another planet, compelled as a dire punish-

[15] In *Calculated Risks: A Century of Arms Control, Why It Has Failed, and How It Can Be Made to Work* (New York: Simon and Schuster, 1987), Bruce D. Berkowitz entitles a chapter, "Does Arms Control Control Arms?" and finds by and large in the negative. It is more relevant, more fundamental at least, to ask whether or not it matters for the prevention of war whether arms control controls arms.

[16] A different judgment applies to Japan (allotted the "3" in the 5 : 5 : 3 ratio in capital ship standard displacement).

[17] Albert Carnesale and Richard N. Haass, "Conclusions: Weighing the Evidence," in Carnesale and Haass, eds., *Superpower Arms Control: Setting the Record Straight* (Cambridge, Mass.: Ballinger, 1987), p. 329.

ment for some heinous crime to monitor the Earth persons' debate about arms control, could hardly help but be struck by the passion brought to the debate, the detailed technicality of the discussion, and the endurance in the polar orientation of the policy positions of individuals from one arms control issue to another.

Tolerance of diversity of view, which is to say of believed error, is not a hallmark of the American public debate on arms control. That debate can become painfully, even embarrassingly, personal, as, for example, in 1977 when Paul H. Nitze challenged Paul C. Warnke's fitness to be director of the Arms Control and Disarmament Agency (ACDA).[18] Arms control frequently triggers examples of a strong belief or disbelief in a particular position that virtually guarantees dysfunctional incivility in debate. As with intense theological disputation, so with arms control many people see the stakes as being so high (divine providence for the security of the state, admission into heaven, or peace and war) that everyday decency and civility, rules of evidence, and risk-benefit calculations simply do not apply.

In the minds of many people in many countries, arms control is believed to be the high road to peace—a belief or item of faith, which vote-seeking Western politicians of all political stripes do not dare or care to challenge. A concern for peace made manifest through public agitation for progress in arms control can assume theological intensity. Indeed, divine sanction can be asserted and exploited for the cause. Needless to say, rational discussion may not be possible when one or more camps of opinion defines its purpose as a cause. Causes embody solutions; they have found the truth. In practice, the cause may be very much an end in itself for bored or alienated people who have lost faith in traditional religion, or whatever. This book does not seek to engage arms control as theology; that would be a hopelessly unprofitable task. It is important to recognize here at the outset, however, that arms

---

[18] Strobe Talbott, *The Master of the Game: Paul Nitze and the Nuclear Peace* (New York: Alfred A. Knopf, 1988), quotes the more unpleasant personal attacks on p. 152. Paul H. Nitze (with Ann M. Smith and Steven L. Rearden) discusses his motives in *From Hiroshima to Glasnost: At the Center of Decision—A Memoir* (New York: Grove Weidenfeld, 1989), p. 335, and explains how his attack on Warnke's views unfortunately was misspoken as an assault on his patriotism.

control is not a subject strictly for civilized discourse among professionally licensed cognoscenti.

Because this book is about arms control, it is necessarily about questions of peace and war. Those questions, though potentially forbidding in their technical aspects, are of the greatest public significance and interest. Moreover, because there is always a large potential clientele or audience for arms control ideas, ideas asserted to be *peace*-relevant, the temptation for experts to oversimplify and play irresponsibly to a public gallery at a bumper-sticker level is permanent. For example, rational debate is not greatly aided when knowledgeable people, seeking to fuel a mass movement (in this case called "ground-zero"), write a popular primer with the appalling title *Nuclear War: What's in It for You?*[19] A process of debate, even among supposed experts for supposed experts, can easily generate new rigidities and resort to lawyers' tricks. When experts debate arms control before the jury of public opinion, the pressure to emphasize theater at the expense of substance is all but irresistible.

Many times in this century generally scrupulous and certainly honest and sincere people have presented arms control, and particularly disarmament, as a panacea for the complicated problems of international security. In 1984, for example, four distinguished Americans presented the public with a stark choice between Star Wars or arms control,[20] while back in 1930 President Herbert Hoover told the U.S. Senate that "the question before us now is not whether we shall have a treaty with either three or more 8-inch cruisers or four less 6-inch cruisers, or whether we shall have a larger reduction in tonnage. It is a question of whether we shall move strongly towards limitation and reduction in naval arms or whether we shall have no limitation or reduction and shall enter upon a disastrous period of competitive armament."[21]

[19] "Ground Zero," *Nuclear War: What's in It for You?* (New York: Pocket Books, 1982). The part and chapter titles are collector's items (e.g., "The Bomb That's Coming to Dinner" and "You Ain't Heard Nothing Yet").

[20] McGeorge Bundy, George F. Kennan, Robert S. McNamara, and Gerard Smith, "The President's Choice: Star Wars or Arms Control," *Foreign Affairs*, 63 (Winter 1984–85), 264–78.

[21] Quoted in Christopher Hall, *Britain, America and Arms Control, 1921–37* (New

The first prize for dramatic overstatement of the century, however, must go to Bernard Baruch. On June 14, 1946, he introduced
the plan that, albeit inaccurately, bears his name, in the following
manner:

> We are here to make a choice between the quick and the dead.
> That is our business.
> Behind the black portent of the new atomic age lies a hope which,
> seized upon with faith, can work our salvation. If we fail, then we
> have damned every man to Fear. Let us not deceive ourselves: We
> must elect World Peace or World Destruction.[22]

The authors of these stark choices had in common both an un-
questionable sincerity and an appalling lack of grasp of the character and dynamic working of their subject—peace and war in
international relations. Notwithstanding the legal constraints imposed by the 1930 London naval treaty and by the ABM treaty of
1972, the arms control effected over cruiser construction in the
early 1930s and over new strategic missile defenses in the 1980s
was really a control by national budgets and lack of political will.
What is more, had there been an absence of legal constraint over
British and U.S. cruiser building in the early 1930s and had the
legal barriers to U.S. strategic-defensive developments in the
1980s been weakened, the outcome for international security most
likely would have been positive. The point can be argued, admittedly, but the balanced arguments against the 1930 and 1972
arms control treaties were not trivial.

One should beware of adopting an overly tolerant attitude toward the opinion of others on the accomplishments of arms control. As noted already, such tolerance has been rather rare in the
public arms control debate. Nonetheless, in a book of this kind,
which attempts a comprehensive view of the subject, there is an
attraction toward some golden mean. It can be tempting to see, or

---

York: St. Martin's, 1987), p. 107.

[22] "The Baruch Plan: Statement by the United States Representative (Baruch) to
the United Nations Atomic Energy Commission, June 14, 1946," in U.S. Department of State, *Documents on Disarmament, 1945–1959*, vol. 1 (Washington, D.C.·
Government Printing Office, 1960), pp. 7–8.

pretend to see, some merit in all doctrinal camps, and hence, one might hope to coopt the sympathy of most readers, regardless of their prior beliefs.

It so happens that a very great deal of historical evidence is available for study both on arms control and on its field of honor, which is to say interstate security relations. In one form or another arms control has been pursued actively since Tsar Nicholas II called the First Hague Conference in 1899. To the experience with agreements on the conduct of war negotiated before World War I—and variably applied during the hostilities—the interwar decades added: (1) a draconian disarmament regime applied to the principal loser of the Great War in the Versailles treaty of 1919, (2) more than a decade and a half's intensive experience with naval arms control (1922–38), (3) a treaty in which war was renounced as an instrument of policy (the Kellogg-Briand Pact of 1928), and (4) endeavors focused on the League of Nations to discipline the arms trade ("merchants of death") and (in 1932–34) to negotiate a general disarmament regime with particular reference to allegedly "aggressive" arms.

Since 1945, world politics has registered bids (one can hardly say negotiations) to abolish national ownership of atomic weapons, occasionally renewed and thoroughly insincere offers to negotiate general and complete disarmament,[23] and a superpower arms control process that truly began in earnest in 1958 with negotiations—or perhaps exchanges of view—on nuclear testing and the dangers of surprise attack. The 1960s witnessed the limited nuclear test ban treaty of 1963, the "hot line" agreement of the same year, the outer space treaty of 1967, the treaty on nuclear nonproliferation in 1968, and beginning in 1969, the formal, institutionalized dialogue of the Strategic Arms Limitation Talks (SALT), to be renamed START in the 1980s for reasons of public relations. Nearly a decade and a half of alliance-to-alliance talks in

[23] In January 1986 Mikhail Gorbachev made a splashy "offer" to negotiate complete *nuclear* disarmament on a timetable looking to full abolition by the end of the century. Among the practical problems with this offer was the consideration that since the United States did not know exactly how many nuclear weapons the Soviet Union had produced, verification of complete nuclear disarmament would be literally impossible.

[14]

the 1970s and 1980s focused quite fruitlessly on mutual and balanced force reductions (MBFR) in Europe, while the superpowers also negotiated on incidents at sea (successfully, 1972), antisatellite weapons (unsuccessfully), intermediate range nuclear forces (INF) (successfully, 1987), and—son of MBFR—CFE (successfully, 1990) and START (successfully, 1991).[24] One could go on. The point, as this terse and selective litany illustrates, is that arms control and a more or less formal process of discussion about arms control have been either on stage or nearly so for most of the years of this century when the great powers were not actually fighting each other.

It would be difficult to argue that arms control is a novel and untried instrument of interstate relations, or that it represents an experimental approach to issues of national security. One might assert that arms control ideas have yet to be applied properly, or that better ideas would surely produce improved outcomes for national and international security. Nonetheless, while one can readily grant that there is much room and possibly some prospect for an improved arms control record in the future, the one thing that cannot be claimed is that there is a shortage of evidence of the arms control process in action in recent history.

Donald G. Brennan, Thomas C. Schelling, Morton H. Halperin, and others wrote in the late 1950s and early 1960s as if they had just discovered the idea of limited cooperation with potential enemies.[25] Indeed, a sense of theoretical innovation and policy experimentation did suffuse U.S. arms control debate and policy practice in the 1960s and 1970s. Yet what was new to generally ahistorical American strategic thinkers was not really very new at all. Given the depth and breadth of the international arms control experience of the 1920s and 1930s, it is little short of amazing that

[24] The descriptions "successful" and "unsuccessful" are intended not as judgments but simply as registration of the fact of agreement or lack of agreement.

[25] In addition to the Schelling and Halperin book already cited, the core books of modern arms control theory include Donald G. Brennan, ed., *Arms Control, Disarmament, and National Security* (New York: George Braziller, 1961); and Hedley Bull, *The Control of the Arms Race: Disarmament and Arms Control in the Missile Age* (London: Weidenfeld and Nicolson, 1961). Those books should be reconsidered in the light of the evidence and arguments presented in Sims, *Icarus Restrained*.

the modern U.S. arms control community could have believed that it was inventing the arms control wheel in the 1959–61 period.[26] (This is not to deny that the attempt to focus upon crisis stability, albeit a very military version of that concept, was new to the late 1950s.)

Ample evidence is available upon which to base reasoned judgments about the promise or disappointments of arms control. The historical record is so rich that anybody who would claim that the future of arms control will be noticeably different from its past should be weighed down with the requirement of a very large burden of proof. For a painfully pertinent analogy, one could cite the ever uncomfortable subject of the relationship between strategy and the U.S. defense effort. Those who assert that the United States will reduce its armed forces in a strategically rational manner in the 1990s are obliged to explain why a country that in the 1980s did not increase its defense effort in such a manner would perform strategically rationally in a period when politicians cannot discern major foreign threats.

Arms control now has enough of a past that one is entitled to cite that history as a reasonable basis upon which to predict the likelihood of future achievement. Although the history of international relations poses many problems for those who seek causal connections among events, the arms control record is not particularly difficult to read. Much of what passes for arms control theory can no longer be advanced simply as a great experiment. There is no necessity to value arms control according to the quality of faith of its adherents, the benefits promised to flow from its energetic pursuit, or even the apparent elegance of its solutions to security dilemmas. Instead, one can and should simply proceed the old-fashioned way and examine the admittedly ambiguous, but still ample, relevant evidence and see if arms control *works* as advertised.

---

[26] Merze Tate, *The United States and Armaments* (Cambridge: Harvard University Press, 1948), might have been consulted; or perhaps John W. Wheeler-Bennett, *The Pipe Dream of Peace: The Story of the Collapse of Disarmament* (New York: William Morrow, 1935).

In the magic kingdom of arms control the theory and practice of cooperation between potential enemies either function to save the world from war or at the least are clearly modestly helpful toward that end. That is the crux of the claims for arms control. I argue that, alas, the theory of arms control is sufficiently flawed so that its practice cannot help but be flawed to a like degree. Arms control fails to realize the goals set for it, even if my fundamental quarrel with its logic is deemed unpersuasive. This is not to claim cleverly that I am right even when I am wrong. Rather, it is to say that even if a root-and-branch critique of arms control ideas should be found wanting, such nontrivial factors as poverty in strategy guidance, incompetence in negotiation, and a systematic failure to enforce treaty compliance must raise severe doubts about the probability of the United States emerging with net benefit from an arms control process. The arms control paradox is not the only reason why arms control does not work.

I think it useful to enrich the argument at this juncture with the presentation of no fewer than five paradoxes, which bear upon arms control phenomena from different points of view.

The first paradox, dignified throughout the remainder of this book as *the arms control paradox*, postulates that if arms control is needed in a strategic relationship because the states in question might go to war, it will be impracticable for that very reason of need, whereas, if arms control should prove to be available, it will be irrelevant. This paradox is treated in some detail in the next chapter and functions as a leitmotiv for much of the argument. The perils of tautological argument, even of argument by definition, are real but, fortunately, none too serious. This paradox is as important an idea as it is controversial. A Harvard study of arms control has questioned whether "linkage"—which refers in part, if rather crudely, to the idea of the arms control paradox—has been a very potent factor. The editors argue, "Overall, the tie between arms control and the larger relationship [U.S.-Soviet political relations in general] appears weak in both directions: arms control does not tend to lead to improved ties overall, nor does it necessarily require them, although it benefits from them. On balance, other factors appear to account much more in determining arms control prospects."[27]

The arms control paradox certainly can be overstated in unduly rigid form. Nonetheless, it is difficult to find even minor, let along major, cases either from the interwar or the postwar period which plausibly challenge its logic. This paradox provides a robust fit with virtually all twentieth-century experience with arms control or its absence. I write "virtually" not because I know of an exception but rather because reasonable identification of such isolated cases would not constitute falsification of the paradox, and one should allow for a plausible exception.

Though logically neat, even compelling, assertion of this arms control paradox begs the question of just how rigorously it applies. It may be objected, for example, that even if the paradox has great explanatory power vis-à-vis state-pairs locked in a zero-sum competition, surely it has little value for adversaries who have some interests in common? This objection amounts to no more, though certainly no less, than a frontal challenge by standard arms control logic. The objection is useful in that it makes a sharpening of the rival arguments necessary.

The arms control paradox and, indeed, the central postulate of this book hold that arms control *must* fail. I assume that the current and historical cases of significance for arms control analysis are cases wherein interest in cooperation and competition is mingled. Moreover, the argument here is targeted upon precisely those mixed cooperative-competitive cases of interaction among states of interest to arms control theory and practice. This first paradox denies the feasibility and value of arms control precisely in those mixed cases that have been assaulted by arms control efforts. Analytically speaking, cases of very large overlap of political interests or of no overlap at all, which is to say cases of deep peace and of all-but-war, are easy to handle. It is the cases in between that are the challenge.

Several answers are appropriate to the objection that this first paradox may not meet the challenge posed by the complex, and

---

[27] Carnesale and Haass, "Conclusions," p. 342.

typical, cases of mixed interests in cooperation and competition. The first response is that this objection yet again propagates the error that weapons and arms relationships have a significant, autonomous meaning for high policy. Second, the logic of the arms control paradox does not have anything very interesting to say about conditions of intense political hostility. The paradox is an obvious truth in such contexts. Much more interesting is its claim that even conditions of international rivalry "as usual" can render infeasible the negotiation of an arms control regime with teeth, while the value of such agreements that can be negotiated will be negated by the standard workings of international security politics. Third, to extend and perhaps help clarify the second point, the arms control paradox shows that plausible potential belligerency in itself suffices to thwart the theoretical promise in arms control to help abate the risks of war. This fatal logical flaw in the theory of arms control explains why its practice must fail.

The arms control paradox has been developed logically against the backcloth of a relevant historical record wherein the interests of high contracting parties have rarely been zero-sum in character. The objection to the arms control paradox that charges it falsely with an inappropriate focus solely upon conditions in which state interests are completely at odds thus misses the mark comprehensively. This objection, to repeat, is but a restatement of the standard claim for the opportunity and need for arms control, which I find to be without merit. At this juncture the last word in support of the logic of the fatal paradox of arms control will be allowed to former Soviet Deputy Foreign Minister Alexei Obukhov, who said: "It is with this process [of greatly improved political relations] that the history of the [START] treaty is linked. In my view, a strategic offensive arms treaty in its present form was simply impossible under the conditions of the Cold War. Its symbolic and political significance lies precisely here."[28]

The second paradox is the central insight upon which arms control theory is constructed. Potential enemies require the (limited) cooperation provided by arms control to help them avoid waging

---

[28] Alexei Obukhov, "START treaty is a critical step in disarmament" [Letter to the Editor], *Washington Times*, 1 August 1991, p. G2.

a war that neither of them desires. Obviously, the first and second paradoxes could be treated as posing antithetical ideas. It can appear as if one has to choose which paradox to endorse. On closer inspection, however, one discovers that these paradoxes are not in opposition. After all, the first paradox claims that antagonistic states which need the services of arms control to help them avoid unwanted war, are unable to secure those services because of their antagonism. The second paradox only claims that states which might fight each other *should*, for that reason, explore the potential blessings of arms control. Paradox No. 2 is correct in its reasoning that the danger of war points toward the benefit of cooperation. Error creeps in when the desirable is confused with the possible or probable.

In practice, the political tensions that fuel the urge to compete in armaments and generate fears of war deny an arms control process the ability to achieve results important for the goals of peace with security. This is not to rule out the generality of mixed policy motives to compete and to cooperate. It is to claim, however, that the competitive incentive has terminal consequences for the practical prospects for arms control. It must not be forgotten that my subject is the feasibility and value of cooperation through arms control, not the feasibility and value of political cooperation between partially hostile states. The argument here is that politics is supreme and that the control of armaments by interstate agreement cannot have a major independent value for peace. Antagonistic states can decide to express their joint interest in the avoidance of war by the signing of an arms control agreement. That possibility, however, would not itself have any great importance for the prospects for peace—those prospects being political in nature.

The third paradox holds that a formal arms control process has a tendency to defeat the higher purposes it should serve. Negotiations on armaments focus both upon an extremely sensitive area of state activity and highlight and give political significance to military-technical relationships that may have little strategic meaning outside the context of the negotiations. Furthermore, the dynamics of a protracted process of negotiation will motivate both sides to design, or redesign, arms programs for the purpose of securing diplomatic leverage. In search of victory or perhaps simply to deny victory to the adversary-partner—in SALT or INF or START—a government can lose sight of what it should be about. Arms control can lose its way and become an end in itself. A SALT II or INF treaty, for example, is defended not on the grounds that it accomplishes important positive things for U.S. and, more generally, Western security, but rather on the basis of the claim that a favorable and allegedly verifiable deal was struck. One must add that just as a long passage or negotiating arms has the effect of focusing political attention upon instruments of policy which express anxiety or fear, so too can a treaty regime provide fallow ground for bitter charges and countercharges of treaty violation.

The fourth paradox holds that, as the sophisticated (or "elegant")[29] solution to the problems posed by competitive armaments, an arms control process itself is a panacea not obviously superior in relevance and effectiveness to its rival, the panacea of unilateral military-technical effort. Arms control, approached as diplomacy rather than a branch of defense planning, has every appearance of comprising a political panacea. One does not have to beat the bushes of the U.S. defense community very energetically before one flushes out, on the one hand, a flock of people whose instinctive reaction to any new weapon is to negotiate about its control and, on the other hand, a flock of people whose visceral response to a new weapon idea is to urge its acquisition. Each of these camps shares a detestation for the other's panacea and typically is blissfully unaware of the panacea character of its own preference.

The fifth paradox is what Bruce D. Berkowitz has called the "arms race paradox."[30] This paradox draws upon insight derived from the mathematical theory of games. The argument is that although both parties to an arms race would be better off were they able to cooperate in reciprocated restraint, appreciation of the potentially disastrous costs of strictly unilateral restraint drives both

[29] I borrow here from Berkowitz, *Calculated Risks*, chap. 7.
[30] Ibid., p. 146.

[21]

sides prudently to continue to race effectively unconstrained. Allegedly, arms control provides an institutionalized elegant solution to some or all of the problems posed by arms competition. Arms control, with this logic, provides a way off the treadmill of competitive armament.[31] Chapter 2 explains that paradox No. 5 and its close relatives can only be as valid as the model of arms race dynamics which they postulate. *If* arms races, or weapons more generally, do not bear causal responsibility for the outbreak of war in any meaningful sense, then arms control is in deep trouble indeed.

THE ARGUMENT AND THE INDICTMENT

Arms control is a house of cards whose promise and reality have always been, *and must remain*, far apart. This chapter has introduced the ideas and charges key to the argument, or indictment perhaps. By way of lowering the drawbridge further for the forthcoming analysis, some critical threads of the argument can be highlighted.

- Countries in conflict that need arms control cannot achieve arms control for the same reasons, and roughly to the same degree, that they need it. (Chapters 1 and 2)
- Weapons do not *cause* war, therefore the control of weapons is unlikely to *cause* peace. (Chapter 2)
- As a master concept for the guidance and assessment of arms control activity, *stability* lacks useful meaning. (Chapter 2)
- Revisionist and would-be revisionist states cause wars as they seek to realize their ambitions and as other states mobilize to thwart them. (Chapters 2 and 3)
- The historical record shows clearly that even on its own terms *arms control does not work*. (Chapters 4, 5, and 7)
- Just as arms control policy must lack integrity in the absence of clarity in defense planning, so its near-term goals should be selected with a view to desirable destinations well down the road in the future. For example, if a fair intellectual grasp of what might constitute a beneficial

[31] See Paul C. Warnke, "Apes on a Treadmill," *Foreign Policy*, 18 (Spring 1975), 12–29.

START II or CFE II is lacking, how can START I or CFE I be designed soundly? (Chapter 5)
- In the absence of well-crafted, authoritative, and effective national grand and military strategies, arms control is a mystery tour. (Chapter 5)
- Western insistence upon strict verification of arms control treaties is little more than a sham because there is an unbroken pattern from the interwar decades to the present of Western democracies failing to design and implement sanctions and safeguards policies for noncompliance. (Chapter 6)
- Arms control is not a harmless irrelevance. At the least it absorbs large amounts of scarce time and energy on the part of already overburdened policymakers and their staffs for little if any net benefit to national security.[32] Arms control ideas have a way of substituting for strategic thought—a serious matter for a country that has never been strongly inclined toward strategic reasoning. (Chapter 8)
- Orthodox wisdom holds that the devil is in the details with arms control. That nugget of wisdom is wrong, or only half-correct. More accurately, the devil is in the *trends*. The details of a treaty do not much matter if that treaty accomplishes the wrong things anyway. (Passim)
- Arms control can restrict the ability to cope flexibly and effectively with the unpredicted and unpredictable needs of the future. Defense planners are not very good at technological prediction. Some arms control treaties oblige policymakers and defense planners to predict rather narrowly what their distant successors would like to inherit from today. Competence in the design of arms control regimes can require the impossible of bureaucratic foresight. The impossible is rarely achievable and hence should not be required. (Chapters 3, 7, and 8)

Each of these threads to the argument translates into an item in an indictment of the theory and practice of arms control. The problem is with arms control, it is not with any particular approach to the subject. The concept of a sound arms control policy

[32] A view endorsed strongly in Kenneth L. Adelman, *The Great Universal Embrace: Arms Summitry—A Skeptic's Account* (New York: Simon and Schuster, 1989), passim. Adelman argues, "Conservatives contend that arms control deludes the public or saps the will of the West by lulling us into a false sense of security, but this is not the worst of it. Rather, its main liability is the staggering drain on presidential and other top-level time for matters of little or no relevance to keeping the peace or strengthening the nation" (p. 34).

is an oxymoron. By analogy, the unlovely USSR of the past had to change into something very different, but it could not be reformed. In other words, the USSR itself was the problem, as Soviet political leaders came to recognize in 1991. This book explains why and how arms control itself is the problem, and therefore why attempt to improve arms control policy are doomed to fail.

[2]

Weapons and War

The focus on vulnerability and first-strike incentives is excessively mechanistic. States start wars for political objectives, not because they see an opportunity or fear that the other side does. . . . Both the danger of aggression and the possibility of long-run spirals of hostility and fear have been more potent causes of war than has crisis instability.

—Robert Jervis, 1991

As Peace Breaks Out, Can Arms
Control Be Far Behind?

War is waged with weapons, but in what sense do weapons make war? Governments choose peace or war: does it much matter for that choice how well they are armed? Or perhaps there are no general truths, no general theory to be achieved; perhaps some weapons, in some hands, at some times, encourage the outbreak of war.

The relationship between weapons and war is as seemingly self-evident as the relationship between weapons and peace provokes endless debate. The central question here is whether the control of weapons can contribute usefully to the control of war. The world at large, including the governments of what used to be distinguished as East and West, already has answered this question with ringing positive acclamation—else what can the burgeoning array of arms control institutions and regimes be all about?

Assertion by word and deed of the significance of arms control expresses the belief that the absence, or limitation, of weapons somehow contributes to the cause of peace. The logical corollary is the proposition that weapons make war. The logic of these two arguments is so tightly entwined, that weapons make war and that the absence of weapons makes for peace, that falsification of either one would falsify the other. The transmission belt from weapons to war often is characterized by the metaphor of an *arms race*.[1] The argument is that the process of competitive armament turns weapons and weapon support systems into fuel for war, just as an arms control process should help render military systems relatively innocuous as instruments of policy.

Through arms control, allegedly, the conditions for stability should be advanced. Stability long has been identified as the holy grail of arms control and of defense preparation more generally. Unfortunately, stability can prove to be an elusive goal. Moreover, that elusiveness flows in good part from an absence of precise meaning which allows capture and employment of the concept by any and all defense arguments in need of added dignity. If no one can be sure wherein stability resides, then no one can be sure wherein stability does not reside. In short, the claim that a favored weapon, strategy, or arms control proposal would advance stability is beyond authoritative refutation. That fact should limit severely the value of the term "stability," but so positive a view is taken by so many people of this slippery concept that it remains a staple of debate.

Consider the apparent wealth of arms control negotiating prospects, or negotiated regime benefits, which beckons in the 1990s. Can it be that Americans and Russians (inter alia) belatedly have learned the value of formal cooperation? Or can it be that far from illustrating the relevance of arms control theory and policy, the contemporary abundance of offerings in that field instead illustrates exactly the reverse. If peace is breaking out on the political front, what—if any—are the important functions of arms control?

FIVE PROPOSITIONS

Five propositions guide the argument in this chapter.

(1) *Governments, not weapons, make war.* In a classic confusion of means with ends, particular kinds of weapons often are defined

---

[1] See Charles H. Fairbanks, Jr., "Arms Races: The Metaphor and the Facts," *National Interest*, 1 (Fall 1985), 75–90.

as the villains that promote the onset of war. There is no intention to suggest here that the kind and numbers of weapons are unimportant for decisions on war or peace; nor is it implied that accidental war or war through misperception of the meaning of precautionary mobilization procedures is literally impossible. The point rather is that the importance of weapons or military behavior per se typically is swamped in relative significance as a trigger for war by the policy drives of governments. Marc Trachtenberg is close to the mark when he argues that

> The purely military side of war causation, as Brodie later complained, became the focus of analysis, as though war itself were not in essence a political artifact—as though the basic insight of Clausewitz, whom they [the strategists] all respected, was somehow obsolete. It was not that the issues they focused on were meaningless or irrelevant. The problem, for example, of "accidental war" resulting from the "reciprocal fear of surprise attack" was certainly worth thinking about. *It was simply a question of balance, of not allowing the tail to wag the dog,* and this depended on the sophistication of one's theory of war causation.[2]

(2) *Arms control regimes worthy of the name are achievable only between states who do not need them.* This is the arms control paradox already introduced in Chapter 1, which suggests that the central assumption of arms control theory—that potential enemies, ipso facto, should be motivated to cooperate—generally is wrong: worthy and well-meriting investigation by policy but still, alas, wrong. The motive to cooperate is overridden by the motive to compete. The arms control paradox argues that the reasons why states may require the moderating influence of an arms control regime are the very reasons why such a regime will be unattainable.

(3) *The concept of an arms race is a confused and confusing metaphor.* It poses problems of different kinds, and there is the question of significance. Even if there is a "race" in armaments, what is its importance for the course of international relations? There is also

---

[2] Marc Trachtenberg, "Strategic Thought in America, 1952–1966," in Trachtenberg, *History and Strategy* (Princeton: Princeton University Press, 1991), p. 45, emphasis added.

the difficulty of internal integrity. Does the phenomenon under enquiry have racelike qualities and, if so, what are the implications?

(4) *Stability is so variably value-charged a concept that it has no utility as a yardstick.* Ideally, the concept of stability would be banished from public discourse, so readily does it lend itself to seizure and employment by any purpose in strategic argument. Absence of clarity, however, has yet to terminate the vitality of a word, particularly when that absence of clarity is important for the concept's utility in debate or narrowly framed analysis. Strategic theorists know how malleable is the concept of stability, but most legislators and other would-be opinion leaders, let alone the general public, certainly do not.

(5) *The character of a weapon (e.g., stabilizing/destabilizing, offensive/ defensive) is determined by the purposes to which it is put, not by its technical properties.* By traditional definition some military systems are labeled offensive and others defensive. Such common usage is not unreasonable: shields, city walls, and anti-aircraft artillery, certainly appear to be unambiguously defensive in character. If concern is focused not upon technology and tactics, however, but rather upon strategy and policy, then the question of purpose becomes paramount. A shield protected the body of both a farmer-militiaman and a Viking raider. But the former used his shield synergistically with a sword to defend his land, the latter to raid and ravage other people's land.

The following sections examine the merit in the propositions introduced above.

THE CAUSES OF WAR

Scholarly literature on the causes of war is a great deal thinner in library shelf length than is the literature on the decline and fall of the Roman Empire, but it is no less inconclusive. It seems probable that more and more scholarship on both subjects will yield an ever richer menu of possibilities. It is interesting to note that a recent first-rate collection of essays on *The Origin and Prevention of*

Major Wars has a brief introductory chapter but, perhaps wisely, no chapter of conclusions.[3]

The purpose here is not to review critically the leading theories of the causes of war, let alone to pick a winner. Rather, the purpose is to see if there are any near-term prospects for enlightenment by general theory and, specifically, to explore the idea that weaponry, or competition in weaponry, may be a strong candidate for a leading cause of war. The conditions for peace and the causes of war are always to a greater or lesser degree a matter for speculation. If scholars are thoroughly disunited on the subject of why Rome declined and fell fifteen hundred years ago, it is not difficult to understand why the causes, origins, and important precipitating events of war and conditions for peace in 2000 or 2020 are more than a little obscure.

Joseph S. Nye, Jr., has observed that "history is the study of events that have happened only once; political science is the effort to generalize about them."[4] Historians can always explain why a particular war happened. Given that great events usually have great origins, though not necessarily great triggers, it is a safe assumption that when there is a war there are origins to be unearthed and traced. It is troublesome to appreciate that although every historical period lends itself to research into the causes of major wars, such wars did not occur in some of those periods.[5]

---

[3] Robert I. Rotberg and Theodore K. Rabb, eds., *The Origin and Prevention of Major Wars* (Cambridge: Cambridge University Press, 1989). In addition, see Geoffrey Blainey, *The Causes of War* (London: Macmillan, 1973); Keith L. Nelson and Spencer C. Olin, Jr., *Why War? Ideology, Theory, and History* (Berkeley: University of California Press, 1979); Michael Howard, *The Causes of Wars and Other Essays* (London: Unwin Paperbacks, 1983); and for the best analytical summary of the literature, Jack S. Levy, "The Causes of War: A Review of Theories and Evidence," in Philip E. Tetlock et al., eds., *Behavior, Society and Nuclear War*, vol. 1 (New York: Oxford University Press, 1989), pp. 209–333. Amid the vast literature on the alleged causes of the decline and fall of the Roman Empire, see A. H. M. Jones, "The Decline and Fall of the Roman Empire," *History*, 40 (October 1955), 209–26; and J. J. Saunders, "The Debate on the Fall of Rome," *History*, 48 (February 1963), 1–7.

[4] Joseph S. Nye, Jr., "Old Wars and Future Wars: Causation and Prevention," in Rotberg and Rabb, eds., *Origin and Prevention of Major Wars*, p. 3.

[5] Those readers who favor precise definitions (when is a war a major war?) are invited to consult Jack S. Levy, "Theories of General War," *World Politics*, 37 (April 1985), 344–74.

An illustration of this phenomenon would be a series of case studies of successful deterrence. Unfortunately for progress in political science, a nonwar outcome, ipso facto, is not proof of success in deterrence.

The fact that history offers a rich menu of tempting causes of major war is both interesting and unhelpful. Fortunately, perhaps, strategy is a subject wherein truth is always pragmatic. Policy asks of grand and military strategy not that they be aesthethically pleasing, elegant, and subtle, or that they be true in some absolute sense. Strategy and statecraft more broadly just has to work well enough. If U.S. policymakers were to cease to conduct statecraft pending the conclusive results of scholarly investigation into the truth about the causes of war, they would be on permanent hold.[6] No particular piece of scholarship, no unique selection of actual or hypothetical wars, will provide policymakers with certain knowledge of how to avoid war in historically unique circumstances tomorrow.

There are any number of ways in which the causes of war can be studied, but five sets of nonexclusive distinctions are particularly useful, if only to underline the complexity of the subject. The causes of war may be sought in:

- underlying conditions or immediate events;
- general or specific (typically territorial) issues in contention;
- offensive or defensive policy intentions;
- political, economic, cultural, religious, or possibly military motives (military motives could be instrumental, for example, only in improving a state's military position for the future or in securing glory, civic reward, and perhaps loot from plunder);
- either simple or complex reasons;
- the views and intentions of an individual or of a state functioning in a unitary way or in a range of views and intentions among many individuals and institutions of state;
- constant or dynamic views of the desirable and the necessary.

It is all too obvious that history provides a well-stocked warehouse of examples to support every favored theory of the causes

[6] It is ironic that the University of Chicago's monumental study of war, begun in the very deep peace of 1926, finally was published in 1942. See Quincy Wright, *A Study of War*, 2 vols. (Chicago: University of Chicago Press, 1942).

of war. It is a poor proposition indeed that would defy attempted provision of illustrative historical support. Strategic theorists looking forward thus have two problems. First they have to decide what it is that historical study might be able to tell them. Second, they have to judge what should be the future relevance of the lessons or, more likely, just the insights and apparently enlightening questions derived from the disciplined contemplation of the past.

The logic of statecraft and of strategy qua logic is truly general and eternal.[7] But, statecraft and strategy are eminently practical activities and wisdom in their regard always has to pertain to what works well enough at tolerable cost. Joseph Nye makes appropriate reference to what he calls the "crystal-ball effect."[8] Statesmen who endeavor to proceed in a consequentialist manner—which is to say, who behave rationally—should be discouraged from taking actions which they have good reason to believe would lead to a great deal more pain than gain. Before the nuclear age it was relatively easy for statesmen to persuade themselves, or to allow themselves to be persuaded, that war could yield a better outcome than nonwar. In Nye's words: "An elementary knowledge of the physical effects of nuclear weapons serves as today's crystal ball."[9]

The relations within and among the five sets of distinctions bearing upon the causes of war are unhelpfully indeterminate. For example, consider the first distinction cited, that between underlying conditions and immediate, or triggering, events. The semi-anarchy that is the states' system is always a general war waiting to happen, but without a powder trail and a match war will not occur. Or will it? For example, were the two world wars of the twentieth century inherent in the structure of the modern great-power system—rather like a statue waiting to be revealed or liberated from a block of marble by Michelangelo—with the precise details of their precipitating crisis slides being matters of no essential significance? It is easy to persuade oneself that although

---

[7] See Edward N. Luttwak, *Strategy: The Logic of War and Peace* (Cambridge: Harvard University Press, 1987), passim. On this central point Luttwak is resoundingly correct.
[8] Nye, "Old Wars and Future Wars," p. 11.
[9] Ibid.

a particular great war or set of wars (the Peloponnesian, the Punic, the occasional wars between Persia and Rome, the world wars of this century) necessarily had a unique historical trail to detonation, in fact, the war in question probably would have occurred one way or another. In other words, some diplomatic or military historians may be convinced that this or that detail of a meeting, formal note, or mobilization plan was critically important, but the wiser scholar of international conflict recognizes that many roads can lead to war or peace.[10] One need hardly add to this discussion a caveat against deterministic reasoning. It is one thing to assert that there were probably many roads that could have been taken to the First and Second Punic Wars or to World War I and II; it is quite another to claim that those wars had to occur more or less when they did.[11]

It is necessary to ask what the statesman, the defense planner, and the strategic theorist should understand about this vitally important subject that might actually help in the prevention of war in the future. What follows is not, alas, a terse summary of a body of knowledge of the kind that professors of international relations can profess. Rather, these eclectic propositions and insights simply fit better with important historical data than do other propositions and insights, and they are chosen for their relative tolerance of fault. In short, these points are not advanced as being true but as being apparently true enough to be useful. Also, the argument should be read with general reference to the purposes of this chapter, to explore the relationship, if any, between weapons and the causes of war and conditions of peace—with a view to understanding what relevance, if any, an arms control process can have.

[10] One should approach Donald Cameron Watt's masterly *How War Came: The Immediate Origins of the Second World War, 1938–1939* (New York: Pantheon, 1989), with this caveat in mind. There is much to recommend P. M. H. Bell's view that "unless German expansion halted of its own accord without breaching the limits set by the vital interests of other strong and determined states, then war was bound to come." *The Origins of the Second World War in Europe* (New York: Longman, 1986), p. 300.

[11] For a thoroughly nondeterministic judgment on the outbreak of the First and Second Punic Wars, see Brian Caven, *The Punic Wars* (London: Weidenfeld and Nicolson, 1980). Also useful is William V. Harris, *War and Imperialism in Republican Rome, 327–70 B.C.* (1979; rpt. Oxford: Clarendon Press, 1985).

A "sense of general rivalry" pervades the policy calculations of adversary-partners in a threat system.[12] The rivalry will always find some concrete expression in litmus-test issues that have some enduring irritation value. For example, throughout much of the eighteenth century Anglo-French relations were exacerbated by the issue of French fortification of the Port of Dunkirk (a major base for French privateers).[13] English irritation on that subject provides a direct parallel with American irritation over the Krasnoyarsk radar in the mid- to late 1980s. Both physical installations were illegal by treaty (Treaty of Utrecht, 1713; ABM Treaty, 1972). A leading historian of Anglo-French relations in the eighteenth century has offered a characterization of his subject that should be generically familiar to readers: "The principal difference in opinion [in Britain] throughout the century was not over whether to trust France, but over what to do about her."[14]

But, what are the roots of this "general sense of rivalry?" Why did, for example, Athens and Sparta, Rome and Carthage, Byzantium and Sassanian Persia, Spain and France, France and Britain, Britain and Russia, Germany and Britain, and most recently the Soviet Union and the United States identify each other as enemies? The answer is that each of these opposed pairs found in their strategic relationship a potentially deadly threat at most to survival and independence and at the least to well-being, including dignity and self-esteem.[15] In principle one can distinguish between anxiety over possible loss of power, and hence security, and an urge to become yet more powerful virtually as an end in itself (although a security rationale can always be found). The

[12] Jeremy Black, *Natural and Necessary Enemies: Anglo-French Relations in the Eighteenth Century* (London: Gerald Duckworth, 1986), p. 145.

[13] See J. S. Bromley, *Corsairs and Navies, 1660–1760* (London: Hambledon Press, 1987), pp. 72–101 ("The Importance of Dunkirk Reconsidered, 1688–1713"); and David Aldridge, "The Navy as Handmaid for Commerce and High Policy, 1680–1720," in Jeremy Black and Philip Woodfine, eds., *The British Navy and the Use of Naval Power in the Eighteenth Century* (Leicester: Leicester University Press, 1988), pp. 61–63.

[14] Black, *Natural and Necessary Enemies*, p. 120.

[15] See Richard Ned Lebow and Barry S. Strauss, eds., *Hegemonic Rivalry: From Thucydides to the Nuclear Age* (Boulder, Colo.: Westview 1991), for a relevant set of essays.

practical distinction between offensive and defensive motives need not be a firm one. After all, the logic of both motives in policy action could lead a polity to attempt to forge a global imperium.

Actual or potential enemies are identified on the basis of their capabilities, modified *in either direction* by considerations of geopolitics and ideology. For example, capabilities analysis and trade rivalry promoted Anglo-American rivalry in the 1920s, but the geography of Anglo-American strategic relations and the measure of shared political values, not to mention the memories of the Great War and the financial impracticality of a conflict for London, all but guaranteed that this particular relationship of conflict would not deteriorate into war.[16] Although it is a general truth that anxiety over the predicted loss of relative power is a potent, perhaps even the most potent, cause of war, it is by no means certain to have consequences which must lead to war. Countries, even once-mighty empires, have been known to acquiesce in a process of decline and to elect not to contest by force of arms slippage in the hierarchy of states.

Nonetheless, the reasons why well- or ill-founded anxiety over national decline can be dangerous to international peace are obvious. The "sick man of Europe" in the nineteenth century, the Ottoman Empire, was denied a graceful decline by the great powers and the subject nationalities, who sought as much of the spoils of the erstwhile empire as they could seize and hold. Austria-Hungary, by contrast, was unwilling to fade gracefully from the ranks of the great powers, a fact with consequences in 1914 that fulfilled a pessimist's worst fears.

[16] Christopher Hall, *Britain, America and Arms Control, 1921–37* (New York: St. Martin's, 1987), takes an overly gloomy view of Anglo-American rivalry, which naturally sets the stage for a fairly positive judgment on the Anglo-American dimension to the Washington treaty system. Although referring to an earlier period (1917–18), David F. Trask was very much to the point when he wrote: "Wrangling between the United States and Great Britain was relatively restrained because the British could simply not afford to antagonize the Americans beyond a certain point and because there was certainly at least a broad correspondence of political viewpoints between the two nations." *Captains and Cabinets: Anglo-American Naval Relations, 1917–1918* (Columbia: University of Missouri Press, 1972), p. 364. Stephen Roskill, *Naval Policy between the Wars*, vol. 1: *The Period of Anglo-American Antagonism, 1919–1929* (London: Collins, 1968), is valuable.

Next, statesmen need to recognize that vacuums of power truly can be a menace to order and peace. The *cordon sanitaire* of new independent states in Eastern Europe created by Allied statesmen at Versailles in 1919 in order to separate German from Russian power instead was a zone of weakness into which the Third Reich duly expanded. Anxiety over relative loss of power (for which read security, appropriately or otherwise), or perhaps over the actual or anticipated rise of some challenger to the balance of power, finds in power vacuums forward positions for the advance protection of embattled core values. Almost regardless of original policy motives, a power vacuum attracts great-power influence and hence often great-power conflict. The post-Ottoman Balkans was just such a zone of insecurity in the decades prior to 1914, while east-central Europe more broadly was all but designed in 1919 to detonate great-power conflict.

One may lament Eurocentric analyses masquerading as global theory, but the fact remains that in modern times there has been a discernible pattern of bids for continental hegemony by the greatest land power of the day. In their turn, Habsburg Spain, France, Germany, and the USSR all posed more or less credible threats forcibly to reorganize the security order of Europe in their favor. The geopolitical theories of Sir Halford Mackinder and Nicholas John Spykman, with some useful early contributions by Alfred Thayer Mahan, serve well enough to explain why the United States has chosen to play an active role in the Eurasian balance of power three times in this century (1917–18, 1941–45, 1947 to present).[17]

It is possible that the pattern of five hundred years of sea-led coalitions for the thwarting of continental hegemony is now past.[18] However, the potentially explosive mixture of a declining Russia, a reviving Germany, a retiring United States, and an exceedingly weak east-central Europe looks alarmingly like a familiar scenario, notwithstanding the value for general security of the "crystal-ball

[17] Halford J. Mackinder, *Democratic Ideals and Reality* (New York: W. W. Norton, 1962), title essay written in 1918–19; Nicholas John Spykman, *The Geography of the Peace* (New York: Harcourt, Brace, 1944); and Alfred T. Mahan, *The Problem of Asia and Its Effect upon International Policies* (Boston: Little, Brown, 1905).

[18] An argument resolutely rejected in George Modelski and William R. Thompson, *Seapower in Global Politics, 1494–1993* (London: Macmillan, 1988).

effect" of nuclear weapons. Policymakers in search of understanding why states fight can cover a great deal of the relevant historical terrain with appreciation of the salience of bids to secure and deny hegemony. First Britons then Americans have waged war to deny continental hegemony to France and to Germany, lest a continental hegemon should free itself of landward distraction and be able to pursue *weltpolitik* from the base of an effectively united Europe.

It is interesting to note how little weapons have intruded in this discussion thus far. Military strategy and posture should express the policy intentions of their political masters. This logical point certainly can be breached in reality. Germany in the years when Alfred von Schlieffen and Helmuth von Moltke (the Younger) were chiefs of the general staff is an example of war plans and the military means being developed in more isolation from policy than was desirable.[19]

Even the German case of an army with a country, however, is not quite as blatant an example of the military instrument making for war as might be supposed. One should not forget Germany's basic geopolitical condition or dilemma, a danger of war on two fronts. Agile diplomatic footwork à la Bismarck and dynastic solidarity could not provide permanent guarantees of a secure eastern border. Furthermore, that geopolitical condition helped fuel a popular political enthusiasm for the idea of a hegemony in Europe and empire overseas. German geopolitics and a popular lust after national greatness provided a permissive environment in which military technicians could ply their trade.

Governments, or perhaps peoples in this democratic age, make war with weapons, but the sense or senses in which weapons

[19] Useful studies include Larry H. Addington, *The Blitzkrieg Era and the German General Staff, 1865–1941* (New Brunswick: Rutgers University Press, 1971); L. C. F. Turner, "The Significance of the Schlieffen Plan," in Paul Kennedy, ed., *The War Plans of the Great Powers, 1880–1914* (London: George Allen and Unwin, 1979), pp. 199–221; and Jehuda L. Wallach, *The Dogma of the Battle of Annihilation: The Theories of Clausewitz and Schlieffen and Their Impact on the German Conduct of Two World Wars* (Westport, Conn.: Greenwood, 1986). For a valuable corrective to overstatement of the case for the isolation of military planning in Imperial Germany, see Marc Trachtenberg, "The Coming of the First World War: A Reassessment," in his *History and Strategy*, pp. 47–99.

make war is none too obvious. Unquestionably, the announcement of plans by the greatest continental power of the day to build a High Seas Fleet will catch the attention of an insular maritime power.[20] Nonetheless, there was more to Anglo-German antagonism and to British policy reasoning than simply the fear of the new German fleet, important though that was. The exit point for this section of the discussion is the proposition, to repeat, that a "sense of general rivalry" provides focus and meaning for military assessment. Countries arm in order to deter, to defend if they must, and sometimes to secure the assets of others, but they do not fight because they are armed.

THE ARMS CONTROL PARADOX AND THE ARMS RACE METAPHOR

The propositions behind the title of this section comprise challenges to the sides of the same counterfeit coin. The arms control paradox introduced in Chapter 1 assaults the idea that the control of arms can make any useful contribution to peace. The argument that the concept of an arms race is a confusing metaphor challenges the inchoate yet still popular notion that arms races cause wars. This is not to deny that some arms races *lead* to wars (while some do not). Indeed, it would be surprising were most wars not preceded by competitive armament between the protagonists.

Attitudes toward arms control cluster into four schools of thought. With some minor element of caricature perhaps, these are (1) the savior of mankind, (2) the marginally useful, (3) the marginally not useful, and (4) the snare and delusion. The argument here comprises a mix of No. 3 and 4. The two propositions that light this section are consistent with the "root and branch" criticism of

[20] See Arthur J. Marder, *From the Dreadnought to Scapa Flow: The Royal Navy in the Fisher Era, 1904–1919*, vol. 1: *The Road to War, 1904–1914* (London: Oxford University Press, 1961); and Holger H. Herwig, *"Luxury Fleet": The Imperial German Navy, 1888–1918* (London: George Allen and Unwin, 1980). Incredible though it may seem, Tirpitz's High Seas Fleet was supposed to pass through its long period of military vulnerability, which is to say until it attained a strength in capital ships two-thirds that of Britain's Royal Navy, without Britain noticing that it was coming as a deadly serious challenge.

school No. 4. My argument, however, is that arms control theory is fundamentally flawed, rather than that malicious or opportunistic adversaries might use an arms control process to lull Americans to sleep over their prudent security needs.[21] The heartland of the U.S. arms control community, contrary to its theories of twenty years ago developed to challenge the Sentinel/Safeguard ABM system, has come to recognize the logic, if not the full implications, of the argument outlined here. In a primer titled *Crisis Stability and Nuclear War*, an all but official statement from the community of arms control advocates recognizes the following:

> For many years the superpowers' strategic forces have projected a degree of mutual threat that has provoked progressively more threatening deployments. A large body of informed opinion that spans most political and national boundaries has emphasized the need to escape from this vicious circle. Nevertheless, arms control, the only visible means to that end, has not yet broken the impasse. *Obviously the adversarial relationship between the two alliances is the fundamental hurdle*, but there is also discord within the United States and NATO as to what would be in their own best interest.[22]

The authors at least recognize the problem. They do not, however, recognize just how severe is that problem for their favored solution. Full appreciation that politics truly is the master and that the strategic relations among great powers cannot be transformed into a branch of administration, continues to elude the arms control community. To quote again from *Crisis Stability and Nuclear War*:

> The risk that ongoing competition between the superpowers could lead to crisis and then to war *is ultimately governed by politics, not technology*. Nevertheless, technology can create new military capa-

---

[21] Almost excessively balanced judgment pervades the useful analysis in Sean M. Lynn-Jones, "Lulling and Stimulating Effects of Arms Control," in Albert Carnesale and Richard N. Haass, eds., *Superpower Arms Control: Setting the Record Straight* (Cambridge, Mass.: Ballinger, 1987), pp. 223–73.

[22] Kurt Gottfried and Bruce G. Blair, eds., *Crisis Stability and Nuclear War* (New York: Oxford University Press, 1988), p. 193, emphasis added.

bilities that could exacerbate a crisis. Furthermore, technology can also provide new capabilities that could enhance stability if they were to be embedded in an appropriate political framework. To that end we shall advocate arms control agreements that contribute to crisis stability.[23]

That all sounds very reasonable, plausible, prudent, and responsible. But, how many of the key assumptions are true? Could new military capabilities exacerbate a crisis? Would such exacerbation be significant, compared with, say, the political will to protect vital interests? If potentially significant, could arms control measures help? Can new military capabilities be developed that "could enhance stability if they were to be embedded *in an appropriate political framework*?" The qualifying phrase I emphasized subverts the sense in the argument. It is precisely the political framework that is the problem; it cannot be assumed away as though it were just a matter of administrative redesign. In the international political framework of the early 1990s, arms control is as relatively easy to achieve as it is close to irrelevant. Indeed, that relative ease is proof of its irrelevance.[24]

With a strong caveat necessary concerning definitions, it would be only a modest exaggeration to argue that arms control is without substantial value for the principal purposes for which ostensibly it is pursued. One must say *ostensibly* because arms control activity can proceed more from the fact that governments have no practicable political alternative rather than that they have powerful ideas on how national and international security might be advanced thereby. For example, if there is a security rationale for proceeding from a START I treaty allowing 6000 treaty-accountable nuclear warheads to a START II allowing 3000 such warheads, that rationale remains a well-kept secret. The necessary caveat referred to above is that arms control can be defined with reference to behavior bearing upon its objectives and not solely

---

[23] Ibid., p. 160, emphasis added.

[24] This is an expression of the arms control paradox, it is not a tautology—appearances to the contrary notwithstanding, perhaps.

with regard to more or less formal diplomatic institutions.[25] This distinction is important because, as the founding fathers of modern arms control theory appreciated very well, the objectives of arms control can, indeed must, be pursued by traditional defense activity. Arms control differs from military preparation above all else in that it requires some cooperation with a putative enemy. But if arms control is about reducing the risks of war, limiting damage in war, and minimizing peacetime economic and social burdens, it might be subsumed wholly within the realm of the defense policy of the state.

The argument here is not that measures of arms control have proved to be utterly without merit. Instead, the proposition is advanced that the formal processes of arms control have not delivered and *cannot* deliver upon the promise in the theory, let alone live up to the frequently overheated promises in the political rhetoric of statesmen and officials. Because wars do not spring from weaponry, the negotiated control of that weaponry—even on the subject of the operation of armed forces in time of crisis[26]— is not important for the prevention of wars.

The fact that I am not arguing that arms control is utterly without merit should not be viewed as an important preemptive concession to potential critics. The two dominant positions taken here, that the arms control paradox precludes the possibility of important success and that weapons do not make war, so far control the argument that whether or not a favorable mention is warranted for this or that arms control measure is really unimportant. What is not unimportant is my claim that arms control *must* fail to generate the political and strategic effectiveness which theory and

[25] A view expressed forcefully in Kenneth L. Adelman, "Arms Control with and without Agreements," *Foreign Affairs*, 63 (Winter 1984–85), 240–63; and Thomas C. Schelling, "What Went Wrong with Arms Control?" *Foreign Affairs*, 64 (Winter 1985–86), 219–33.

[26] The perils of crisis-time military behavior are emphasized in Scott D. Sagan, "Nuclear Alerts and Crisis Management," *International Security*, 9 (Spring 1985), 99–139, and *Moving Targets: Nuclear Strategy and National Security* (Princeton: Princeton University Press, 1989), chap. 4; and Ashton B. Carter, John D. Steinbruner, and Charles A. Zraket, eds., *Managing Nuclear Operations* (Washington, D.C.: Brookings, 1987), passim.

aspiration requires of it in difficult cases. States can find arms control agreements useful to help seal a political bargain which has been struck already and to help cover a retreat and save face, as with the formal British retreat from naval superiority in 1922. But arms control cannot be useful as an intended means to change policy. Arms are the tail, not the head, of the dog.

In theory, vast and complex rival military organizations operating in alert conditions in the fog of crisis could trigger war by accident. Through accident, inadvertence, and misperception surely it can be argued that weapons make war. There can always be a first time, but it is an impressive fact that there are literally no familiar examples of states stumbling into war because of military accident or misperception. In the great storehouse of military history there should be an example or two that could be unearthed, but the exceptional case, if it can be found, really proves the rule. The argument here is not that superpowers could not blunder into war. Instead, the point is that such a remote possibility is quite overwhelmed in significance by the quite conscious political purposes of states. *If* arms control, with such instruments as the Accidents Measures agreement of 1971 and the Incidents at Sea agreement of 1972, can minimize the possibility of potentially dangerous military acts, well and good.

To summarize on what analysts have come to call the logic of accidental war: first, an arms control process that encouraged states to think more carefully about the accident or misperception-proneness of their military alerting procedures *might* be of some positive benefit—though still that potential benefit would be dwarfed by the politics of war causation. Second, arms control theorists in quest of robustly crisis-stable or war-proofed military operating procedures have a distressing habit of forgetting that peril is an inherent characteristic of crisis. States do not wage crises for the purposes of avoiding war; rather they wage crises in defense of or to advance vital interests, and they hope to secure some minimum level of security satisfaction short of war. By definition, a crisis is a political condition wherein war is perceived either to be imminent or at least in sight. While statesmen and military planners certainly should seek to avoid both genuinely

[41]

accidental clashes of forces and military actions that positively beg to be misunderstood (e.g., precautionary alerting activity being mistaken as plain evidence of an intent to attack), one should not forget that military posturing, threatening gestures, even a measure of "brinkmanship," are endemic to acute international crises.

Third, arms control regimes that constrain military behavior are not likely to endure when they become very inconvenient. Arms control of the confidence-building genus concerning timely information transmission on military movements, deployment restrictions, and the like are all but certain to fall early victim to military expediency when the policy context alters for the worse. Finally, people who would erect arms control fences against allegedly crisis-unstable kinds of military behavior, have to recognize that the very existence and inevitable crisis-time fracturing of arms control–derived rules of benign military conduct actually would exacerbate an already tense situation. Overall, because war could be triggered by an accidental clash of arms, it is fitting that all available avenues, including arms control diplomacy, be explored to reduce the danger. However, states worry about this class of potential problem quite assiduously on a unilateral basis. It is not self-evident that crisis-stabilizing measures themselves would be crisis-proof. It happens to be a fact that none of the major wars of history—ancient, medieval, or modern—have been caused, in the sense of triggered, by behavior plausibly characterizable as accidental.

One hesitates to assert that weapons and the processes of competitive armament are not a factor in the political and strategic relationships which can become crisis slides to war. But unlike the authors of *Crisis Stability and Nuclear War*, the temptation should be resisted nominally to coopt opposing arguments and then neglect their implications. All things are possible, if not equally probable. It is possible that some arms control regime might have a modest net technical effect which would have massively immodest benign consequences for the prevention of war. History, common sense, and strategic logic, however, suggest the contrary.

Indeed, the case against arms control is so strong that the persistence of governments in its formal pursuit is difficult to explain

[42]

on rational grounds. Five negative points in particular command respect.

- The contribution of formal arms control processes to peace and security in the twentieth century has been either trivial or negative.[27]
- Arms control, being a variable dependent upon the political context, falls an early victim to a severe worsening of interstate relations.
- The claims, even most of the more modest claims (e.g., that arms control usefully enhances predictability), advanced in defense of an arms control process, are either readily falsifiable or distinctly arguable.
- Arms control, which entails a greater or lesser measure of technology prediction, typically has the effect for democracies of constraining the range of choice among possible solutions to problems that are left unaddressed or underaddressed.
- Finally, to come full circle, the signing of a bevy of arms control treaties and agreements in the 1990s is proof not of the wealth of the arms control instrument but rather of its poverty. Where were you when we needed you? By analogy, the arms control paradox is reminiscent of the banker's credit paradox: to secure a large loan one must first prove that one does not need it.

Despite brutal historical, conceptual, and statistical assaults over the past twenty years,[28] the arms race metaphor continues to decorate public debate and to be taken seriously by scholars who should know better. For many years a body of well-meaning but historically ill-equipped policy advocates argued that through suitable arms control measures the dynamics of the arms race could be interdicted. The action-reaction process that allegedly fueled the process of competitive armament could be halted or at least greatly retarded if a critical link in the simple and predictable

[27] Even Carnesale and Haass conclude that "what emerges above all is the modesty of what arms control has wrought. Expectations, for better or worse, for the most part have not been realized. . . . If the history reveals anything, it is that arms control has proved neither as promising as some had hoped nor as dangerous as others had feared." "Conclusions: Weighing the Evidence," in Carnesale and Haass, eds., *Superpower Arms Control*, p. 335.

[28] Albert Wohlstetter, *Legends of the Arms Race*, USSI Report 75-1 (Washington, D.C.: United States Strategic Institute, 1975); Fairbanks, "Arms Races"; Patrick Glynn, "The Sarajevo Fallacy: The Historical and Intellectual Origins of Arms Control Theology," *National Interest*, 9 (Fall 1987), 3–32.

causal chain could be removed. This elementary theory of employing arms control surgically to cure the arms race disease was deployed explicitly in aid of the campaign to halt the ABM program of the late 1960s and early 1970s.[29]

Without revisiting the merit or otherwise in the Sentinel and Safeguard ABM systems, the subsequent history of Soviet-American strategic relations demonstrated as plainly as a reasonable person could request that the dominant model of arms race dynamics much favored by the anti-ABM camp of circa 1967–72 was wrong. The ABM and associated arms control debate of the 1960s and early 1970s stirred some scholarly as well as obviously policy-motivated interest in the subject of arms races. It transpired, with no noteworthy dissenting voices from any side of the public policy debate, that people did not know what they were talking about when they referred casually to an arms race. Not only was there no consensus on a workable definition of the phenomenon, but it was not even clear that the metaphor of an arms race was anything more than a politically powerful concept. Even if there were such phenomena as arms races, which remains an open question, neither scholars nor public policy controversialists knew how they worked, if indeed they worked in any tolerably standard way at all. Following the distinctly ex post facto and exculpatory musings of the former British Foreign Secretary, Sir Edward Grey,[30] as well as registering what seemed to be common sense, many people have believed that somehow arms races *cause*

[29] George W. Rathjens, "The Dynamics of the Arms Race," *Scientific American*, 220 (April 1969), 15–25. Action-reaction theories are roughly handled in Colin S. Gray, *The Soviet-American Arms Race* (Lexington, Mass.: Lexington Books, 1976). Also see Barry Buzan, *An Introduction to Strategic Studies: Military Technology and International Relations* (New York: St. Martin's, 1987), part 2.

[30] Viscount Grey of Fallodon, *Twenty-Five Years, 1892–1916* (New York: Frederick A. Stokes, 1925). "The moral is obvious: it is that great armaments lead inevitably to war" (1:89). Also see 2:279–87. As Marc Trachtenberg suggests persuasively ("Coming of the First World War"), the quest for a robust peace settlement generated a powerful vested interest in the theory "that no one had really been responsible for it [the war]. The conflict could readily be blamed on great impersonal forces—on the alliance system, on the arms race and on the military systems that had evolved before 1914" (p. 97).

wars. Such study as there has been over the past decades, however, does not support this proposition.[31]

In principle, a process of competitive armament, whatever the
precise dynamics of interaction might be, should fuel political
anxieties that could prompt a more belligerent policy. In practice,
even the degree of fit between a fairly intense process of competitive armament and the outbreak of war is none too impressive, let
alone a fit between competitive armament and a *decision* for war.
To cite three examples: World War I did not occur because of the
competitions in land and naval armaments but rather because of
the Austrian wish to teach Serbia a very sharp lesson and the
German desire to change the status quo; World War II was caused
by the German determination to reverse the verdict of 1918; and
the Cold War was caused by the Soviet threat to the balance of
power in Europe and Asia.

There is quite widespread agreement today with the proposition that arms races are more a substitute for, than a cause of,
war—"almost a necessary surrogate for war," in Michael Howard's words.[32] In a powerful study published more than thirty
years ago, Samuel P. Huntington speculated that quantitative, in
contrast to qualitative, arms races, were prone to lead to war.[33] A
qualitative arms race is perpetually inconclusive: the military
instrument in question is always in the process of significant improvement, meaning that a much improved performance is promised for *tomorrow*. A quantitative race places a heavier burden on
society than does a qualitative one, to the point where the load
can become intolerable. In Huntington's view, the growing burden of competitive armament requires relief either by war or

[31] See George W. Downs, "Arms Races and War," in Philip E. Tetlock et al.,
eds., *Behavior, Society, and Nuclear War*, vol. 2 (New York: Oxford University Press,
1991), pp. 73–109. The state of the art in understanding the arms race–war relationship is captured nicely by Downs when he writes: "The low correlation between arms races and war . . . does not signify that arms races have no impact on
the probability of war, simply that they have a highly contingent impact" (p. 103).

[32] Howard, *Causes of Wars*, p. 21.

[33] Samuel P. Huntington, "Arms Races: Pre-Requisites and Results," in Carl J.
Friedrich and Seymour E. Harris, eds., *Public Policy, 1958* (Cambridge: Graduate
School of Public Administration, Harvard University, 1958), pp. 40–86.

agreement. Moreover, one side of a quantitative race is almost certain to win the competition and find itself armed with an instrument of prospective decision. This distinction is popular, but not particularly useful or historically well-supported. Notwithstanding its promise, it fails empirically to rescue even the much modified assertion that some kinds of arms races cause, or significantly contribute to, the outbreak of wars. There is little sense today in attempting to distinguish between a qualitative and a quantitative competition. Technological advance is a cultural fact and not merely a matter of periodic policy choice.

The notion that arms races *cause* wars rests upon a whole set of fallacies.

- Because wars are waged with weapons, the latter are presumed, in some mysterious but still significant fashion, to cause the former.
- Arms competition often precedes war; therefore, it seems self-evident that such competition *leads to war*.
- Mutually identified political foes do watch each others' defense preparations closely. Competitive military activity reinforces with military proof a threat postulate that originally may have been almost wholly political.
- An arms race, so the argument proceeds, is a distinctive phenomenon with a dynamic functioning that makes narrow military, but not necessarily policy, sense. References to the mad momentum of the arms race or similar descriptions convey the idea that the arms race system is running out of political control, driven by its own logic, rather than by any controlling policy.

Even the fallacies just cited fail to secure a grip on an explicit, historically researchable connection between an arms race and the outbreak of war. Both historians telling their unique stories and political scientists engaged in generalization are confounded by the sheer redundancy of candidate explanations of the causes of war. If the land and naval arms races were in some sense *causes* of World War I (and how could one demonstrate that they were not?), how do those races, as causes, relate to such other long-term or underlying possible causes as militarism; imperialism; nationalism; racism; social Darwinism; the alleged decay in the political structures of Imperial Austria-Hungary, Germany, and Russia; and the structure of countervailing alliances?[34] If one then proceeds to introduce or overlay the candidate near-term or immediate causes of war, a quest after the causes of World War I appears as quixotic as a search for the *real* reasons why Rome declined and fell, or endured so long. Plainly one should not neglect the love life of the Austro-Hungarian chief of the general staff (General Franz Conrad von Hötzendorf), the political division within the British cabinet on the necessity for aiding France in the field,[35] the implications and consequences of the Schlieffen-Moltke Plan, and a myriad of other immediate factors of some consequence in late July and early August 1914.

REVISIONIST STATES

Just as much of the recent theorizing about crisis stability is wont to forget what crises are about, so the theory of arms control is liable to neglect the fundamental subject of why states choose to compete in armaments.[36] One can only speculate about why the all-important subject of the urge to compete remains so neglected. Plausible candidate answers include the thoughts that (1) policy motives are soft, complex, and liable to change, which make them resistant to social-scientific enquiry; (2) many researchers are really interested in the possible mechanics of arms regulation (as a technically intriguing set of problems), not in the reasons why the arms exist in the first place; and (3) many arms control theorists

[34] See Samuel R. Williamson, Jr., "The Origins of World War I," in Rotberg and Rabb, eds., *Origins and Prevention of Major Wars*, pp. 225–48.

[35] Britain's liberal government faced domestic defeat unless it avoided the cabinet split that was threatened by Edward Grey's insistence that the country fully stand by France. See K. M. Wilson, "The British Cabinet's Decision for War, 2 August 1914," *British Journal of International Studies*, 1 (July 1975), 148–59. Also see Imanuel Geiss, ed., *July 1914, The Outbreak of the First World War: Selected Documents* (1965; rpt. New York: Charles Scribner's Sons, 1967); and Zara S. Steiner, *Britain and the Origins of the First World War* (London: Macmillan, 1977).

[36] See Colin S. Gray, "The Urge to Compete: Rationales for Arms Racing," *World Politics*, 26 (January 1974), 207–33; and Barry Buzan, *Introduction to Strategic Studies*, pp. 90–93.

and even a fair number of would-be practitioners do not feel the need to revisit a topic upon which they already have deeply settled beliefs. After the fashion of a classic British mystery story, the culture of arms control encourages the view that the equivalent of the butler is the arms race, merchants of death, the military-industrial complex, offensive military doctrines, "destabilizing" weapons, and so forth.

Leaving aside the difficult and easily misleading issue of arms as bargaining chips, two important truths about competitive armaments need to be accorded their full due. First, as a general rule, states do not acquire arms for the purposes of facilitating an arms control process. States may acquire arms to forward the objectives of arms control, but that is quite a different matter. Second, no state wants *its* arms to be controlled through a process of interstate regulation. After all, except economically, the problem is not *my* armament, it is *your* armament!

In an era of good feeling it may appear Neanderthalic to remind people that armaments have security functions which transcend their roles as players in arms-control theater, or perhaps simply as currency in the transactions that occur. President Bush has performed his rhetorical duty in affirming that "arms control is a means, not an end; it is an important component of a broader policy to enhance national security."[37] But only the historical record of the 1990s will tell whether these admirable words are anything more than dutiful rhetoric. If the past is any guide, there are solid grounds for skepticism.

A number of states in this century have sought to employ arms control as a powerful and expedient diplomatic process for national security ends a light-year removed from the character of the magic kingdom envisaged by modern American arms controllers. There is absolutely no doubt that the founding tyrant of the evil empire of the USSR, V. I. Lenin, had nothing but contempt for the "bourgeois pacifists" who took the idea of disarmament seriously. As a matter of tactical expediency the USSR was always

---

[37] George Bush, *National Security Strategy of the United States* (Washington, D.C.: White House, March 1990), p. 15.

willing to outbid political rivals in its rhetorical commitment to peace through disarmament and, more recently, arms control. As a bid for foreign popular approval and as a diplomatic instrument to inhibit the military preparation of materially better endowed potential enemies, Moscow was never confused over the fact that arms control was but one instrument of its grand strategy. Idealistic or sentimental attachment to notions of disarmament and arms control was a distinctively Western affliction. The Soviet Union that in 1990–91 could inflict widespread food shortages upon its citizens in noticeable part because the railroads were tied up transfering military equipment out of CFE-accountable territory, remained a Soviet Union only uncertainly attached to the culture of arms control.[38]

Some of the more unsavory polities of this century have signed on to participate in arms control regimes. As an interesting hypothesis, at least, one can suggest that, whatever it was about arms control that attracted them, such tyrannies as the Japan of the early 1930s, fascist Italy, Hitler's Germany, and the Soviet Union of recent decades shared little intellectual common ground with the ideas of Western arms control theorists. This is not, at least not quite, to suggest that these states named were bent upon villainy through arms control but rather that such a notion falls far short of being outrageous. After all, it is precisely because rogue states are roguish that their accession to arms control regimes renders such regimes important. If it is only the sheep who regulate their defenses by formal agreement, little will be achieved for farmland security.

---

[38] By the close of 1990 as many as 70,000 treaty-limited items of military equipment reportedly had been transported beyond the Urals. Strictly, most of this was quite legal. It had the effect, however, of negating a notable fraction of the strategic value of the CFE treaty to the non-Soviet signatories. See (Anonymous), "The CFE Treaty: Missed Opportunity?" *Global Affairs*, 6 (Summer 1991), 1–23. The political dissolution of the Soviet Union in 1991, subsequent to the signing of CFE, underlines with unusual clarity the impracticality of arms control. Just what is the political order that CFE should support? Indeed, whose armed forces in the East are to be reduced? An answer to the latter question certainly will emerge in due course, but the fact that it needs to be posed should encourage second thoughts on the part of those who seek to use arms control to engineer political outcomes.

By and large, it has only been Western arms control theorists who regarded new weapon systems as arms control fodder. Most statesmen and defense planners, and even a few high officials, tend to regard the arms control process and resulting agreements as necessary evils. Necessary because it is believed or hoped that foreign armament of great concern can be regulated usefully through arms control; evil because the price that must be paid for the attempted control of others' arms is the acceptance of control over one's own arms. The great U.S. debate over the Strategic Defense Initiative (SDI), and hence over the ABM treaty in the 1980s, was conducted very much in the shadow of the principle of "two powers [licensed to deploy extensive missile defenses] or none."[39] The policy question did not bear simply upon the attractiveness to the United States of new *U.S.* missile defense deployments. The question also had the inescapable dimension of the new or additional Soviet missile defenses which a serious U.S. move toward SDI deployment must legitimize.

It is modish even in Moscow now to recognize what has been called the security dilemma.[40] The dilemma postulates that my search for increased security can lead to increased insecurity for others. That insecurity felt abroad will tend to trigger prudent policy responses which must work, in due course, to fuel new insecurity for me. The anticipation of future insecurity promotes the preemptive urges that can find expression in the "prisoner's dilemma" of game theory, and allegedly it is the crazily rational policy thinking behind an arms race spiral.

In theory and even in practice, as the Soviet experience of the 1970s and 1980s attested, there is much worth saying in praise of recognition of the security dilemma. The policies pursued by Leonid Brezhnev's USSR fueled so great a feeling of insecurity in the United States at the beginning of the 1980s that the Reagan administration directed (loosely speaking) a quantity and quality of political-military response such that Moscow plainly could pre-

[39] See Albert Carnesale, "Reviving the ABM Debate," *Arms Control Today*, 11 (April 1981), p. 8.
[40] See Robert Jervis, "Cooperation under the Security Dilemma," *World Politics*, 30 (January 1979), 167–214.

dict a growing inferiority as its certain future.[41] At some point in the mid- to late 1970s, the Soviet Union proceeded beyond its culminating point of victory in search of influence abroad through the support of local clients and by competitive armament. The current turmoil in the former Soviet Union and in its military doctrine relates directly to the strains of a broad-fronted superpower competition that Moscow unwittingly kicked into a higher gear at the turn of the last decade (1979–80). The problems the Soviet commitment to offensive counterforce programs were giving the United States in the early 1980s, led President Reagan to the rediscovery and relegitimization of ballistic missile defense. U.S. domestic politics, fed in part by the kind of arms control ideology criticized in this book, would blunt SDI of much near-term competitive leverage, but SDI had alarming long-term and broad-fronted implications for Soviet security.[42] Russian President Boris

[41] In the 1980 U.S. presidential election, both candidates ran against the USSR. Ronald Reagan's promises to wage the Cold War tenaciously were more credible than were Jimmy Carter's. As with the emergence of the Third Reich from the ashes of Weimar Germany in 1933, so the collapse of the extended Soviet imperium in 1989 and then the dual demise of the USSR itself and even of the Russian empire in 1991 is so much easier to comprehend with hindsight than it was to anticipate with wise foresight. Great empires tend not to expire for a single reason. It could be a mistake, however, to succumb too readily to the current fashion in belief and uncritically endorse the notion that the Soviet Union was so rotten at the core that the slide to catastrophe of the late 1980s and very early 1990s truly was inevitable and hence irresistible. U.S. statecraft and Mikhail Gorbachev's errors in judgment played major roles in the Soviet, and Russian, collapse of empire.

[42] Senior U.S. officials repeatedly issued reassuring words such as (variants upon) the following: "in pursuing SDI, we do not seek superiority, but to maintain the strategic balance and place deterrence on a more stable basis." Prepared statement of Paul Wolfowitz, Under Secretary of Defense (Policy), in U.S. Congress, Senate Committee on Armed Services, *Department of Defense Authorization for Appropriations for Fiscal Years 1990 and 1991, Hearings, Part 6, Strategic Forces and Nuclear Deterrence*, 101st Cong., 1st sess. (Washington, D.C.: Government Printing Office, 1989), p. 492. Soviet officials could not believe that their American counterparts purposely would eschew strategic advantage. The SDI threatened to accelerate Western development of whole families of military-relevant technologies. Indeed, the SDI has helped fuel the advance of a new revolution in military affairs. Strategically, even modestly proficient, multilayered (and preferential) U.S. ballistic missile defenses (BMD) could raise the entry price dramatically for a technically and tactically reliable Soviet response to controlled and limited first nuclear use by the United States. Even distinctly imperfect strategic defenses enhance the

Yeltsin's announcement in January 1992 that Russia and the United States should "jointly devise a global system for protection from space," while—strangely—abiding by the terms of the ABM treaty, tells us a great deal about the changing political climate but not very much about the benefits of arms control. If anything, sensible and long overdue amendment of the ABM treaty in favor of a GPALS (global protection against limited strikes) system would amount to the conclusion that the best way to control the missiles of regional powers is to render them militarily ineffective.

Strategic and other kinds of theory always require assessment in concrete historical and geopolitical terms. The security dilemma is a general truth; *my* security can translate into *your* insecurity, and so forth. It is also a general truth that statesmen and defense planners are obliged ultimately to tend the garden of national, not international, security. Following the better part of three centuries of territorially predatory behavior, Americans in most of this century generally have been resolutely, smugly, and even arrogantly sophisticated in their obeisance to the cautionary tale that can be read in the security dilemma.[43] However, there have been and are polities much less wise than the contemporary United States. That is to say, in this context, that they did not orchestrate a national history of continental empire building against typically slight opposition, defensible by oceanic distance. These unwise

---

credibility of the U.S. nuclear guarantee of the security of distant friends and allies. The SDI has been restructured to provide global protection against limited strikes (GPALS). See Keith B. Payne, *Missile Defense in the 21st Century: Protection against Limited Threats, Including Lessons from the Gulf War* (Boulder, Colo.: Westview, 1991), and Charles L. Glaser, *Analyzing Strategic Nuclear Policy* (Princeton: Princeton University Press, 1990), for statements of the cases respectively for and against ballistic missile defenses. Glaser's book predated the formal shift of focus for the SDI from the Soviet threat to accidental or third-party missile perils.

[43] The uninvited European immigrants to the North American continent in the seventeenth and eighteenth centuries found a land relatively (relative to Europe) empty of people but which most emphatically was not uninhabited. Americans wont to wallow in their ideology of freedom should not forget that their ancestors *took* much of their country the old-fashioned way, by fire, sword, gunpowder, pestilence, bribery, and trickery. What was done was not uniquely wicked by historical standards; indeed, in retrospect the taming of the moving frontier from the Appalachians to the Pacific coast had more the appearance of the action of a force of nature than a protracted crime against native peoples.

polities, atavistically perhaps, either do not care about the insecurity of others or believe that that insecurity cannot fuel effective countervailing policies.

As a practical matter, the general truth of the security dilemma does not operate as by a hidden hand to render all competitive armament necessarily futile. Arms races, crises, wars, and even arms control negotiations, can be won (and of course, lost). Under the terms of SALT II, for example, the Soviet Union was not required to count its Backfire bombers against the delivery vehicle ceiling, these allegedly not being heavy bombers, whereas antique and terminally nonoperational B-52s were held to be SALT-accountable. SALT II counted some B-52 wrecks and failed to count Backfires which, with aerial refueling, could attack North America. More significant was the 5 : 5 : 3 ratio established at the Washington Conference (1921–22) for capital ship standard displacement as among the United States, Britain, and Japan. Japan won the negotiations in Washington because 5 : 5 : 3, in operational and strategic fact, yielded to her a clear superiority over the U.S. or the Royal Navy in the western Pacific. The nonfortification clause of the Washington treaty denied Britain and the United States the ability to develop naval bases within 3000 miles of Japan. Whatever Britain's Royal Navy pretended to the contrary for reasons of public dignity, the 5 : 5 : 3 ratio which translated into Japanese superiority where it mattered, also translated into U.S. naval superiority over Britain because of the contrasting geostrategic terms of operation for U.S. and British naval power.[44] The Washington force ratios certainly provided a robust mutual security for the high contracting great powers at home. Unfortunately for international order, however, security against invasion by treaty partners was not the key problem for the period. Instead, the Western powers needed to be able to extend deterrence to protect China from Japanese imperialism. The arms limitation treaties denied the United States and Britain that margin of naval superiority necessary to face down, or defeat, Japan in the western Pacific. The kind of stability enhanced by the Washington

[44] See Christopher Hall, *Britain, America, and Arms Control, 1921–37* (New York: St. Martin's, 1987), pp. 198, 202.

system was not conducive to international security. Reasoning on arms limitation was divorced from consideration of regional security in east Asia.

Statesmen compete in arms, foment crises, and wage wars for their vision of security, no matter how pernicious or sensible that vision may seem in retrospect to others. For example, on 17 February 1800, British Prime Minister William Pitt (the Younger) was challenged to define the real object of the war with France and "in one sentence to state, if he can, without his *ifs* and *buts* and special pleading ambiguity what this object is." Pitt replied, "I know not whether I can do it in one sentence; but in one word I can tell him that it is *security*: security against a danger, the greatest that ever threatened the world. It is security against a danger which never existed in any past period of society. It is security against a danger which in degree and extent was never equalled; against a danger which threatened all the nations of the earth.[45]

Most of the states historically key to the prospects for general peace sought energetically to secure unilateral strategic advantage. This is not to deny the general proposition that cooperation as well as competition can generate security. It is, however, to underline the point that states committed by high policy to the alteration of the geopolitical status quo, tend to be less than overwhelmingly attracted to the potential blessings which could be conferred by an arms control process. It would be difficult to exaggerate the importance of this axiom penned by Christopher Hall: "Limitation by agreement first requires a desire for limitation. Such a desire was singularly lacking in most powers in 1935–36 [or 1981–82, and so forth]."[46] Had Hall proceeded to apply the logic of the arms control paradox, he could have made his point more forcefully still. When the will to limit arms is available in abundance, such limitation is unlikely to be significant for the conditions for peace. But Hall recognizes that "naval limitation may indeed have contributed to the harmonious international cli-

---

[45] *The War Speeches of William Pitt the Younger* (Oxford: Clarendon Press, 1915), pp. 284–85.

[46] Hall, *Britain, America and Arms Control, 1921–37*, p. 191.

mate of the 1920s. It could do nothing for the problems of the 1930s."[47] When arms control was needed it could not work.

In conditions of international hostility, which really are the only conditions of interest to the arms control theorist or practitioner, the state players will be interested in military gain. They will compete with a view to their being likely to win in arms rivalry, crisis, and war. To most statesmen at most times, although the prospective benefits of the limited cooperation that is arms control will not be wholly unattractive, those benefits pale to insignificance when compared with the rewards of a military advantage earned of necessity by competitive effort. The urge to compete for national advantage does not preclude arms control as a tool of grand strategy. Italy, Japan and Germany in the 1920s and 1930s, and the Soviet Union since 1945 have all illustrated the point that predatory regimes, bent upon the radical revision of their national security circumstances, can find value in, among other things, the cover of respectability provided by a formal arms control framework. The objectively revisionist policy goals of a state or states do not preclude what can appear to be the successful practice of arms control diplomacy—witness the Washington and London treaty system of 1922–38, the Anglo-German Naval Agreement (AGNA) of 1935, and SALT I of 1972. It is even possible that some very modest benefit to international security will accrue as a result of arms control diplomacy. But there is next to no prospect that an international political system containing polities very deeply dissatisfied with their security lot, can provide substantial bulwarks against the outbreak of war via an arms control process. Arms control registers political facts, it does not change them.[48]

If the world was not troubled by states governed by regimes with revisionist policy goals, then there would be little need for arms control. Whenever and wherever one looks, historically and geopolitically, there is a revisionist state or two. There will be periods, even long periods, when the leading would-be revision-

[47] Ibid., p. 203.

[48] See Henry Kissinger's testimony on this point in U.S. Congress, Senate Committee on Foreign Relations, *The SALT II Treaty, Hearings, Part 3*, 96th Cong., 1st sess. (Washington, D.C.: Government Printing Office, 1979), p. 166.

ist of the era has no choice but to misbehave discretely (e.g., Weimar Germany vis-à-vis the disarmament and arms control provisions of the Versailles treaty of 1919).[49] But when the ideas and the practice of arms control are handed a direct and major challenge by a determined revisionist state, such as the World Disarmament Conference by Germany in 1933 and the Washington-London (naval) treaty system in 1934 by Japan, arms control *inevitably and invariably* must fail.

For a more recent case, the strategic arms control process between the superpowers, now more than two decades old, comprehensively has failed to forward the goals of arms control. SALT and START I have not controlled and will not control what the U.S. government has sought to control in pursuit of some facsimile of the still dominant Western theory of crisis stability. From 1969 to the end of the Cold War the process of strategic arms control negotiation was not able to inhibit the Soviet (and also the U.S.) quest for war-fighting advantage. The extensive degree to which Soviet nuclear strategy was not matched with a fully competent tactical and operational military instrument is not plausibly attributable to benign interdiction by arms control.

Arms control should be assayed only with reference to admittedly hard cases. There should be little interest in the one-foot putt. Virtually every state would like to see some revision of the terms of its national security. Obviously, that is not what is meant by a revisionist state. A tight definition would risk being overly exclusive. Nonetheless, a revisionist state is one whose general line in statecraft is intended *radically* to alter the terms of national security in its favor. Those terms may alter as a result more of the course of events than of purposive national statecraft, an outcome that will trigger, or reinforce, old as well as some new hostile sentiments abroad. The rise of the United States to superpower status and, by default, to a global guardianship role, is a leading case in point. Whatever the preferred definition, revisionist states on any reasonable understanding have rarely been in short sup-

[49] But see Michael Geyer, "The Dynamics of Military Revisionism in the Interwar Years: Military Politics between Rearmament and Diplomacy," in Wilhelm Deist, ed., *The German Military in the Age of Total War* (Dover, N.H.: Berg Publishers, 1985), pp. 100–151.

ply in the history of international politics. The phenomenon of the revisionist state is not just a limiting factor for the prospects for arms control; instead, it is a fatal challenge. The intensity of political commitment to change, or resist change in, the distribution of power translates into states willing to praise, and even participate in, the arms control process, provided that process is believed to function to net competitive advantage.

If arms control cannot help prevent or contain the damage to international security that can be caused by an Imperial or Nazi Germany, an Imperial Japan, the former USSR, or a contemporary Syria, Libya, Iran, or Iraq—the regimes whose policies provide the most dangerous fuel for interstate conflict—then what help can it offer? Just as the policies of revisionist states are the leading cause of war, so those policies and the countervailing policies they trigger abroad are the leading reason why arms control is Mission Impossible.

STABILITY: A CONCEPT WITH MANY FACES

It is easier to agree on the general merit of stability than it is to secure agreement on the meaning and real-world implications of this slippery concept. The desirability of stability is rarely in question, rather its virtue is a truth by definition. In its several incarnations, stability refers to a condition wherein war is prevented from occurring or escalating. In the context-free and bloodless world of abstract strategic theory, the prevention of war and the control of escalation are necessarily praiseworthy outcomes to processes of conflict.[50] The broad purpose here is not to subject the concept of stability to rigorous philosophical examination but rather to explore its practical utility as a key to the design of policies, programs, and procedures intended to help generate peace with security. A narrower purpose is to comment on the uses

---

[50] The strategic literature, which is prone to analyze the requirements of deterrence at the expense of considering what would need to be done should deterrence fail, also is prone to forget that the prevention of war cannot be an overriding goal of policy. Countries seek peace with security, not just peace. Victim societies can achieve peace of a sort, if they decline to resist aggression.

[57]

made of the concept of stability to promote what would amount to a technological, or perhaps a defense-analytical, peace.[51] Although a belief in stability would be required as the principal item in an arms controller's creed, it is remarkable how little careful philosophical or empirical examination the concept has attracted. The explanations are probably that: (1) busy policy-minded people do not have time for apparently idle thought; (2) the merit in stability is held to be so obvious that it does not require study; (3) since everyone appears to agree that stability is a, even *the*, master concept, why debate the subject; and (4) while even a modest level of enquiry serves rapidly to reveal that further conceptual work raises unwelcome questions about assumptions and evidence. Therefore, the concept of stability remains overemployed and little comprehended.

Stability comes in at least four distinctive varieties in the strategic and arms control literature.[52]

- *Crisis stability* refers to the likelihood that an acute political conflict will explode into war even though both sides would prefer to remain at peace. Some theorists like to distinguish between crisis stability and *first-strike stability*, with the latter referring rigorously to a context wherein the strategic forces of neither party are vulnerable to preemp-

[51] This point is illuminated perfectly by Henry Kissinger when, commenting upon the problems of political authority and democracy in the former Soviet Union, he writes that "the key issue is not whether nuclear weapons are under central control—which they seem to be—but whether the military structure in Moscow that controls them is subject to responsible political leadership. "Russian Minefield," *Washington Post*, 17 September 1991, p. A19. True to form, the abortive left-wing coup (not right-wing, as the American media sought to insist) in Moscow in 1991 encouraged the U.S. arms control community to parade its standard litany of technical and administrative fixes for the political problem of the security of the former Soviet nuclear arsenal. Adhering to their very nature—a point familiar to students of animal behavior—arms control advocates respond to each bend in the road of the unfolding of current history with arms control solutions to the challenge of the hour. In addition to the Soviet case just cited, it is interesting to observe both liberal- and conservative-minded arms controllers rising to the challenge of regional security in the post–Gulf War Middle East. Apolitical ideas on the control of the arms trade which have seventy years of failure behind them are paraded yet again.
[52] For an earlier reconnaissance in force into this particular conceptual swamp, see Colin S. Gray, *Nuclear Strategy and National Style* (Lanham, Md.: Hamilton Press, 1986), chap. 5.

ive destruction.[53] This distinction leaves crisis-stable conditions as meaning a situation wherein the military balance cannot be shifted by a preemptive strike. This distinction is not particularly enlightening or useful and therefore is not employed here.

- *Arms race stability* refers to the rate of change in competitive armaments and to the strength of the incentives discerned by each "racing" party to introduce new, or more, armaments.[54]
- *Weapon-system stability* is the claim that particular types of weapon systems (e.g., MIRVed ICBMs and ASATs) have detectable, even calculable, qualities and quantities of stability or instability inherent in their technical nature.
- *Political stability* is recognized as the intensity of incentive to fight in particular international relationships. This nominally master form of stability frequently is treated as though it were a variable, in uncertain though important measure dependent upon the emerging military-technical context.

Crisis stability and political stability overlap but are not synonymous. Indeed, the relationships among all four categories give each of them some of their specific meaning. Recall the earlier statement that the central question is whether the control of weapons can contribute usefully to the control of the outbreak of war. In operational form, that question may be presented in the following manner: *if* stability is the key quality for the control of war (its outbreak or conduct), wherein does it lie? Philosophical answers are not very helpful. Of course, crisis stability is generally desirable, but how is it to be secured?

War is such an uncertain realm that political will is invariably more important than the various ways in which the military balance could be calculated. Policymakers, not the military balance as a factor on its own, decide upon war or peace.[55] Victory is

---

[53] For example, Walter B. Slocombe, "Strategic Stability in a Restructured World," *Survival*, 32 (July–August 1990), pp. 304–6.

[54] Arms race stability is a term that is at least 3½ decades old, but—for the overall hypothesis—what can be meant by a stable arms race? The idea of stability in arms racing challenges any reasonable definition of an arms race. Colin S. Gray, "The Arms Race Phenomenon," *World Politics*, 24 (October 1971), particularly p. 41.

[55] For an example of thoroughly misguided analysis, see Dean Wilkening et al., *Strategic Defenses and Crisis Stability*, N-2511-AF (Santa Monica, Calif.: Rand Corporation, April 1989). The authors explain that "this analysis assumes that one of the

rarely truly assured, and obviously even less so in the nuclear age than in previous military-technical eras. The arms control community is certainly right in principle to seek to ensure that the intended military engine of deterrence does not function inadvertently as the engine for war. The arms control literature provides stern warnings against the perils of provocation that can lurk underrecognized in alert procedures, for example. Because of the scale of evil consequences that could flow from error, it is probably sensible to pay more attention to the speculations of technically minded stability analysts than to what one really believes they warrant.

An important point in the arms control literature on crisis stability bears upon the speed with which war could be fought today, the allegedly unprecedented advantage which surprise assault could convey in the nuclear missile age and, hence, supposedly the uniquely perilous potential of reciprocal fears of attack. The logic of this point is as dubious as is its purported historical support. There is no question that a great war could be launched, conducted, and completed at a pace not even remotely approached in all of history to date. But it so happens that fears of surprise attack were a hardy perennial in British contemplation of its French problems for more than two centuries and that an initial lead in mobilization in 1914 was expected to yield noteworthy advantage. Also, fear of a surprise knock-out blow from the air was a familiar feature of British defense debate in the 1930s.[56] Of course, the nuclear age is different in absolute terms, but it would

---

most important determinants of crisis stability is the correlation of nuclear forces." They proceed to note that "many other exogenous factors influence crisis stability, for example, the political climate and diplomatic skills relating to crisis management, not to mention idiosyncratic factors having to do with the political and military leadership" (p. 1). Notably lacking is any recognition of the importance of what the crisis is about. What are the policies of the participants, and how attached are they to them? Narrow defense analysis along the all too familiar lines of this report is really worthless, or worse: it actually impedes understanding à la Gresham's law—poor analysis can drive out useful analysis.

[56] See the essay, "The Bolt from the Blue," in John Gooch, *The Prospect of War: Studies in British Defence Policy, 1847–1942* (London: Frank Cass, 1981), chap. 1; and John Terraine, *A Time for Courage: The Royal Air Force in the European War, 1939–1945* (New York: Macmillan, 1985), chap. 6, "The Knock-Out Blow."

show little respect for history to argue that only in the nuclear age has crisis stability loomed as a topic pregnant with implications of winning or losing a war.

With respect to the claim that structural and operational arms control measures might play a critical role as safety engineering for military machines that otherwise could detonate too expeditiously, a friendly skepticism is in order. Sensible though this aspect to crisis stability theory can appear, on close examination it reveals the characteristic errors of arms control reasoning. The speed with which war machines can initiate and conduct an opening, perhaps the only, campaign, is very much a function of the political context. Given a protracted acute political crisis, even two antagonistic reserve-dependent military machines will be ready to fight on next to no notice. The argument that peace is threatened by armed forces which would wage war too rapidly founders in its alleged significance both on the general truth that what passes for progress cannot be repealed and on the familiar point that politics cannot be neutralized by administrative or technical subversion. The problem lies with politics, not with weapons. It can be difficult to break into the mental universe of the arms controller and make the point that states acquire and operate military capabilities primarily for serious reasons of defense. Governments are at least as concerned to ensure that weapons will work when ordered, as to insure against the outpacing of policy by military events. States willing to allow safety engineering to affect such military qualities as speed and economy in communications, and speed in weapons execution, accuracy, and lethality in action do not need arms control at all.

In its military-technical guise, the concept of crisis stability is both an oxymoron and a strategic fiction. Of course, military power is important in time of crisis and even more so in war, but that is not to concede merit to the concept of crisis stability. Perceptions, even attempted calculations, of net military prowess can function by general and by immediate deterrence to help shape decisions of high policy.[57] So much is but common sense to recog-

[57] See Patrick Morgan, *Deterrence: A Conceptual Analysis* (Beverly Hills, Calif.: Sage Publications, 1977), chap. 2.

nize. A leap of analytical faith must occur, however, if one is to proceed much beyond recognition that the military currency of grand strategy is salient to political choice, to claims for the significance of allegedly crisis-stable or unstable forces. Crisis stability takes one into the historically unpopulated realm of political conflicts which explode into actual war even though both sides would prefer to remain at peace.

Robert Jervis has attempted the most sophisticated and reasonable rescue thus far of the arms controller's concept of crisis stability. He approaches plausibility, while the practical implications of his view are not very dissimilar from those developed here. Jervis advises that "crisis instability can interact with political conflict," and he suggests that "arms controllers never suggested that the former in the absence of the latter would yield war."[58] His argument suffers from a fundamental existential difficulty ("crisis instability can . . . ") and creates, or arguably takes note of, a huge eminently challengeable escape hatch for those arms control theorists much less careful in their analysis over the years than he. Jervis acknowledges that "there is much validity to the old Soviet criticism of American arms control as preoccupied with the military causes of war at the expense of considering the broader relations between the two countries."[59] Arms control theory is not beyond defense. The point is that that defense falls short of being persuasive. Jervis has done his best with a poor case.

Before assaulting the fraternal concepts of crisis, arms race, and weapon-system stability more directly still, it is important to revisit the question of evidence. Although history comprises the only real evidence available concerning strategic behavior, each case is unique and the differences among cases may be at least as significant as the similarities. Having said that, it is worth noting that weapons, their control or lack thereof, have played no more than a supporting role in all of the slides to war of modern times.

[58] Robert Jervis, "Arms Control, Stability, and Causes of War," *Daedalus*, 120 (Winter 1991), p. 178.
[59] Ibid.

- *The Cold War* was about the respective domains of superpower political influence in an essentially bipolar system.
- *World War II* was about the renewed German bid for continental hegemony in Europe.
- *World War I* was about both Austria-Hungary's survival and standing as a great power, and Imperial Germany's (defensively or offensively motivated, no matter) bid for continental hegemony.
- *The Wars of the French Revolution and Empire* were about the French bid for continental hegemony (to cite a case which precedes industrial-age conditions, at least in continental Europe).

If one includes the more restricted conflicts of the past two centuries (the Crimean War, the American Civil War, the Wars of German Unification, the Sino-Japanese War, the Russo-Japanese War, and so forth up to the present day), it becomes even more evident that Charles S. Maier is correct when, although referring specifically to 1914, he affirms, "The irreducible primacy of political determinants of war [is] political in the assessment of the respective threats to security . . . and political in the failure of mediation."[60]

The historical argument for the importance of a military posture designed so as not to promote an undesired war outcome to an acute crisis, in practice reduces to the 1914 case and to speculation about a World War III. The 1914 case tells us what we know already. Acute international crises, particularly very complex international crises, can lead to war. The military postures and plans of the great powers in the crisis of 1914, especially in the German regard, arguably inhibited freedom of political choice at a critical moment.[61] But it is not plausible to argue that the military strate-

[60] Charles S. Maier, "Wargames: 1914–1919," in Rotberg and Rabb, eds., *Origin and Prevention of Major Wars*, p. 263.

[61] It should not be forgotten that although the pace of events was very rapid in the final days of the 1914 crisis, and particularly on July 29–30, the principal players behaved with great deliberation for nearly a month between the assassination on 28 June and the delivery of the Austro-Hungarian ultimatum on 23 July. Austria-Hungary and Germany, and even Serbia, Russia, and France, had ample time in which to shape and reshape their policies in a distinctly purposive manner. By far the most persuasive analysis to date is Trachtenberg, "Coming of the First World War."

gies, let alone the military tactics or weapons, of the great powers in some critical sense *caused* the war in 1914.[62] It may seem as if the Schlieffen-Moltke Plan turned what was about to be the Third Balkan War into a general war, but really it was the rival alliance systems which, *by 1914*, mandated, if anything did, that a war would not be localized.[63] The alliance systems, let it be noted, were expressions of the most careful political calculation.

What was destabilizing about German armaments in 1914 and again in 1938–39 was not anything to do with their technical characteristics, for example, the relationships between tactical and operational offense and defense directed, respectively, by timetables of railroad mobilization as far as the enemy's frontier and by the operational, but not strategic, concept of blitzkrieg. Rather the problem for stability was the fact that those armaments were German. German and, in 1914, Austro-Hungarian policy was the leading problem for European security, not the weaponry or fashion in offensive military doctrines. This is not to endorse Fritz Fischer's exaggerated claim for Germany's war guilt.[64] In the final analysis at the end of July 1914, Germany was content to allow the war to occur, but she had not set out to wage an "aggressive war."

Historically speaking, the conceptual emperor of a technically oriented stability has no clothes. The idea of arms race instability lends itself to ready dismissal. Not only is there a conceptual and historical missing link between arms races and wars, but also it can be argued plausibly that arms competitions help defer, or even substitute for, wars, and can function to promote an instability healthy for peace and security. In support of the last point one could cite the current time of troubles in the former Soviet Union. Against the backdrop of an unexpected resurgence of

[62] The thesis of Jack Snyder in "Civil-Military Relations and the Cult of the Offensive, 1914–1984," *International Security*, 9 (Summer 1984), 108–46; and *The Ideology of the Offensive: Military Decision Making and the Disasters of 1914* (Ithaca: Cornell University Press, 1984).

[63] Scott D. Sagan, "1914 Revisited: Allies, Offense, and Instability," *International Security*, 11 (Fall 1986), 151–75, overstates a good case.

[64] Fritz Fischer: *Germany's Aims in the First World War* (1961; rpt. New York: W. W. Norton, 1967); and *War of Illusions: German Policies from 1911 to 1914* (1969; rpt. New York: W. W. Norton, 1975).

American military competitive effort, Soviet military doctrine in the early 1980s anticipated a new "revolution in military affairs." The traditional Soviet Union could not compete in knowledge-based weapons for information-age warfare.

In order to register a Soviet claim to continued recognition as a superpower, Mikhail Gorbachev was obliged to abandon literally whatever needed to be abandoned (including the divine right to rule of the CPSU) if *perestroika* was to stand any prospect at all of success. The events of 1991 were to show that the USSR could not be reformed and that *perestroika* was envisaged for a terminally sick system. Wherever the untrackable truth may lie precisely, there can be little doubt that the massive U.S. increase in military investment in the early 1980s helped considerably to spur Soviet recognition that their traditional way of doing business would lead inexorably to defeat in the new information age. An impending arms race *instability* contributed most usefully to the basis for a growing political stability in superpower relations.

It may be that "the dynamics of mutual alarm,"[65] precautionary alert procedures, mobilization steps, and the like could provoke rather than help deter war. To recall Nye's "crystal-ball effect," however, certain knowledge of just how catastrophic a nuclear war could be has functioned as a self-negating prophecy. It is appropriate that the probably very small, but nonetheless possible, danger of inadvertent, or genuinely accidental, war should be minimized to the uncertain degree possible by purposive official action. But the prudent if minor anxiety that a military posture itself might unintentionally detonate a war should not be expanded into the rococo intellectual edifice which is the contemporary theory of crisis stability. The argument advanced here can be reduced to a caricature by those so disposed. My thesis is not invalidated by the possibility that truly heedless military behavior in time of crisis could persuade the adversary, incorrectly, that war was certain—triggering as a result a desperate preemptive strike. It is difficult to develop a theory fully proof against refutation by folly on the truly grand scale. In recognition of the distant

[65] Thomas C. Schelling, *Arms and Influence* (New Haven: Yale University Press, 1966), chap. 6.

possibility of such folly, I endorse the idea that military forces should be operated very carefully in times of crisis. That is not a theoretical concession; it is simply a step toward fault-tolerance in argument.

Caricatures aside, particular military postures, doctrines, and types of weapons inherently are neither stabilizing nor destabilizing. What makes for stability or instability is the policy intention of the political owner of the posture, doctrine, and weapons in question. Crisis stability, in common with its stablemate, arms race theory—indeed, in common with the still dominant school of thought on arms control—would replace policy choice and political values with a reductionist approach to security approximating astrategic administration. In worst Jominian style,[66] universal truths of stability are applied as technical surgery to cure the war-causing disease of competitive armament or menacing crisis posturing. This view of the world has a list of villainous destabilizing weapons: that is to say, accurate weapons, weapons that could not ride out an attack, and weapons rapid in mission execution. In this world where a yardstick of stability can be applied to assay any weapon, deployment mode, or operating practice, the political character and policy purposes of states can be rendered all but irrelevant. No matter that a tank battalion or system of fortification is French or German, that a MIRVed mobile ICBM is American or Russian. If weapons or military postures make for war, there is no need to muddy the waters with political value judgments.

The principal problem for security in Europe since 1945 has not been Soviet arms; rather it has been the policy behind those arms. Military strength of any and every kind on the Western side has been a force for stability because that Western side sought only to protect the existing order. As some Russian leaders now admit, explicitly or implicitly, it was the evil empire of the USSR that menaced stability in Europe. The idea that an arms control proc-

---

[66] Baron Antoine Henri de Jomini, who in his voluminous writings on the Napoleonic art of war sought to distill the essence of that art for general application. See John Shy, "Jomini," in Peter Paret, ed., *Makers of Modern Strategy from Machiavelli to the Nuclear Age* (Princeton: Princeton University Press, 1986), pp. 183–85.

ess could contribute usefully to the cause of peace by "placing constraints on new technologies that threaten stability"[67] expresses either a thorough misunderstanding of the nature of stability and the causes of wars, or comprises a desperate and failing bid to assert some vitality in a technological approach to peace discredited by events and analysis.

Claims, for example, that the MX ICBM or an anti-satellite (ASAT) weapon program would contribute to crisis instability, must imply, if they mean anything, that deployment of these weapons makes war more likely. The crisis instability claim has to mean that. One is required to believe that a superpower would choose to wage central nuclear war, a class of conflict reached presumably in one military leap from a condition of deep peace, otherwise the enemy would be on maximum alert at least, because fifty or more MX ICBMs would have to be launched in a prompt second-use mode or lost in their silos. A reasonable person might be excused from thinking that anticipation of receiving a strike back by MX ICBMs very promptly would be a healthily deterring prospect.

Alternatively, because ASAT weapons could assault valuable, but generally nonstrategic, platforms in low earth orbit, thereby sending an unambiguous calling card for war, one is requested to believe that crises could become less stable. Instead, what makes for instability in crisis is when an Austria-Hungary wants war and its powerful ally by and large, if somewhat erratically, elects to allow events to take a war-prone course. Or for a speculative case, crisis instability certainly would be generated by Russian determination to support Poland against a reunited Germany's pressure for the return of Silesia and Pomerania, were Germany, for its part, very determined to win on the territorial issue. When policy goals expressing perceived vital national interests are incompatible, the prospects for peace or war are unlikely to be impacted noticeably by the character of the adversaries' armaments.

One can distinguish offensive from defensive polices and strategies, but those distinctions have little or no meaning for operations, tactics, individual weapons, or weapon technologies. The

---

[67] Gottfried and Blair, eds., *Crisis Stability and Nuclear War*, p. 293.

reason is that the same operations, tactics, and weapons can be applied either to offensive or defensive policy and strategy purposes. In 1939, French frontier fortifications (the Maginot Line) served an overall defensive purpose, while German fortifications (the Siegfried Line) served an overall offensive purpose. Passive defenses, say the Theodosian walls of Constantinople, could serve both defensive and offensive purposes simultaneously. In 627 the Byzantine emperor Heraclius was able to strike offensively at the very heart of the Sassanian Empire, leaving his capital city besieged by an alliance of Avars and Persians.[68] Offense and defense are not so much qualities in particular weaponry but rather purposes in the hearts and minds of policymakers.

THE IRRELEVANCE OF ARMS CONTROL

Peace and war are political; they are not technological or administrative via apolitical and astrategic theories of arms control and stability. Sometimes, important truths need stating in such a loud voice that minor untruths can intrude, perhaps as sins of omission. Overwhelming evidence of all kinds argues for the irrelevance at best of the arms control process. Nonetheless, provided the costs do not include damage to policies and military strength, potentially credibly significant for the prevention of war, it is well to be generous even to arms control arguments and ideas of stability that appear to lack merit. After all, one could be wrong. This is a matter of fault-proofing theory. Provided the hedge against possible error cannot imperil necessary policy performance, a belt and suspenders approach is favored here. I am entirely unconvinced by both the thin literature on accidental and inadvertent war and by the promise of technical forms of arms control to alleviate the alleged dangers of such wars. Nonetheless, if there are nearly cost-free ways to cover even these unconvincing perils, by all means let them be adopted.

Great wars have not begun by accident, or even by inadvertence, but there could be a first time. The kind of arms control

---

[68] See George Ostrogorsky, *History of the Byzantine State* (1940; rpt. New Brunswick, N.J.: Rutgers University Press, 1969), pp. 102–3.

most responsive to the highly theoretical, if unlikely, perils of accidental or inadvertent war is the kind that states should apply unilaterally, as indeed generally they have. It is a matter of record that with one arguable exception, none of the more important military-technical and procedural safety measures introduced by the superpowers over the course of the past three decades owe anything of note to formal processes of interstate negotiation. That exception is the idea of permissive action links (PALs) for nuclear weapon safety.

Since weapons do not make war in any causal sense, neither can the formal control of weapons make for a more peaceful world. More arms control agreements will be signed in the 1990s. But that fact will have no importance for what arms control primarily is supposed to be all about—the prevention of war. It is the reciprocal policy judgments that war is very unlikely for years to come that render arms control strategically painless and hence politically possible, even though actually irrelevant.

[3]

Dragons Live Here:
How the Real World Makes
Life Difficult for the Theorist

The problem with a good theory is that facts sometimes get in
the way.

—Bruce D. Berkowitz, 1987

THE DRAGONS CANNOT BE SLAIN

This chapter introduces the dragons of politics in the form of
the policy motives of states determined to oppose revisionist
drives and the complex relationships among uncertainty, prediction, and the regulation of technology. There are many reasons
why arms control does not work, but these broad, yet deep, factors explain much of the difficulty. The dragons of politics and
technology cannot be slain, tamed, or incarcerated by arms control negotiation. What is wrong is not politics or the march of
technology, but rather the endeavor to resolve or alleviate political difficulties by some administrative method to a neatly reductionist conclusion. If the quest for strategic arms control truly can
be guided by the twin axiom that "killing people is good; killing
weapons is bad,"[1] then SALT or START can be pursued "as an
intellectual problem in need of a solution rather than as a process
of negotiation that seeks out the basis for a deal or bargain."[2] Ad-

[1] John Newhouse, *Cold Dawn: The Story of SALT* (New York: Holt, Rinehart and
Winston, 1973), p. 176.
[2] Hedley Bull, "The Scope for Soviet-American Agreement," in *Soviet-American*

[70]

mittedly, this is an extreme, though historical, case of a particular arms control doctrine influencing statecraft.

The arms control process seeks to reduce policy intentions and geopolitics to administration by experts. There is a large and important place in defense behavior for management skills and security engineering, *once policy has decided what is in need of achievement and strategy has determined which objectives should be pursued.* Diplomats, like lawyers, can perform admirably in defense of their clients, once they are told what constitutes success. Diplomacy, even arms control diplomacy, like legal skills, is inherently hollow of content. A country cannot in effect turn vitally important matters of security over to a policy *instrument* (i.e., diplomacy) for resolution or alleviation. Arms control negotiators have to be told by policymakers what is and is not negotiable and why. Genuinely technical and administrative problems can impede negotiations that policymakers already have concluded in broad principle. In such cases "arms control expertise" indeed might rescue a negotiation that should be concluded with a treaty. But if policymakers are agreed on high principle, on broad parameters, and on the political desirability of a treaty, actual consummation of the agreement is unlikely to score very high on the Richter scale of security significance. This excludes those common cases where an announcement of agreement in principle translates as a soft landing for real disagreement.

Arms control can be a highly technical subject. For example, a START negotiating process which defines the precise percentages of change in missile throwweight (21 percent) and length (5 percent) which would render a project a "new" missile, plainly is not very friendly to detailed control by technically inexpert politicians. Arms control experts, like lawyers, can tell their clients what a deal means but not which deal to judge acceptable. To adapt Clausewitz's dictum about war, there is a "grammar" to arms control but not a policy "logic."[3]

The central problem is politics. It is precisely because different

---

Relations and World Order: Arms Limitations and Policy, Adelphi Papers no. 65 (London: Institute for Strategic Studies [ISS], February 1970), p. 10.

[3] See Carl von Clausewitz, *On War* (1832), ed. Michael Howard and Peter Paret (Princeton: Princeton University Press, 1976), p. 605.

polities can harbor very different ambitions that a common arms control reasoning cannot reliably be applied to regulate their armaments. Arms control experts could function as philosophers to princes were the problems and opportunities posed by competitive armaments friendly to management, as broadly understood. But, the more demanding cases for arms control attention are never those primarily in need of the skills of the arms control diplomat and the arms competition administrator.

In the bad old days of the Cold War, as in the Middle East today and probably in east-central Europe tomorrow, the problem is the balance, or imbalance, of power. The grammar of arms control all but mandates the appearance of military parity, but its logic often requires massive military advantage on the side of the established order. Similarly, arms control experts may believe that they can identify uniquely destabilizing weapons and weapon technologies, but it is geopolitics and dependent geostrategy which must establish how new weapons will function with respect to political stability.

Illusions persist. The arms control doctors today urge application of their skills and remedies to nothing less than the snake pit of the Middle East.

> The bitterness of the Arab-Israeli dispute is not necessarily a block to useful arms negotiations—no more than was the once bitter enmity between the West and the Soviet bloc. Indeed, arms control has often been more effective between adversaries than allies, because its potential payoff is most obvious and the interest of the parties is correspondingly intense.[4]

The usual bundle of confidence-building fixes is recommended: hotline agreements, risk reduction centers, establishment of keep-out zones, demilitarization of critical terrain, and so forth. How would they work?

> Collectively these measures would go a long way toward making the use of war a far more difficult course of resolving political differ-

---

[4] Michael Nacht, Jay Winik, and Alan Platt, "What about Arms Control? We Shouldn't Wait for the Peace Process before Trying to Curb Mideast Weaponry," *Washington Post*, 22 September 1991, p. C3.

ences. Over time, states in the region would have greater confidence in the diplomatic process and would also have greater incentives to make concessions for peace. Moreover, in due course arms-reductions agreements that could lend further stability to the region would have a better chance of success.[5]

But arms control cannot substitute for policy choice. The application and administration of arms control measures might have some minor prophylactic value for peace. It is very likely, however, that any political context capable of being prodded toward a nonwar outcome by arms control would not be in critical need of such assistance anyway. The problems in the Middle East are, first, the political antagonisms and ill-will on many sides and, second, the necessity to keep the party of the status quo (Israel) militarily superior to its would-be revisionist Arab foes. A new "order" might be imposed on the Middle East in a more benign variant of the "order" which Germany and the Soviet Union successively imposed upon the Balkans from 1940 to 1990. But such an order cannot be applied with arms control remedies comprising the cutting edge for unaddressed political difficulties.

My reasoning here is neither cynical nor despairing. Rather, the time is long overdue for arms control quackery to be exposed. The idea that arms control can be applied usefully to the quarrels of the Middle East is about as sensible as the notion that astrology should be consulted as a guide to statecraft. The fact that many statesmen have believed in astrology is not, alas, a powerful testimonial.

MILITARY ADVANTAGE FOR THE CONTROL OF ARMS

Arms control theory and much of Western arms control practice can be inappropriately evenhanded in its definitions of, and approaches to, problems. As Chapter 2 explained, the villains tend to be allegedly destabilizing weapons and, again allegedly, arms race dynamics. With the quantity, quality, or operating practices of arms as its currency, arms control sidesteps the political ques-

[5] Ibid.

tions that serve to explain the weapons at issue. The idea noted above that the political differences between states can be evaded by what amounts to administrative or managerial wisdom, as when the management doctrine of strategic stability is applied through arms control, is as naive as the speculation that "if the habit of cooperation can be established in the field of armament policy, it may well prove 'catching' in other, nonmilitary areas."[6]

Arms control negotiations have political problems with outcomes other than some formal appearance of parity. Since the meaning of armaments for peace or war is dominated by the policy intentions of states, like-looking forces can have very different implications for international security. To resort to a favorite Soviet concept, "equal security" regularly has been claimed in support of arms control treaties. Unfortunately, each country's national security circumstances are geostrategically unique.

Parity, though typically necessary as the only workable solution for successful arms control negotiations, fails to capture what at least one party to the process truly requires by way of prudent armament. Because potentially significant passages of arms control negotiating experience typically will involve a revisionist, even rogue, polity—some close facsimile to parity is unlikely to control armaments in any very useful way. The parity in question is almost bound to be of the optical kind, even if it takes the form of supposedly balanced asymmetries among force categories. One cannot prudently ride the tiger of sharing a *joint* arms control enterprise with a revisionist state, because (inter alia) such a state cannot reliably be discouraged by a rough equality in forces. An oxymoron is an oxymoron: tigers cannot be ridden safely—period. Also, numerical parity in forces translates into advantage-disadvantage according to the political geography of prospective conflict (e.g., 5 : 5 between Britain and the United States in capital ships or "double zero" for both superpowers in the INF treaty of 1987). If a would-be aggressor requires a notable preponderance of force in order to succeed, then the parity principle could be

---

[6] Donald G. Brennan, "Setting and Goals of Arms Control," in Brennan ed., *Arms Control, Disarmament, and National Security* (New York: George Braziller, 1961), pp. 40–41.

useful for peace. Unfortunately, a state prepared to fight for gain is unlikely to be a state willing to be constrained to equal force levels by treaty. Also, tactical, operational, and strategic skills often can substitute for absent numbers.

The arms *control* that truly works for a while is that imposed by the victor on the vanquished, as in 1919 and 1945, and that which flows inescapably from a radical process of political change. The notion that "the establishment of arms-control programs might therefore have a catalytic effect on the political problems and tensions" exactly reverses the dominant terms of the relationship.[7] Arms control is *about* politics; politics is not *about* arms control.

Those visible arithmetical relationships between different countries' armed forces which tend to be the focus for negotiation and verification, typically are an affront to the lessons of military history as well to the logic of policy motives. Ships, aircraft, and missiles do not wage war. Rather, war is waged by navies and air forces across a wide spectrum of tactical and operational effectiveness. Mass is always potentially important in war, particularly in a long war, but it is the prospective use of mass at the decisive point that sparks hope of military success in the breasts of war planners.[8] It is the quality of higher direction of a fighting force as well as that force's tactical effectiveness that brings victory.[9] Briefings on the theme of victory is certain/probable/possible tend to be unaffected by the kinds of constraints imposed by the formal interstate regulation of arms. Parity is a political, not a military or even a genuinely strategic, concept. The rich history of twentieth century arms control folly has witnessed a politically inevitable, if strategically absurd, focus upon parity as the prominent solution to arms relationships not only between potential enemies but even between functional political allies. In his classic study of *Sea Power in the Machine Age*, Bernard Brodie wrote that

[7] Ibid., p. 41.

[8] Clausewitz, *On War*, p. 204.

[9] Different kinds of effectiveness are assessed systematically in Alan R. Millett and Williamson Murray, eds., *Military Effectiveness*, 3 vols. (Boston: Allen and Unwin, 1988). Such distinctions also pervade the argument in Colin S. Gray, *War, Peace and Victory: Strategy and Statecraft for the Next Century* (New York: Simon and Schuster, 1990).

Three years before the London Naval Conference of 1930, Jellicoe [former First Sea Lord], in listing Britain's needs had put the irreducible minimum for cruisers at seventy [allegedly, an absolute British requirement, driven by the length of the country's maritime trade and imperial security routes]. Yet for motives of political expediency, the Prime Minister of the day [Ramsay MacDonald] instructed the British delegates at the Conference to accept the American quota, which reduced the total of British cruisers to fifty. Nine years later the British had the same convoy problem as in 1917 with half the cruiser resources. *Great Britain and the United States, between whom no antagonism worth mentioning existed, proceeded to disarm each other in an unsettled world,* relying completely, as Admiral Beamish put it, "upon faith, hope, and parity, with parity said to be the most important of all."[10]

This quotation offers a number of oversimplified judgments and is true more as a cartoon can be true than in detail. Nonetheless, Brodie pointed accurately enough to the bizarre fact that in the 1920s and 1930s the two countries above all others whose armaments by policy definition provided leverage for international order, resolutely sought to discourage each other's force-building. Ultimately, Washington and London were somewhat saved from themselves by the unalterable Imperial Japanese determination by 1933–34 to repudiate the nominally unequal force ratios imposed by the Washington (1922) treaties. President Roosevelt was determined to outbuild the Japanese and welcomed the domestic economic benefits of renewed competitive effort.

Two conclusions follow. First, the prospects for arms control are thwarted not only by the policies and competitive military activity of revisionist states, but also by the policies and military programs of those states who seek to deny the revisionists achievement of their goals. Virtually by definition, revisionist states will not sign on for arms control regimes which, *if applied rigorously in practice,* would have the net effect of blunting their competitive edge (shortening their swords). Broadly, status quo powers, such as Britain and the United States in this century, serve the objectives of arms control by declining to offer would-be revisionist

[10] Bernard Brodie, *Sea Power in the Machine Age* (Princeton: Princeton University Press, 1941), p. 336.

[76]

polities arms control frameworks likely to be harmful for international order. If success or failure in arms control is measured by the achievement of agreement, then the U.S. refusal to concede mathematical parity to Imperial Japan over naval armaments in 1933–34, or to endorse a START regime in the late 1980s, which would have conceded a Soviet right to veto SDI deployment, was in large measure responsible for arms control failure. The logic is similar to that which notes the responsibility for war of a victim state which chooses to resist aggression.

Second, it has always been the case that the cause of peace, though not necessarily of justice, is best served when there is a healthy disproportion of competitive armament in favor of the established order. Contrary to much of the logic of arms control theory, with its focus upon weapons and alleged arms races, the danger of war lies overwhelmingly in the ownership of armaments by polities motivated to use them for self-aggrandizement.

One must take note of the propositions that power corrupts and that disproportionate power corrupts disproportionately. It is true that policy appetite grows with national capability. In their turn both Britain and the United States were guilty of imperial hubris and both were humbled: Britain in South Africa (1899–1902)[11] and the United States in Vietnam (ca. 1960–73). Notwithstanding the occasional abuse of power by a dominant state, overarmament by the United States would be a policy error that international order could tolerate very well. It would be difficult to overstate the point that U.S. armament—as with British, French and (again) U.S. armament in the 1930s—does not pose a threat to the kind of peace that is worth endorsing or, indeed, to peace at all. Arms control policy, and particularly heated public debate about such policy, easily can lose sight of the fact that Western arms do not need to be constrained in the interest of stability by the administrative approaches of arms control man-

[11] See Aaron L. Friedberg, *The Weary Titan: Britain and the Experience of Relative Decline, 1895–1905* (Princeton: Princeton University Press, 1988). For superior analyses of the British Empire in the twentieth century, see Correlli Barnett, *The Collapse of British Power* (1972; rpt. Gloucester, U.K.: Alan Sutton, 1984); and Anthony Clayton, *The British Empire as a Superpower, 1919–39* (Athens: University of Georgia Press, 1986).

agers. Those arms are controlled suitably by nonmartial Western policy developed in defense of nonmartial societies.

Obviously, this argument can be overstated. In objecting to the apolitical evenhandedness of much of the stability theory which chooses to be blind on the question of policy goals, one must take some account of the small danger that a would-be revisionist state could misread Western capability for Western policy intention. By far the best way to discourage adventure on the part of deeply fearful revisionist-dreaming polities, however, is to deny them plausible theories of victory. Clear military advantage on the side of order is a force for peace. Far from being troubled by the logic of that security dilemma explained above, one should be delighted to frustrate the demands for more security expressed in the policies of most would-be revisionists. The political relativism that lurks underrecognized in arms control theory, as well as in much attempted arms control practice, needs to be exposed as dangerous folly. An astute British historian has noted how the British delegation to the World Disarmament Conference of 1932 "adopted their favorite post of umpire. 'Britain had the difficult role,' wrote Simon [Sir John Simon, British foreign minister] in his memoirs, 'of trying to be fair to each.' For what was at stake, in the British view, was not a matter of grand strategy, but moral justice."[12] It matters who owns weapons. For an extreme example, an Iraqi ICBM force would not be the same as the U.S. ICBM force, no matter how similar the two forces might be in their technical characteristics and standard practices of operation.

When a status quo power enjoys great military advantage, the consequence is control over the threat or use of arms by would-be revisionist states. Secretary of Defense Dick Cheney was right in affirming that "America's global military posture and leadership promotes an international environment in which free peoples and those seeking freedom can prosper. . . . Not only does our presence deter Soviet influence, it also can dampen regional arms competition and discourage local powers from seeking to dominate their neighbors."[13] Describing the goodwill with which traders

---

[12] Barnett, *Collapse of British Power*, p. 339.
[13] Dick Cheney, prepared statement in U.S. Congress, House Committee on

and pilgrims were treated in the Eastern Mediterranean in the middle of the eleventh century, Sir Steven Runciman has written that "this goodwill was guaranteed by the power of Byzantium."[14] Runciman and Cheney register the same point: international civility prospers in the presence of a well-armed guardian. This is a theory and practice of benign hegemony, of a pax Romana, pax Britannica, and pax Americana.

Although one needs to beware of excessive zeal, not to mention the pursuit of unduly private agendas, on the part of armed policemen, nonetheless, an imbalance of power in their favor vis-à-vis potential criminals is a healthy condition. The point is not that a particular police force is incapable of errors in judgment, incompetence in performance, or even of plain venality. Rather, the leading alternatives to regional or global guardianship by a reasonably benign hegemonic power, tend to compromise a state of chaos or a strong bid for a dominant position by a malign would-be hegemonic power.

In statecraft and strategy beauty is a matter of what works. An "immoderately great" United States, to borrow a turn of phrase from Edward Gibbon,[15] is a source of irritation to envious and underappreciative foreigners, but the general as well as regionally specific benefits of American hegemony to international order have been, and remain, of inestimable value. Would that an arms control process could accomplish as much for its classic objectives as does a somewhat preponderant United States.[16]

PERIL IN PREDICTION

In addition to the dragon of antirevisionist states, whose determinedly military-competitive endeavors can work to thwart the

Armed Services, *National Defense Authorization Act for Fiscal Year 1991—H.R. 47 39, Authorization and Oversight, Hearings,* 101st Cong., 2d sess. (Washington, D.C.: Government Printing Office, 1990), p. 11.

[14] Steven Runciman, *A History of the Crusades,* vol. 1 (Cambridge: Cambridge University Press, 1951), p. 51.

[15] Edward Gibbon, *The History of the Decline and Fall of the Roman Empire,* vol. 4, ed. J. B. Bury (London: Methuen, 1909), p. 173.

[16] Samuel P. Huntington, "The U.S.—Decline or Renewal?" *Foreign Affairs,* 67 (Winter 1988–89), 76–96, is an outstanding treatment.

ambitions of arms control theory, there is the dragon which variously may be labeled as uncertainty, simply the future, or the necessity for prediction.

In February 1932, the U.S. ambassador to Belgium, Hugh Gibson, proposed to the World Disarmament Conference in Geneva that "offensive," or "aggressive," weapons should be abolished.[17] Among other specific suggestions—to ban tanks and heavy mobile artillery, for example—he advocated the abolition of submarines. On April 22, 1932, President Herbert Hoover recommended the abolition of all bombing aircraft. A decade later, the submarines of the U.S. Navy achieved all but decisive success in severing the sea lines of communication of an overextended Japanese empire which had neglected to provide effectively for the defense of its maritime transport.[18] Also a decade later, the U.S. Army Air Forces (USAAF) achieved arguably independently decisive results in the strategic bombing of Japan.[19] With respect to the war in Europe, the USAAF believed officially that if properly supported and used it could defeat Nazi Germany with little need for U.S. or

[17] The best study is Marion William Boggs, *Attempts to Define and Limit "Aggressive" Armament in Diplomacy and Strategy*, University of Missouri Studies, 16 (Columbia: University of Missouri, 1941), particularly pp. 54–55. More recent endeavors to grapple with the offense-defense relationship generally have been less successful than Boggs. See George H. Quester, *Offense and Defense in the International System* (New York: John Wiley and Sons, 1977); Jack S. Levy, "The Offensive/Defensive Balance of Military Technology: A Theoretical and Historical Analysis," *International Studies Quarterly*, 28 (1984), 219–38; and Lawrence Freedman, *Strategic Defence in the Nuclear Age*, Adelphi Papers no. 224 (London: International Institute for Strategic Studies [IISS], Autumn 1987). These three authors are all skilled and experienced theoreticians, but they are all defeated by the complexity of their subject.

[18] In his magisterial study of the Pacific war, Ronald H. Spector claims persuasively that "the U.S. submarine offensive against Japan was one of the decisive elements in ensuring the empire's defeat. A force comprising less than 2 percent of U.S. Navy personnel had accounted for 55 percent of Japan's losses at sea." *Eagle against the Sun: The American War with Japan* (New York: Free Press, 1985), p. 487. An excellent account is Clay Blair, Jr., *Silent Victory: The U.S. Submarine War against Japan* (1975; rpt. New York: Bantam Books, 1976).

[19] "The Twentieth Air Force got the job done before the Allied armies had to do it, but it was touch and go." General Curtis E. Lemay and Bill Yenne, *Superfortress: The Story of the B-29 and American Air Power* (1988; rpt. New York: Berkeley Books, 1989), p. 156. For a very different perspective, see Michael S. Sherry, *The Rise of American Air Power: The Creation of Armageddon* (New Haven: Yale University Press, 1987).

allied ground forces to conduct other than mopping-up operations.

Neither for the first nor for the last time, in 1932 U.S. policymakers advocated draconian measures of control—abolition, no less—of kinds of weapons which, a few years later, the United States itself was to wield with the most deadly strategic consequences for the country's enemies. From time to time, policymakers in search of exciting-sounding diplomatic initiatives can forget that, even if an idea might fly in the magic kingdom of arms control, that idea also needs to fly for U.S. national security policy. As a country obliged by strategic geography to organize its defense preparation around missions of distant power projection,[20] the United States in the early 1930s should have been more respectful than it was at the highest level of the value of strategic airpower and of the merit in potential submarine harassment of the sea lanes of the Japanese Empire. To be fair, in the early 1930s the U.S. Navy did not anticipate waging a protracted struggle against Japanese sea lines of communication.[21] At that time the orthodox view was that the American battle fleet would traverse the central Pacific, fight a climactic battle for command of the western Pacific, relieve the garrison in the Philippines, and then blockade the Japanese home islands.

More recent illustration of the point that one should be careful in predicting the utility of types of weaponry was offered by Ambassador Henry F. Cooper, then chief U.S. negotiator at the Space and Defense Talks, who advised wisely that "given the complexities of still embryonic military activities in space, the United States should take care in keeping its associated arms control initiatives modest in scope while sorting out its national security objectives."[22]

[20] A work of lasting value is Samuel P. Huntington, "National Policy and the Transoceanic Navy," U.S. Naval Institute *Proceedings*, 80 (May 1954), 483–93.

[21] A point noted appropriately in Robert Gordon Kaufman, *Arms Control during the Pre-Nuclear Era: The United States and Naval Limitation between the Two World Wars* (New York: Columbia University Press, 1990), p. 17. Gerald E. Wheeler, *Prelude to Pearl Harbor: The United States Navy and the Far East, 1921–1931* (Columbia: University of Missouri Press, 1963), is useful.

[22] Henry F. Cooper, "Anti-Satellite Systems and Arms Control: Lessons from the Past," *Strategic Review*, 17 (Spring 1989), p. 45.

Unless one has excellent reason to believe both that arms control policy can substitute for defense policy, and that what is intended through arms control actually will come to pass, arms control policy must pass muster for its implications for foreign policy and strategy. Arms control will be an activity subordinate to politics and strategy. As Lawrence Freedman notes, "Arms control can therefore mark important changes, but by and large it serves to consolidate and reaffirm the status quo against change."[23]

The cases of submarines and bombing aircraft in the early 1930s, and of space-based missile defenses and ASAT systems more recently, all illustrate the potential of an arms control process to run ahead of strategic reasoning, defense planning, and national security policy. In the name of arms control and often with the best of intentions, statesmen and officials have a long history of engaging almost casually in what amounts to the most radical guesswork about future technology, tactics, operations, strategy, and policy.

Functioning actively in shaping their security futures, states need to decide which trends in military technology they prefer to see accelerated or retarded. So much is not at issue. States, as with individuals, naturally seek control over their own destinies. But frequently on the basis of little strategic analysis, statesmen try to construct an arms control house with bricks but without mortar. Prediction in international security matters is exceedingly difficult, as virtually all of the experts on the former Soviet Union and the German problem (or is it the German opportunity?) rediscovered in 1989–92. The argument is not that forward planning, even prediction, can be avoided by a government behaving prudently; of course, that cannot be avoided. Rather, arms control theory asks impossible prescience of policymakers, while arms control practice demonstrates that the impossible is indeed just that. The dragon of uncertainty is a complex beast comprising a number of interdependent arguments.

Arms control negotiations tend on the part of Western de-

---

[23] Lawrence Freedman, *Arms Control: Management or Reform?* Chatham House Papers No. 31 (London: Routledge and Kegan Paul [for the Royal Institute of International Affairs], 1986), p. 72.

mocracies to be about arms control negotiations and not about security. Negotiability is a quality not to be despised in a policy position. But negotiability can subsume consideration of the strategic implications of what proves expediently to be negotiable. It is always difficult to make defense decisions today that will not be regretted tomorrow. It is additionally, even gratuitously, difficult when a government has to plan for the future around the terms of an arms control regime that was not crafted (by us, at least) for its net strategic benefit.

Political, strategic, operational, tactical, and technological prediction is exceedingly difficult to effect with a good average for accuracy. Political and military history is littered with the corpses of polities and politicians, generals and armies, who got it wrong. There is a distinctly poor track record of official prescience concerning such nontrivial topics as "the next war," "tomorrow's enemy," "tomorrow's enemy's leader," and "strategy for the next war." Adolf Hitler in the 1920s and Winston Churchill before May 1940 were regarded more as figures of fun than as serious statesmen, while Mikhail Gorbachev's name was not exactly on the lips of every prominent Western Sovietologist prior to 1984–85 and Boris Yeltsin virtually had to be blessed by the global media in 1991 before "expert" Washington would take him at anything close to face value. The point is not that history has been dominated by incompetent statesmen and military theorists who were distinctly imprudent in their predictions; rather, it is that the future cannot be foretold. For that reason even sensible guesses about the future are difficult to make, and statesmen and defense planners frequently are surprised by the course of events.

The history of arms control regimes shows that although an arms control process is not *the* villain of the piece, on balance it functions in ways unhelpful for Western-oriented visions of international peace and security. The relevant villains, if that is the correct description, are would-be revisionist states and simply the uncertainties of an unknown and unknowable future. The theory and practice of arms control is not responsible for the problem of uncertainty. But that theory is guilty of promising a great deal more predictability about the future of competitive armaments than it can possibly deliver. Also, the net effect of arms control regimes is to hinder rather than help the ability of generally status quo powers to live in tolerable security with enduring problems.

Whether or not an arms control process can deliver upon its promise of "enhancing predictability in the size and structure of forces in order to reduce the fear of aggressive intent"—for the purpose, what else, of "strengthening international stability"[24]— the predictability in question may have a content that policy-makers some years in the future will come to regret. The fault here does not lie with erroneous strategic prediction. To err is but human, and official. Instead, the error lies in the acceptance of constraints that are likely to inhibit agility in strategic adaptive-ness, either directly or indirectly via the domestic political mood they can encourage. In the memorable words of Laurence Martin: "The rigidity you legislate today may deny you the evasive man-oeuvre you want to take tomorrow."[25] And "Entering into over-simplified agreements about particular aspects of a complex strategic environment, where politics and technology interact in ever-changing patterns, entails the danger of losing the flexibility with which to adapt to change."[26]

It may be objected that the restrictions upon flexibility against which Martin warns are a price well worth paying for the security of balancing restrictions upon the flexibility to adapt on the part of others. This objection is important and from time to time will be correct. The warnings against the rigidity that arms control can impose are warnings against a strongly undesirable tendency; they are not dogmatic claims for absolutely all-case error though arms control. As a general rule, however, formal arms control regimes have an unhelpful impact upon the ability of status quo polities to adapt prudently to changing circumstances.

Notable among the fallacies which make up much of the folk-lore of arms control is the argument that it does not matter why countries are able to agree upon a particular arms control treaty because each can cooperate and be content for its own distinctive

---

[24] George Bush, *National Security Strategy of the United States* (Washington, D.C.: White House, August 1991), p. 14.
[25] Laurence Martin, *The Two-Edged Sword: Armed Force in the Modern World* (London: Weidenfeld and Nicolson, 1982), p. 73.
[26] Ibid., p. 72.

reasons. This tolerantly liberal and highly relativistic doctrine is as attractive and expedient as it is faulty. Policy intentions matter when democracies are wont to shy at the hurdle of verification of treaty noncompliance (see Chapter 6); when treaty regimes, though constraining, in effect constrain unequally because their very existence provides powerful excuses for democracies not to build or modernize to treaty limits; and when weaponry inherently is technologically, tactically, and even operationally ambivalent in its meaning.

On the last point, for example, former Soviet officials and theorists stated that their military doctrine was unequivocally defensive in both its political-social and military-technical dimensions.[27] Unfortunately for the reassurance that might be drawn from that claim, the proposition also was advanced that the traditional technical distinction (bearing upon range and agility) between offensive and defensive weapons is becoming ever less valid. If defensive forces also are offensive forces, then how can one verify reliably a shift to the defense in the military-technical aspect of doctrine? The question answers itself.

Arms control can encourage innovation. It tends to impose regulation upon the dominant weapons of the day and provides incentives to develop capabilities that are totally or relatively unrestricted. For example, the Washington treaty system had the originally unintended consequences of encouraging the construction of large aircraft carriers (on battlecruiser hulls) and very large cruisers ("treaty cruisers"), while the SALT process rewarded the

---

[27] See Army General D. T. Yazov, "On Soviet Military Doctrine," *RUSI Journal*, 134 (Winter 1989), 1–4, for a representative explanation. The events of summer 1991 brought General Yazov's career to an abrupt close. Raymond L. Garthoff assures us that "since 1985, and especially since the announcement of a new defensive doctrine at the military-technical level in 1987, that whole concept has drastically changed. By 1989 there could be no doubt that the change was real and not rhetorical." *Deterrence and the Revolution in Soviet Military Doctrine* (Washington, D.C.: Brookings Institution, 1990), p. 159. But note the caution expressed on pp. 184–85. In 1990–91 there was some scope for Western choice between being impressed by the scale of the very adversely asymmetrical reductions required of the USSR by the CFE treaty or being impressed by the scale and flagrancy of the Soviet measures taken to avoid the worst military consequences of that treaty. Conceptually, the dethronement of Marxism-Leninism should be traumatic in its impact upon Russian military science.

[85]

developer of cruise missiles and of large ballistic delivery vehicles. If launchers, not warheads, are limited, there is an obvious advantage in maximizing the firepower concentrated on each vehicle.

Overall, the innovation (and cheating) encouraged by arms control tends to be opportunistic rather than necessarily prudent, let alone strategically rational. The journey into an unknown future that is the forward course of national policy and strategy is rendered difficult enough by the uncharted terrain to be traversed. It is not useful to dignify guesses about the future by translating them into legislation that cannot help but impair flexibility in defense planning. As argued already, arms control regimes cannot make for peace any more than their absence can make for war. But as one factor among many, arms control regimes can impact negatively upon the ability of states to generate the strategic effectiveness necessary for success in deterrence in crises and for advantage in wars that they could not help prevent.

Finally, the demands of arms control place burdens of foresight upon individuals and bureaucracies that typically they are not adequately equipped to bear. Prudent arms control planning is probably an oxymoron because the future is unduly uncertain in too many aspects and the more rigorous arms control regimes (the ABM treaty, for example) are at least as likely on balance to do real harm as to do good on some favored "stability-meter." Arms control can reduce or perhaps ascend—depending upon the point of view—to a form of "security engineering," with all of the problems that that pejorative concept implies.

One could object that to cite the problems posed by politics, which is to say the urge to compete against revisionist states, by the uncertainties of the future, and by technology, is really to make the generic case for an arms control process. Indeed, if the dragons of politics, future unknowns (possible perilous crisis slides to the abyss of war, the possibility of inadvertent conflict, and the like), and military-related technology truly were tamed, there would be no need for arms control. Although the dragons of politics, uncertainty, and technology highlight an objective need for arms control action, each functions to thwart the transition of arms control theory into arms control practice effective for outcomes friendly to peace with security.

It was said of Britain's Royal Navy in the age of "fighting sail" that the genius was in the system so that genius was not required, literally and unreasonably, of any particular individual at any particular time. An average competent and courageous captain or admiral would tend to perform well enough, because all his various tools—including tactical and strategic ideas—were sound. By way of contrast, a U.S. administration peopled by only average talents cannot be trusted to perform well enough in an arms control process. There is no genius in the U.S. arms control system or in the theory behind it. Nothing about arms control compels genuinely strategic assessment; indeed, in practice quite the reverse is true. An arms control process does not provide a sturdy vessel for those who aspire to evade the logic of political conflict and the perils of a deeply uncertain future.

[4]

History:
What Does the Record Show?

It is a curious fact that, in the many discussions on disarmament after the war of 1914–18, little, if any, investigation was made of the root question whether, or within what limits, it was really desirable, either as a general proposition or from the point of view of the British Empire in particular. The blessings of disarmament were, for the most part, assumed as a self-evident proposition.

—Lord Hankey, 1946

BEYOND EXPERIMENT

Kenneth L. Adelman has noted that "to believe the old line that arms control can save gobs of money is akin to Dr. Samuel Johnson's calling second marriages a triumph of hope over experience."[1] So, what has been the arms control record? I believe there is a unity to arms control experience: prenuclear and nuclear-age history is all of a piece. Some of the combat vehicles and the weapons they carry are very different in the 1990s from their predecessors in the 1920s and 1930s. But the political incentives, many of the strategic (and astrategic) ideas, and certainly most of the major problems, have been either identical or very similar. Overall, arms control has failed since 1945 for very much the same reasons that it failed before 1945.

It is sad to note that the editor of the bible of modern arms

---

[1] Kenneth L. Adelman, *The Great Universal Embrace: Arms Summitry—A Skeptic's Account* (New York: Simon and Schuster, 1989), p. 179.

control enquiry, Donald G. Brennan, could advise in 1960 "that the entire subject of arms control should be approached in something of an experimental, 'try-it-and-see' spirit."[2] The reader who knows no history would be amazed to learn that the United States already had experimented with arms control for no fewer than seventeen years (1922–38) between the wars. The 1936 (second) London Treaty for the Limitation of Naval Armament was scheduled to expire on 31 December 1942. In practice, however, the Washington-London arms regulation regime was defunct as of 29 December 1934, when Japan gave formal notice that it would leave the treaty system as of 31 December 1936. Nonetheless, although the second London treaty eschewed quantitative regulation all of the naval powers were rearming by 1935–36. The treaty, albeit with escalator clauses, imposed significant qualitative limits as well as provided what a later era euphemistically would call confidence-building measures. For the United States and the European naval powers, at least, naval arms control had some half (perhaps quarter) life from 1936 to 1938.

Like statistics, history can be used to further any argument. I am under no illusion that I can cite historical evidence and prove my case against the theory and practice of arms control to the satisfaction of people strongly disposed to believe otherwise. Seeking only to accomplish the possible, this chapter and the next provide specific and extended historical illustration of the thesis that arms control generally has been harmful at worst and irrelevant at best to the objectives widely agreed to be its guides. The discussion here focuses upon the great-power record with naval arms limitation in the interwar years. The next chapter focuses on the extant SALT and START process, which the superpowers began formally in 1969.

---

[2] Donald G. Brennan, "Setting and Goals of Arms Control," in Brennan, ed., *Arms Control, Disarmament, and National Security* (New York: George Braziller, 1961), p. 41. On a personal note, Brennan was a deeply respected colleague of mine for four years. His views on what he regarded as the perversion of arms control by the arms control community and the U.S. administration of the day may be gauged accurately from his vigorous testimony in 1972 and 1979 opposing both SALT I, particularly the ABM treaty, and SALT II.

EVIDENCE

Even in writing a book designed to expose the errors in arms control theory and the irrelevance or worse of arms control practice, I can feel "the pull of the trivial," the sheer technicity and diplomatic minutiae of the subject. A great deal of the literature on and public debate about arms control is singularly naked of a sense of strategic purpose. The complexity and indeterminacy of the near-term and underlying factors which produce war render the task of war prevention, *the primary mission of arms control*, a much less than scientific enterprise.

Unfortunately, there is no science of peace, and—*ab extensio*—arms control is not the sharpest sword in the arsenal of such pretensions to a science as exist. Some colleges and universities teach courses on Peace Science, but that fact reflects praiseworthy, if naive, good intentions and lax academic standards.[3] It is as difficult to be certain that one is judging past arms control endeavors fairly, as it is to be certain that one is not, through arms control effort, worsening the condition that is being treated. Readers are reminded, yet again, that the causes of war, unlike the causes of particular historical wars, remain obscure and uncertain just as the causes or conditions of peace are not precisely known. That being the fairly noncontroversial case, it would be unreasonable to ask very much of arms control policy. One might argue, however, that people in high office should recognize what they do not know and should cut the clothes of chosen policies according to their knowledge, or lack thereof, concerning the properties of their cloth.

Governments are held responsible for the consequences of their policies, not for the moral or political attractiveness of their intentions or even for the quality of the ideas that helped shape policy. My purpose in this and the next chapter is simply to seek some empirical guidance from the two most protracted, far-reaching,

[3] See the section on "The Nature of Peace Science," in Walter Isard, *Arms Races, Arms Control, and Conflict Analysis: Contributions from Peace Science and Peace Economics* (New York: Cambridge University Press, 1988), pp. 7–13. With its wealth of social science jargon and elaborate methodologies, peace science tends to be as unreadable as it is abstruse and arcane.

and evidence-rich cases of arms control in action—the Washington and London naval agreements and the SALT and START regimes. People unfriendly toward my thesis might try to argue that this chapter assaults a hill no one is defending, but the historical record all but mandates careful treatment of naval arms control between the wars. Indeed, from that period the leading alternative would be the League of Nations' World Disarmament conference of 1932–34, a barrelful of fish for this book's argument. The Washington-London system has been selected because it was by far the best performance by arms control policy in the 1920s and 1930s and so is the hardest case from those years for the merit of my argument.

What about the regimes for naval and strategic arms limitation has been beneficial and what has been harmful for international peace and security? Were the Washington treaty and the SALT and START regimes (to date) a good thing? This crudity of phrasing, reductionism even, is useful if discussion of arms control is to be rescued from experts who understand a great deal about the topic except what it is all about. Statesmen and citizens who must judge a Washington treaty on the limitation of naval arms, an ABM treaty, or a treaty on Conventional Forces in Europe (CFE) should ask *strategic* questions; which is to say questions about means-ends relationships. Whatever one's preference among theories on the causes of war and conditions of peace, a pending arms control regime should be subjected to rigorous examination in light of that preference. A senator will ask, for example, if a regime is equitable, if it is verifiable, and how far the United States shifted the goal-line defining policy success in the course of the negotiations. But that senator should vote on the basis of an overall judgment of whether or not the control regime will help advance the interest of peace with security.

History lends itself to abuse by the scholar or the polemicist who knows what he is looking for. With that peril in mind, here are seven points which help explain my attitude toward both the historical record of arms control and the admittedly selective employment of that record for the purposes of this book.

First, beliefs about what an arms control process is likely and unlikely to achieve may rest upon an extensive empirical basis.

[91]

Much of nuclear-age strategic theory rests strictly upon deductive logic and was invented by skilled logicians. There has been a theory and practice of deterrence throughout history,[4] but modern deterrence theory rests scarcely at all upon prenuclear evidence.[5] Modern arms control theory, coming from the same intellectual stable as deterrence (and limited war) theory,[6] also bears deductivist stigmata.

Yet the twentieth century provides a rich and varied record of arms control endeavor. Statesmen have never sought to restore deterrence through the tightly controlled coercive use of nuclear weapons; nor have they attempted to terminate a nuclear conflict. By way of contrast, statesmen have negotiated quantitative and qualitative limits on armaments. Moreover, even when arms control has failed to secure agreement it has tended to leave a well-marked trail of intriguing argument and counterargument.

Second, war-gamers and other experts in simulation can run "alternative 1930s" or "alternative 1970s," but history provides only a single passage of experience. Both the Washington naval arms limitation and the SALT regimes have attracted backhanded praise of the kind that compares an admittedly flawed reality of arms regulation with a hypothetical, unregulated 1920s and 1930s or 1970s. Mere quantities of weapons are not particularly significant for the objectives of arms control, though many people believe that *the rate of change* in quantities, which is to say arms race instability, can be significant.[7] Nonethless, it is a sobering experi-

---

[4] For historically very wide ranging, if superficial and suspiciously "social-scientific," study, see Raoul Naroll, Vern L. Bullough, and Frada Naroll, *Military Deterrence in History: A Pilot Cross-Historical Survey* (Albany: State University of New York Press, 1974).

[5] Or even much upon nuclear-age cases. A major path-breaking attempt to render deterrence theory empirically better founded is Alexander L. George and Richard Smoke, *Deterrence in American Foreign Policy* (New York: Columbia University Press, 1974). Also see Paul Huth and Bruce Russett, "What Makes Deterrence Work? Cases from 1900 to 1980," *World Politics,* 36 (July 1984), 496–526; "The Rational Deterrence Debate: A Symposium," *World Politics,* 41 (January 1989), 143–237; and Richard Ned Lebow and Janice Gross Stein "Deterrence: The Elusive Dependent Variable," *World Politics,* 42 (April 1990), 336–69.

[6] As I explain in detail in *Strategic Studies and Public Policy: The American Experience* (Lexington: University Press of Kentucky, 1982), chaps. 4–6.

[7] For example, see Charles Fairbanks and Abram Shulsky, "From 'Arms Control'

ence to compare the Soviet strategic weapons count (known to be deployed) in mid-1972 with the figure for mid-1991. Specifically, the SALT era has accommodated a growth in the Soviet strategic arsenal from *very* approximately 2620 warheads to 10,841. As always on the subject of Soviet arsenal accounting, beware of apparent precision.[8] The comparable figures for the United States reportedly are 7430 warheads in 1972 and approximately 12,061 in mid-1991. It is less than obvious that a SALT-unregulated 1970s and 1980s would have witnessed a more substantial build-up of offensive weapons. Although the ABM treaty of 1972 is of indefinite duration, strategic offensive arms have been subject to formal, though not treaty, regulation only for the five-year period, 1972–77.

There are no completely satisfactory tests for the claimed merit of an arms control regime. It is argued that the Washington and London treaties of 1922 and 1930 were important in reducing the possibility of war between Britain and the United States.[9] The 1922, 1930, and even 1936 treaties probably had positive political value for Anglo-American relations. But few people then and now believe that an Anglo-American war was at all likely as an alternative to arms control.

---

to Arms Reductions: The Historical Experience," *Washington Quarterly*, 10 (Summer 1987), pp. 60, 63–5.

[8] The mid-1991 figures are reported in David Hoffman and John E. Yang, "U.S., Soviets Reach Pact Reducing Nuclear Arms," *Washington Post*, 18 July 1991, p. A28. The official START data base, a memorandum of understanding incorporated into the START treaty, lists a total of 10,563 *accountable* warheads for the United States and 10,271 for the Soviet Union as of 1 September 1990. U.S. Arms Control and Disarmament Agency, *Fact Sheet, The Strategic Arms Reduction Treaty: START Data Base*, 1 August 1991.

[9] The major defense of the Washington-London system advanced in Christopher Hall, *Britain, America and Arms Control, 1921–37* (New York: St. Martin's, 1987). The author never quite commits himself on the subject of just how dangerous he believes an unregulated Anglo-American naval competition would have been, but he does talk about a "precarious balance of Anglo-American relations," and he claims that "the Washington system eliminated the possibility of conflict between these two 'superpowers' of the interwar period—a conflict that was certainly envisaged from time to time by naval officers and planners on both sides of the Atlantic" (p. 218). Hall would seem to exaggerate the peril of war and he is more than a little naive in taking what was "envisaged" by some "officers and planners" as prima facie evidence of anything very significant.

One must beware of interpretations of the historical record which allege there was a leading alternative that certainly would have been much more dangerous for peace with security. Virtually any arms control regime can be retailed to the credulous on the grounds that the supposed principal alternative must be much worse in its consequences.

An example for the ages has been identified by Wesley Wark in his outstanding study of British intelligence on Nazi Germany in the 1930s. Wark shows how the British Admiralty supported the Anglo-German Naval Agreement (AGNA) of 1935 with powerful-seeming, though actually monumentally flawed, quantified argument. The Admiralty argued in a July 1936 paper for the Committee on Imperial Defence that, for example, an AGNA-constrained Germany could complete only 8 capital ships, 15 cruisers, 38 destroyers, and 44 submarines by December 1942. It was claimed that, if unconstrained by the AGNA, respective German numbers by that date could well be 14, 30, 135, and 118.[10] Those who recall the official arguments in defense of SALT I and SALT II will find the British Admiralty's claims familiar. The Royal Navy believed what it wanted to believe and took no steps to seek out evidence that might provide contradiction. It was believed, as German spokesmen had stated repeatedly, that the *Kriegsmarine* was not built against Britain; that Germany would comply with the terms of the AGNA; and—as just noted—that Germany readily could build beyond her AGNA limit (of 35 percent of the Royal Navy) should she so desire. Also, the British Admiralty in 1935 was almost desperately eager to endorse any agreement that would radically reduce the Empire's potentially catastrophic strategic vulnerabilities. It was hoped that the AGNA would help politically to keep Nazi Germany off Britain's active enemies' list. The Royal Navy could not cope successfully with a hostile Japan in the Far East, a hostile, rearmed Germany in northern Europe, and a hostile Italy sitting astride the Mediterranean route to India.[11]

In company with the British Admiralty, Admiral Erich Raeder

---

[10] Wesley K. Wark, *The Ultimate Enemy: British Intelligence and Nazi Germany, 1933–1939* (Ithaca: Cornell University Press, 1985), p. 139.

[11] See N. H. Gibbs, *History of the Second World War, Grand Strategy*, vol. 1: *Rearmament Policy* (London: H.M.S.O., 1976), p. 256.

harbored the fantastic notion that a great and balanced German fleet could be built in an orderly and expeditious manner—the vision which justified the AGNA in London. But in the words of Holger H. Herwig, "Unfortunately for Raeder, it was much easier to develop ships on drafting boards than to construct them: shortages of skilled labour, oil, steel, non-ferrous metals, yard space, and dock facilities by 1937 brought the building programme on the average twelve months behind schedule, with some units as much as twenty-two months in arrears."[12]

Neither German naval planners nor the British Admiralty took intelligent account of Hitler's less-than-burning ambition to rebuild a great fleet. Similarly, the glaring limitations of the German industrial base to support simultaneously mammoth rearmament programs for all three services should not have escaped the notice of professional observers.

Third, when trying to understand a particular historical period, one needs to beware both of deterministic interpretation and of preconceived judgments on significance. One can ask if the arms competitions of the 1920s and 1930s, or the 1970s and 1980s, really had to proceed as they did and whether the arms relationships in question mattered very much (and if they mattered, how they mattered). On the latter point, it is obvious that the realm of nominally successful arms control in the 1920s, and even the 1930s, that is to say, the *naval* realm, was of scant relevance to the continentalist machinations of Adolf Hitler who was beyond deterrence by 1939 and anyway was "a Central European landlubber."[13] This is not to say that maritime power was unimportant. On the contrary, German naval deficiencies were to prove fatal as their enemies used their superiority at sea to wage global war with a flexibility and on a scale that the Axis could not match.[14] Also, Hitler understood very well just what the failures in grand strat-

[12] Holger H. Herwig, "The Failure of German Sea Power, 1914–1945: Mahan, Tirpitz, and Raeder Reconsidered," *International Review of History*, 10 (February 1988), p. 91.

[13] Correlli Barnett, *Engage the Enemy More Closely: The Royal Navy in the Second World War* (New York: W. W. Norton, 1991), p. 253.

[14] This topic is treated extensively in Colin S. Gray, *The Leverage of Sea Power: The Strategic Advantage of Navies in War* (New York: Free Press, 1991).

egy and in operational prowess of Grand Admiral Alfred von Tirpitz's High Seas Fleet had meant for Imperial Germany.[15] The point, rather, is that the regulation of the naval relations among the powers in the 1920s and 1930s was colossally irrelevant to the course of the crisis slide to war in 1938–39. Hitler himself took the initiative in abrogating the AGNA on 28 April 1939, following Neville Chamberlain's announcement of the Anglo-Polish Mutual Assistance Declaration on 31 March.[16] The consequences of the Washington system did matter for the Japanese calculation in 1941 to strike sooner rather than later, but that calculation was politically critical only because of the massive distraction of the energy and attention of Japan's possible foes by the war in Europe.

Fourth, it should never be forgotten that the hard cases for arms control are the only cases that really matter for peace with security. A major successful passage of arms control negotiation has to rest upon a permissive political climate. When that climate deteriorates severely, as in the 1930s or by the close of the 1970s, an arms control process cannot prosper. All too often, commentators excuse any arms control process from requirements for achievement in politically difficult periods. They are correct in noticing that negative political linkage killed the World Disarmament Conference in 1932–34, just as it did SALT II in 1979–80. But

[15] There is general agreement among historians that Hitler was obsessed with what he understood to be the lessons of the Great War. In the mid-1930s he endeavored to avoid policy steps that would drive Britain into active opposition to his statecraft. Hitler appreciated that Tirpitz's "risk fleet" helped deliver Britain as an ally of France and Russia, while it could not be developed to the point where it could challenge the Royal Navy for maritime surface command. F. H. Hinsley's *Hitler's Strategy* (Cambridge: Cambridge University Press, 1951) remains an outstanding analysis.

[16] See Charles S. Thomas, *The German Navy in the Nazi Era* (Annapolis, Md.: Naval Institute Press, 1990), p. 180. The AGNA, though not damaging to Germany's naval program in the 1930s, had been intended primarily as a prophylactic for British anxieties, to postpone the old Anglo-German antagonism generated by Tirpitz. However, the German announcement in December 1938 that the U-boat force would be built up to parity with the Royal Navy's submarines and that two new cruisers would carry a main armament of eight guns, when taken in context with the January 1939 decision to build the Z [*ziel*; "target"] Plan balanced fleet and the AGNA denunciation of April, do not suggest a statecraft overly sensitive on naval subjects.

[96]

the apologists are incorrect in arguing that one should not ask arms control to tackle the politically difficult cases. What is the use of an arms control process that yields agreement and general compliance only when the prospects for war are nearly totally absent? Arms control treaties typically overperform on tasks that do not need performing but are thoroughly incompetent in the face of genuine need. The problem does not lie with policy or policymakers but rather with arms control itself.

Fifth, the historical record does not prove in an absolute fashion the validity of the arms control paradox as developed through this book. But the reasoning of the paradox, which amounts to the proposition that an arms control process can cope only with relatively easy cases (or "arms limitation works best when needed least"),[17] is resoundingly consistent with such facts as are beyond dispute. Surely, it is no coincidence that arms limitation was: (1) sustainable in the 1920s but collapsed under the weight of Japanese and German ambition in the 1930s; (2) registered in the early 1970s but languished subsequently during Leonid Brezhnev's late-imperial epoch, only to revive when his successor-but-two decided that external tranquility was mandatory. The flow and ebb of history tells one a great deal less about arms control, or an alleged arms race, than about the course of political relations and domestic political conditions within the actual or possible high contracting parties. When political relations are generally cooperative in tenor, if not actually friendly, an arms control process might provide some positive reinforcement. Further, when political relations turn antagonistic, an arms control process tends to provide fuel for a *worsening* of relations. The currency of arms control is weaponry—a coin concerning which states are wont to be very sensitive indeed.

Thirty-plus years from the rediscovery of arms control theory in the late 1950s and early 1960s, the superpowers have demonstrated what their predecessors already had shown to be true in the 1920s and 1930s. Specifically, states tend to be able to agree not to do those things they had no wish to do anyway. For exam-

[17] Robert Gordon Kaufman, *Arms Control during the Pre-Nuclear Era: The United States and Naval Limitation between the Two World Wars* (New York: Columbia University Press, 1990), p. 144.

[97]

ple, the arms control record of recent decades registers such monumental successes as agreement not to place weapons of mass destruction in orbit or on the seabed, not to continue testing nuclear weapons in the atmosphere, not to behave dangerously in day-by-day encounters of naval forces at sea, and not to assist other states to become nuclear powers. With few honorable exceptions worthy of note, arms control is condemned to be either an instrument of political warfare (an "accoutrement of the Cold War")[18] or a strictly redundant registration of peaceable political intentions. History shows not a single plausible case of an arms limitation regime having an important, or reasonably arguable (e.g., not the Anglo-American case in the 1920s), benign effect upon strategic relationships *that otherwise could have led to war.*

Sixth, there is understandably a wide range of opinion on the strategic merit of the Washington and SALT arms control systems. Moreover, as Kaufman observes correctly with reference to the Washington regime, the balance of opinion tends to be cyclical.[19] In the 1940s, 1950s, and even 1960s, the shadow of World War II hung heavily over judgments upon interwar arms control. By the late 1960s and subsequently, however, the Washington treaty regime came to receive more favorable notice. The quality of scholarship was not notably different in the two periods, but fashion in historical judgment had changed, as fashion will, in this instance expressing new hopes for nuclear-age arms limitation.

I do not claim that the sad history of arms control *proves* my thesis beyond all doubt. I do claim both that the argument of arms control being a house of cards is consistent with the evidence and that all plausible and even some implausible objections to the argument are taken into account.

It is important to be sensitive to the argument that, because the difficult truly is difficult, one should not rush to a neat judgment in a complex case. In other words, before concluding, as opposed merely to speculating, that arms control ideas and attempted practice were irrelevant or worse to progress toward the classic

---

[18] Ken Adelman, "Arms Control Exit Signal," *Washington Times*, 16 April 1990, p. F3.
[19] Kaufman, *Arms Control during the Pre-Nuclear Era*, p. 83.

goals identified for the exercise, one needs to think carefully about evidence for success. Could the arms control record provide evidence, or tentative evidence, which would support the claim that a positive contribution was made toward the prevention of war?

Seventh and finally, there is simply no escaping the fact that history is what historians say it is. Since historians disagree, one has to select the interpretation, or mix of interpretations, that one favors. Not without reason did Oscar Wilde declare that "any fool can make history, but it takes a genius to write it."[20] Careful scholarship is always of value, but one must beware of the scholar's fallacy, which holds that some final truth about events awaits discovery by the spade of the sufficiently diligent archivist. Indeed, there are some subjects, such as the causes of World War I or some aspects of American history concerning which too many professional historians are overinterpreting familiar material, where more and more scholarship actually appears to impede understanding.

History is an art and not a science. The kinds of questions that I am asking of the arms control record cannot be answered from the historical record alone. Complex causal relationships cannot be definitively uncovered by archival research. Even if one knew everything that there was to know about the diplomatic process of naval arms limitation in the 1920s and 1930s, or about the arms control process which brought forth SALT I (1972), SALT II (1979), and START (1991), one would still only be close to the beginning of comprehension of how those protracted exercises performed or failed to perform as candidate contributions to the prevention of war.

THE WASHINGTON-LONDON SYSTEM, 1922–1938

On March 8, 1936, British Foreign Secretary Anthony Eden wrote a memorandum for the cabinet on the subject of British

---

[20] Quoted in Peter P. Witonski, ed., *Gibbon for Moderns: The History of the Decline and Fall of the Roman Empire with Lessons for America Today* (New Rochelle, N.Y.: Arlington House, 1974), p. 15.

policy choices toward Nazi Germany. His advice concerning agreements that should be "safe and advantageous" to conclude contained a truth about arms control which is as important and enduring as it is liable to be ignored by democracies in the periodic bouts of virulent optimism to which they are prone. The telling judgment in Eden's memorandum was his argument that agreements of a "safe and advantageous" kind would have a "durability . . . which might be assumed by reason of the fact that Herr Hitler [*inter alia*] would not be making any concrete concessions or submitting to any inconvenient restrictions."[21] A feature of the interwar years, as of the postwar period, was that the revisionist states—Imperial Japan, Nazi Germany, Fascist Italy, the USSR—did not sign on for "inconvenient restrictions." More often than not, restrictions that could have been inconvenient were simply ignored.

One might try to argue that the policymakers and negotiators on arms control for the *status quo* powers (by and large the United States, Britain, and France) have failed time and again to negotiate a "real arms control" whose power for peace would stem in part precisely from the inconvenience of its restrictions. Such an argument, though apparently logical and reasonable, in fact would be seriously in error. There are systemic reasons why would-be revisionist or rogue states decline to negotiate, or be bound by, restrictions they judge to be inconvenient. Those reasons amount to a restatement of—what else?—the arms control paradox. It is commonplace to notice, and for people to condemn, the scarcely arguable point that neither SALT I nor SALT II, nor even START before the June 1992 agreement, really bit into net war-fighting prowess.[22] Stepping back half a century, it is no less

---

[21] Quoted in Gibbs, *Grand Strategy*, vol. 1, p. 239.

[22] The U.S. Department of Defense noted in September 1989 that "silo conversion activity to replace the current variant of the SS-18 Satan [heavy ICBM]—which is the bulwark of the SRF's [Strategic Rocket Forces'] hard-target kill capability—with a newer, more accurate version (the SS-18 Mod 5) is under way. The increase in the Mod 5's warhead yield, along with improved accuracy, would, under a START treaty, help allow the Soviets to maintain their hard-target kill requirements *even with the 50 percent cut in heavy ICBMs START requires.*" *Soviet Military Power: Prospects for Change, 1989* (Washington, D.C.: Department of De-

plain that the authoritarian would-be revisionist powers of the interwar years did not endorse noteworthy restrictions on prospective net military prowess either.

When all is said and done, the Japanese signed on for, and then quite systematically flouted, arms limitation packages in 1922 and 1930, which amounted to a geostrategic triumph for Tokyo. It was perhaps ironic that Tokyo should choose to cheat on the rules of a system which functioned so much to its strategic advantage. Nazi Germany agreed through the AGNA of 18 June 1935, to restrict her naval construction to 35 percent of the Royal Navy—an agreement whose detailed terms Berlin treated with characteristic contempt[23] but which the *Kriegsmarine* knew would not press restric-

---

fense, 1989), pp. 44–45, emphasis added. The 1990 version of this document noted that "despite this limitation [the 50 percent cut in heavy ICBMs], improvements in the Mod 5's accuracy and yield will allow the Soviets to maintain a credible wartime hard-target kill capability." *Soviet Military Power, 1990* (Washington, D.C.: Department of Defense, 1990), p. 520.

[23] To be fair, the Third Reich's record of disdain for the detail of legal constraint over armaments was of a pattern with the behavior of its Weimar predecessor. See Hans W. Gatzke, *Stresemann and the Rearmament of Germany* (Baltimore: Johns Hopkins Press, 1954). Germany sought to construct superior naval vessels, unit for unit, a determination that inevitably obliged her to exceed the tonnage limits by ship and by class of the Washington-London system. Although the 35 : 100 ratio of AGNA set no practical limit upon German naval rearmament at the level of gross tonnage permitted, the unit by unit limits that the agreement adopted from Washington-London were sufficiently inconvenient as simply to be ignored (and lied about). Recent scholarship does not support D. C. Watt's generous view that the AGNA "was more or less faithfully observed until its denunciation in April 1939." "The Anglo-German Naval Agreement of 1935: An Interim Judgment," *Journal of Modern History*, 28 (June 1956), pp. 155–75. Strongly adverse judgment on Germany's compliance record with naval arms control can be found in Robin Ranger, "The Naval Arms Control Experience," *Washington Quarterly*, 10 (Summer 1987), pp. 53–55; and Kaufman, *Arms Control during the Pre-Nuclear Era*, p. 107. In his war memoirs, Winston Churchill was appropriately scathing on the subject. "The British Admiralty had recently [1935] found out that the last two pocket-battleships being constructed, the *Scharnhorst* and the *Gneisenau*, were of a far larger size than the [Versailles] Treaty allowed, and of a quite different type. In fact they turned out to be 26,000-ton light battle-cruisers, or commerce destroyers of the highest class [and not 10,000-ton armored cruisers]. In the face of this brazen and fraudulent violation of the Peace Treaty, carefully planned and begun at least two years earlier (1933), the Admiralty actually thought it was worth while making an Anglo-German Naval Agreement." *The Second World War*, vol. 1: *The Gathering Storm* (1948: rpt. London: Penguin, 1985), pp. 123–24. The myth of German compliance

tively for the better part of ten years. The AGNA was signed by the British because they were desperate to bind the new Germany *somehow, in some way,* and the experts were convinced that 35 percent was the best, possibly even the only, offer that Hitler would make. The SALT I and SALT II agreements on the limitation of strategic offensive arms, amounted in practice to little more than a license to Leonid Brezhnev's USSR to effect the qualitative improvement of its long-range nuclear arsenal. Moscow drove 300 SS-19 "light" ICBMs through the terms of SALT I and more than 300 SS-25 mobile ICBMs through the unratified SALT II. The former was strictly legal, but flagrantly in contradiction to the explanation of the treaty provided the U.S. Congress and public by the Nixon administration. The SS-25 ICBM has been deployed in what amounts to an insulting disdain for U.S. competence in monitoring and will in verifying noncompliance with the "one new type" (of "light" ICBM) provision in paragraph 9 of Article IV of the SALT II treaty. This is not to ignore the fact of U.S. refusal to ratify the treaty. The point is that Moscow lied determinedly and consistently about the allegedly compliant character of the SS-25.

The Washington-London arms control process and regime, while not "one of the major catastrophes of English history" (to quote Correlli Barnett on the outcome of the Washington Conference),[24] amounted very much to a house of cards. On balance, the

---

with the AGNA was supported in Richard Dean Burns and Donald Urquidi, *Disarmament in Perspective: An Analysis of Selected Arms Control and Disarmament Agreements between the World Wars, 1919–1939*, vol. 3: *Limitation of Sea Power* (Los Angeles: California State College at Los Angeles Foundation, July 1968), chap. 18.

[24] Correlli Barnett, *The Collapse of British Power* (1972; rpt. Gloucester, U.K.: Alan Sutton, 1984), p. 272. It is more plausible to argue, as does John Robert Ferris in an important book, that it was the 1930 London treaty, and not the 1922 Washington one, which had near catastrophic effects upon British security. Ferris argues that signature of the London treaty, set against the backcloth of the government's 1926–30 decisions to deny the Royal Navy the pace of modernization requested, was "Britain's single gravest strategic error of the interwar years." *Men, Money, and Diplomacy: The Evolution of British Strategic Policy, 1919–1926* (Ithaca: Cornell University Press, 1989), p. 181 (also see pp. 100 and 187). Ferris argues persuasively that, in principle, Britain had time in the 1930s to correct her strategic policy course and the naval programs inherited from the 1920s but that the London treaty imposed reductions, deferred building plans, and generally cost five

Washington system should be judged damaging to international security, while at best, it was irrelevant. Before turning specifically to analysis of the historic interwar journey for peace through arms limitation, however, it is important to consider an argument advanced by Paul M. Kennedy. Writing of the 1920s and *early* 1930s, Kennedy claims

> That these few years of "placidity" were to be virtually the last the armed services enjoyed, has made the British government, and its economic and strategic advisers, easy targets for retrospective criticism. It would, however, have taken a prophet of rare sagacity and insight to have foreseen that the international situation would change so swiftly, and that so many *simultaneous* threats to the British Empire would occur precisely at a time when its defenses were weakest and when the public's attention was riveted upon the domestic scene. Probably the government's greatest failure was that it was unlucky, which is always fatal in politics.[25]

No statesman should be faulted for failing to predict the future. Moreover, as Kennedy notes, it was an extraordinary ill fortune for the British governments of Stanley Baldwin and Neville Chamberlain to face simultaneous naval challenges, actual and prospective, in minor and major key in the North Sea, the Mediterranean, and the Pacific. But statesmen can and should be faulted for failing to plan prudently against surprise effect, for restricting knowingly the ability to act with the flexibility that they can predict that

---

years which truly, in retrospect, it was clear that the locusts ate. Ferris's work is useful in the clarity of the distinction he draws between the 1920s and the 1930s, with the world economic crisis of 1929–30 naturally as the watershed, and in his somewhat unfashionable thesis that Britain in the 1920s (and even the 1930s) had the potential, if grand-strategically properly directed, to remain the mistress of her imperial security. In his recent monumental study of the Royal Navy in World War II, Corelli Barnett delivers witheringly negative judgment upon the consequences in wartime of the pursuit of arms limitation in the preceding two decades. Barnett identified "the pernicious influence of the inter-war pursuit of naval arms limitation agreements" as one of "two recurring strands in the twentieth-century history of British seapower." The other strand comprised "weaknesses in the design and technology of major warships." *Engage the Enemy More Closely*, p. 374.

[25] Paul M. Kennedy, *The Rise and Fall of British Naval Mastery* (New York: Charles Scribner's Sons, 1976), p. 279.

their successors may need, and for discounting evidence of many kinds concerning the fragility of the political underpinnings of a particular arms agreement. Charles H. Fairbanks, Jr., has written that "arms limitation agreements, which by their very nature involve precise ratios and numbers of arms permitted to each side, are far more specific and detailed than most treaties. They thus lack the flexibility that enables most international agreements to bend with change and be infused with a new political content."[26]

In the 1920s and 1930s, and again in the 1970s and 1980s, the side of order quite gratuitously denied itself through arms control some of the flexibility it needed in order to be able to adapt strategy to changing times. Arms control could not and cannot address usefully the security problems that lie in the ambitions and anxieties of would-be revisionist states, but it could and does restrict a policymaker's freedom of action to address the problem with military means. The last word on this subject at this juncture will be allowed to Alfred Thayer Mahan. Writing in September 1902, following his personal experience as a delegate to the First Hague Peace Conference (May–July 1899)—called by Tsar Nicholas II for the principal purpose of trying to avoid the necessity of having to modernize his army's antiquated artillery park[27]—Mahan observed that "a tendency arises to seek the solution of difficulties in artificial and sometimes complicated international arrangements, contemplating an indefinite future, instead of in simple national procedure meeting each new situation as it develops, governed by a settled general national policy."[28] Mahan's modest and sensible suggestion found echoes in the 1980s. The case for "arms control without agreements," expressed in a prudent U.S. national security policy, had a small but select body of advocates.[29]

---

[26] Charles H. Fairbanks, Jr., "The Washington Naval Treaty, 1922–1936," in Robert J. Art and Kenneth N. Waltz, eds., *The Use of Force: International Politics and Foreign Policy* (Lanham, Md.: University Press of America, 1983, 2d ed.), pp. 476–77.

[27] See William W. Langer, *The Diplomacy of Imperialism, 1890–1902* (1935; rpt. New York: Alfred A. Knopf, 1968), pp. 582–83.

[28] Alfred Thayer Mahan, *Retrospect and Prospect: Studies in International Relations, Naval and Political* (London: Sampson Low, Marston, 1902), p. 214.

[29] For example, Kenneth L. Adelman, "Arms Control with and without Agree-

In the Washington (1922) and London (1930) treaties the three contemporary High Seas Powers—the United States, Britain, and Japan—agreed: (1) to cease building capital ships (battleships and battlecruisers) for ten years (extended for another five); (2) to a 5 : 5 : 3 ratio among their navies (initially in capital ship and aircraft carrier displacement but extended in 1930 to cruisers, destroyers, and submarines), as measured in the new metric of "standard displacement"; and (3) to a 35,000 ton limit on capital-ship displacement and a 16-inch caliber limit on main armament. The 1930 treaty specified offsetting asymmetries for the United States and Britain in cruiser tonnage between heavy cruisers (particularly favored by a Pacific-oriented and base-poor U.S. Navy) and light cruisers (favored by a Royal Navy that required large numbers of smaller vessels to protect trade worldwide). The European naval powers—France and Italy in the 1920s and 1930s, joined by Russia and Germany in the latter decade—added distinctive complications to a complex naval balance that would be the statistical delight of the U.S. defense-analytical community today.[30]

The Washington Conference of 1921–22 produced a whole package of agreements, actually no fewer than six treaties and one declaration, somewhat analogous to SALT I of 1972. Prominent among the political pillars of the Washington system was the somewhat undignified British abrogation of its 1902 alliance with Japan. This British decision not to renew her bilateral alliance with Japan was to prove to be the critical step on the path to the appeasement policy of the 1930s. Britain abandoned her old partner for security in the Far East but did not secure a replacement (until 7 December 1941). In exchange for the 1902 treaty between Tokyo and London, vague and general multinational pledges were substituted, bearing upon such topics as the security of, and

ments," *Foreign Affairs*, 63 (Winter 1984–85), 240–63; and Thomas C. Schelling, "What Went Wrong with Arms Control?" *Foreign Affairs*, 64 (Winter 1985–86), 219–33.

[30] Writing about the complications of multipolar naval relations with regard to the London Naval Conference of 1930, Kaufman observes that "if the Italians insisted on the right to build a navy as large as that of France, the British would have to abandon the two-power standard in Europe or increase its naval forces substantially. Correspondingly, the Americans and the Japanese would insist on the right to match any British increase." *Arms Control during the Pre-Nuclear Era*, p. 136.

assurance of universal access to, China (the "open door"), and declarations of good intent with respect to consultation over insular possessions in the western Pacific. Article XIX of the naval arms limitation treaty had the greatest significance of any item because it undermined the integrity both of the treaty it marred and of all the other provisions in all of the other treaties. This article prohibited new British fortifications (for naval bases) any closer to Japan than Singapore, and new American fortifications west of Hawaii. One could go on and on. The history of arms control is nothing if not rich in detail. But what did it all mean? What sense was there in the Washington-London system and what were the consequences of that system for the prospects of peace with security?

States are afflicted with the arms control regimes that they deserve politically. If the Washington system for the regulation of naval armament was severely flawed, then that is a judgment not upon some reified arms control process but rather upon the statesmen and the hands they had to play at the time. Even though this discussion is highly critical of the Washington arms limitation venture, I am not peddling the fallacy that if only another arms control policy, or no arms control policy at all, had been pursued, the outcome for international security, and just possibly for peace, might have been considerably happier. The generalization that by and large policymakers agree through arms limitation not to do what they prefer not to do anyway was as true in 1922 and 1930 as in 1972, 1979, and today.

If one argues that an arms control process proved to be nearly irrelevant to the course of critical political decisions and events, all that one need be saying is, first, that the existence of the arms control regime would appear to have had little significance for the prospects of war or peace, and second, that the arms limitation process would seem to have had only a modest impact upon naval doctrine and posture.

This book does not indulge in extensive what-if speculation concerning "alternative" interwar periods and the like. The Washington-London regime is assayed as it was, not as some alternative to it might have been. I am prepared to concede the theoretical, if unlikely, possibility that the treaty navies (which is to say the less-than-treaty navy of the United States and the more-than-treaty navy of Japan) of the powers in the 1920s and 1930s, for all their faults, may have been superior in their implications for international security than would the consequences have been of treaty-unregulated fleets. The central luminous fact about the Washington-London system was that its overall net effect was to constrain either not at all or not at all usefully the navies which in a blessedly uncoordinated fashion came close to defeating the guardians of Western civilization in 1940–43. Fortunately, the Axis had no common grand or military strategy.[31] In the classic American axiom, "the battle is the payoff." Naval arms limitation did not—of course, could not—prevent World War II. But its effects were painfully evident through much of the course of the war. To be specific, the Western maritime allies: (1) had no defensible bastions in the western Pacific; (2) had too few capital ships for the worldwide duties in need of performance;[32] (3) found that too many of their capital ships that were available were overage (courtesy of the fifteen-year building "holiday" [1922–36]) and/or poorly designed; (4) had far too few cruisers and destroyers (which, again, tended to be poorly designed for reason of treaty constraints on displacement); and (5) had allowed too little aircraft-carrier tonnage to permit extensive experimentation (and the treaty-compliant carriers could be of less than optimal size as a consequence of the unit and total displacement limits).

Britain and the United States were obliged to wage literally global, which means thoroughly maritime-dependent, war from

[31] *Axis* grand strategy truly is an oxymoron. In a brilliant essay written in 1945, Herbert Rosinski observed, "Thus we can see clearly in retrospect how, in those critical weeks after Pearl Harbor, the two coalition groups moved in diametrically opposite directions. The two Axis groups remained apart, in spirit no less than in space, each of them expecting the other to carry the main burden, each of them maintaining its own separate strategy and, therefore, envisaging the sea less as a pathway than as a barrier to protect them from counter-blows of their enemies." Herbert Rosinski, *The Development of Naval Thought*, ed. B. Mitchell Simpson, (Newport, R.I.: Naval War College Press, 1977), pp. 99–100.

[32] For example, in December 1939 the fifteen capital ships which the Washington system had allowed the British Royal Navy translated into only nine more or less ready for sea. Those nine somehow had to protect convoys against German surface raiders, watch the still-neutral Italian battle fleet, and contribute to the deterrence of Japan in Asian waters. See Barnett, *Engage the Enemy More Closely*, p. 78.

1939 to 1941 with navies dangerously undersized for their missions until late 1943. The Washington-London system, whatever the harm it inflicted upon Anglo-American seapower, did not inflict like damage upon the prospective strategic effectiveness of future enemies. The Axis center of gravity was *continental*, not maritime. Even Imperial Japan, whose deepest geostrategic ambitions were continental and not maritime, was seeking only a naval competence adequate to enable her to hold the maritime flank of her burgeoning east Asian empire as a defensive perimeter.[33] Japan, it should be recalled, both built her allowed treaty navy and "broke the rules seriously, systematically, and often clandestinely."[34] The Washington-London system specified a floor, not a ceiling, for the Imperial Japanese Navy.

Why did fortress Europe, including a conquered Britain, not become a geostrategic reality in 1940–42? Probably the leading reasons were because Hitler was too dilatory in his U-boat construction program and German operational (radio) signals security was so bad. In 1930 the Western maritime powers limited themselves to 180,000 (U.S.A.) and 146,800 (G.B.) in heavy cruiser tonnage and—of real note for putative trade-protection duties—to 143,500 (U.S.A.) and 192,200 (G.B.) in light cruiser tonnage, with 150,000 tons allowed to each for destroyers. The Nazi submarine force which nearly cost Britain and the United States the war, was permitted by the terms of the Anglo-German Naval Agreement (1935) to achieve parity with the submarine force of Britain. (Since submarines did not fight submarines in those days, the military sense in that provision can pass without comment). It is worth noting that British intelligence on German naval, including submarine, construction in the 1930s was so abysmally poor that it did not much matter what the AGNA permitted or prohibited. That, of course, sidesteps the fact that even when the British gov-

---

[33] Particularly insightful studies are Paul S. Dull, *A Battle History of the Imperial Japanese Navy (1941–1945)* (Annapolis, Md.: Naval Institute Press, 1978); H. P. Willmott, *Empires in the Balance: Japanese and Allied Pacific Strategies to April 1942* (Annapolis, Md.: Naval Institute Press, 1982); and Clark G. Reynolds, "The Continental State upon the Sea: Imperial Japan," in his *History and the Sea: Essays on Maritime Strategies* (Columbia: University of South Carolina Press, 1989), pp. 137–51.

[34] Kaufman, *Arms Control during the Pre-Nuclear Era*, p. 99.

ernment did have thoroughly reliable verification of German treaty noncompliance, to resort to the modern jargon, no appropriate policy response was unearthed by London (a familiar tale, indeed). If a large and important fraction of the government believes that good relations are essential with a treaty violator (e.g., Anglo-German relations in the 1936–38 period or Soviet-American relations much more recently), evidence of noncompliance is ignored. Even when a government does not quite ignore evidence of treaty violation, it can find itself paralyzed with respect to responses. Writing of his years (1983–87) as director of the Arms Control and Disarmament Agency (ACDA), Kenneth L. Adelman informs us that his "greatest disappointment [was that] we didn't do anything, really, about Soviet cheating. Not from want of answers. We never really found anything much *to do* about Soviet cheating. That's the sad truth."[35]

Lest I am accused of abusing the past unhistorically with the wisdom of hindsight, it may be necessary to explain that the argument here bears only upon the bottom line of the consequences of the Washington-London system. Of course, the Royal Navy of 1930 believed that the submarine menace *à la* 1917–18 had been mastered by ASDIC (in the United States, SONAR). Admiral Karl Donitz's U-boat force did not exist at that time, and of course, the Royal Navy could not predict in 1930 that by summer 1940 Donitz's U-boats (which had not yet been built because they were illegal under the Versailles treaty of 1919) would be able to operate from the Biscay coast of France and from Norway. Similarly, to recall Paul Kennedy's thoughts quoted earlier in this chapter, nobody could have predicted in 1930 that, geostrategically, the Royal Navy would face in ten to eleven years what anybody would have agreed was a truly worst-case scenario. The concern at this juncture simply is to note the consequences of arms con-

---

[35] Kenneth L. Adelman, "Where We Succeeded, Where We Failed," *Policy Review*, 43 (Winter 1988), p. 45. There were many things that the United States could do, or cease to do, by way of policy toward treaty noncompliance. To decline to sign-on for new treaties (e.g., INF in 1987) would have been one symbolically significant negative response. As an advisor to the U.S. government in the 1980s, I (in common with many other people, within and outside of official ranks) identified a wide range of possible and, in my opinion, desirable U.S. policy responses to violations (see Chapter 6).

trol, not to condemn well-meaning people who did not know where to order a reliable crystal ball.

It has been suggested above that some of the results of the Washington-London system were unfortunate. Particularly in the British case, there were to be in 1940–42 too few ships for trade protection and evacuation protection when and where they were desperately needed. Making excuses for statesmen and defense planners functioning as arms controllers is so easy that one needs to beware of becoming overly empathetic to their problems. No matter how just one endeavors to be when making historical judgment, there is no way in which one can expunge from the landscape of the mind the knowledge that the most destructive war in history occurred at the end of the period under examination here. Also, there can be no argument that the first and over-riding objective of arms control is the prevention, or direct and indirect assistance in the prevention, of war. In the 1930s something went fatally wrong with the functioning of the security structures that should enforce order. As always, while success has many fathers, failure is an orphan. Those of a more deterministic bent would incline to the view that World War II was so obviously the second round, a replay of the Great War, that the statesmen of the 1930s faced an impossible task in endeavoring to cope with the legacy of 1914–19 (to include the great Peace Conference).

Whatever was "right" for peace with security about the Washington-London system, indeed about arms control efforts in general in that interwar period, plainly it was not right enough. That is an important, even critically important, fact to register. It throws a searchlight beam upon the error in Joseph Kruzel's apparently reasonable argument that "if arms control is to have any productive future at all it must be shielded from the political burdens it has been required to carry in the past."[36] History shows quite unmistakably that arms control cannot be shielded from political burdens. If arms control is to attempt important missions, if it is to make a difference, it has to be thoroughly political. War

[36] Joseph Kruzel, "Arms Control and Arms Competition," in B. Thomas Trout, James E. Harf, and William H. Kincade, eds., *Essentials of National Security: A Conceptual Guide for Teachers* (Menlo Park, Calif.: Addison-Wesley, 1989), p. 128.

and peace are two sides of a political coin. If arms control could not handle the hostile, or at best nonpermissive, political traffic of the 1930s, what value can it have? Political hard times do not excuse the collapse of an arms control process; rather, they demonstrate its irrelevance. There is a considerable practical unity between the arms control experiences of the 1920s and 1930s and of the late 1960s to the present. With a view to locating pointers to some more general wisdom, the Washington-London system is discussed below with reference to its politics and political consequences and with regard to the broader implications of the naval force ratios expressed in the key metric of "standard displacement."[37]

Each of the three High Seas Powers had pressing domestic reasons for a naval arms limitation agreement in 1921–22. As frequently is the case, there is a redundancy of plausible explanations for why the Washington system was feasible, probably uniquely so, in 1921–22. Certainly, there were hard-nosed skeptics in each of the countries, but even the contemporary skeptics, with few important exceptions, judged the Washington treaty on balance to be some variant of a regrettable necessity.

There is no good reason to deny the sincerity of the American and British political leaders most responsible for the treaty. The U.S. Navy's General Board held sensible views on the causes of wars and the dynamics and consequences of arms races, but those views did not move the body politic or government policy

---

[37] In the words of part 4 of the Washington treaty: "The standard displacement of a ship is the displacement of the ship complete, fully manned, engined, and equipped ready for sea, including all armament and ammunition, equipment, outfit, provisions and fresh water for crew, miscellaneous stores and implements of every description that are intended to be carried in war, but without fuel or reserve feed water on board." *Conference on the Limitation of Armament, Washington, November 12, 1921–February 6, 1922* (Washington, D.C.: Government Printing Office, 1922), p. 1601. As Robin Ranger suggests ("Learning from the Naval Arms Control Experience," *Washington Quarterly*, 10 [Summer 1987], p. 48), standard displacement is broadly comparable to throwweight, ceteris paribus (accuracy, reliability), the most important rough indicator of a ballistic missile's military potential. It is not surprising that definition of what is and is not a "new" missile, a definition focused upon throwweight, was the most difficult, and therefore the last, issue to be resolved in the nine-year-long START negotiations which concluded in July 1991.

in 1921. The leading light of the Washington Conference, U.S. Secretary of State Charles Evans Hughes, claimed that the Conference "absolutely ends the race in competition in naval armaments."[38] No one has suggested that Hughes was dissimulating. The affected navies and their lobbying organizations made their several negative cases in terms of realpolitik, but the treaty was retailed to the public as the conclusive solution to an arms race problem that could cause another great war. Peace by conference was very much the vogue in 1921–22. Barely three years from the dreadful events of 1914–18, the prevalence of enthusiasm for nonviolent modes of conflict resolution was understandable, if ultimately unfortunate. As a well-known contemporary commentator argued in 1932, "Throughout history peace conferences have been the grave of reputations and the womb of future wars. The Conference of Paris [1919] has more than justified the first of these attributes and there is no presently apparent reason why it should not fulfill the second function also."[39] The Washington system was to reveal what its nuclear-age SALT successor would have to reveal in its turn to those unable to learn from history. Namely, the easier matters tend to be negotiated first, for the quite unremarkable reason that they are easier. The would-be regulators of virtually all things naval in the 1920s, discovered that 1921–22 (like SALT I in 1972) had been atypical in its relatively permissive political context and in the negotiability of its simple structure. Cruisers, destroyers, and submarines were to prove less readily tractable in the follow-on negotiations, as in a different forum aircraft and land armaments also were to prove.

There is something positive to be said for a Washington treaty that provided legal, or legalistic and even moralistic, cover for the truly historic *formal* surrender of naval superiority by Britain. Britain lacked the economic means to enforce naval superiority over the United States by competition, while any such foolish en-

---

[38] *Conference on the Limitation of Armament*, p. 248. In his next sentence Hughes claimed that "it [the treaty] leaves the relative security of the great naval powers unimpaired."

[39] John W. Wheeler-Bennett, *Disarmament and Security Since Locarno, 1925–1931: Being the Political and Technical Background to the General Disarmament Conference, 1932* (New York: Macmillan, 1932), p. 25.

deavor certainly would have exacerbated trans-Atlantic political antagonisms. Having granted so much, we also need to note that neither Britain nor the United States was able politically (largely Washington) or economically (largely London) to pursue the naval competition that appeared to be pending, and neither country deemed war against the other to be an acceptable option in their security relationship.

Japan acceded formally to the Washington-London system until 1936—and cheated quite systematically, as noted already—not in wide-eyed expectation of the dawn of an era of perpetual peace but because she had no superior alternatives. The terms of the treaties of 1922 and 1930, though nominally damaging to Japanese "face," a fact fatal in Japanese domestic politics in the 1930s, actually yielded her the military superiority that she needed in the western Pacific and hence in China. It is possible to argue that the Washington system was a disaster for international security. One can hold quite plausibly that resentment against the system's apparently discriminatory terms and the voicing, but not pressing, of Western suspicions about Tokyo's possible noncompliance may have been critical in turning Japan from a generally responsible and cooperative player into what amounted to a rogue polity by the early 1930s.[40] It is always possible that maintenance in some form of the Anglo-Japanese Alliance after 1921 might have precluded that poisonous sense of victimized isolation that Japan's leaders later came to feel.

On balance, the argument in the paragraph immediately above is unpersuasive. A principal difficulty was that the three key strategic players (the High Seas Powers) and the fragile state of Japanese-American relations focused as always upon China severely limited London's freedom of choice. London chose Washington over Tokyo because Washington denied London the option of two special relationships: the ally of my antagonist cannot be my friend. Without denying the malign contribution of racism in Japanese-American relations, that antagonism only became serious

---

[40] See Stephen Pelz, *The Race to Pearl Harbor: The Failure of the Second London Naval Conference and the Onset of World War II* (Cambridge: Harvard University Press, 1974); and Michael A. Barnhart, *Japan Prepares for Total War: The Search for Economic Security, 1919–1941* (Ithaca: Cornell University Press, 1987).

when Japanese policy ambitions on the continent of Asia were translated into brutal action in 1931. Japan's military-dominated governments of the 1930s would not accept the continuing humiliation of a legislated, if geostrategically nonexistent, naval inferiority. The core of the problem was Japan's policy intention to construct a great east Asian empire, an ambition that required the securing of an economic underpinning that the Japan of the interwar years obviously lacked. It is plausible to suggest that the Washington-London system overwhelmingly was a political irrelevance, which was unfortunate given that peace and war are political subjects. The consequences of the arms limitation regime were marginally negative on the political side and somewhat more serious in their military-technical aspects. The naval relations of the great powers were not a significant cause of World War II in either Europe or the Pacific, but the material state of those relations as of 1939–42 did have definite implications for the operational feasibility of strategic choices. The Washington system rested upon the continued political preponderance of moderate opinion in Japan, the absence of anarchy in China, and the continuation of the Versailles-Locarno era in Europe. The naval arms control system of the 1920s was fashioned by and for a political context that began to disintegrate rapidly after 1931 with the Japanese invasion of Manchuria.

Writing at the beginning of the SALT era in 1970, Hedley Bull argued that "'parity' has no more strategic meaning now than between 1922 and 1936."[41] Unfortunately, it is as easy to criticize both the parity in the Anglo-American 5 : 5 ratio of the Washington system and the disparity of 5 : 5 : 3, to consider Japan, as it is difficult to suggest any practicable alternative consistent with negotiability. Parity is a political, not a strategic concept. The SALT and START negotiators of recent years have had no more idea how to legislate true strategic parity through arms control than did those of their forbears in the 1920s who inadvertently persuaded strategically ignorant politicians that a yardstick could be

[41] Hedley Bull, "Strategic Arms Limitation: The Precedent of the Washington and London Naval Treaties," in Morton A. Kaplan, ed., *SALT: Problems and Prospects* (Morristown, N.J.: General Learning Press, 1973), p. 50.

invented to assay the worth of each naval unit.[42] Even if two or more governments genuinely wished to regulate their military relations on the basis of a strategically strict parity, they would not know how to do it. Not to mince matters, the job cannot be done.

Aside from the narrowly technical and human-operator distinctions between two countries' arsenals or fleets, such nontrivial matters as national geography and unique geopolitical interests must help determine the value of weapons. The Washington regime with its 5 : 5 : 3 ratio—though Japan was permitted mathematical parity in submarine displacement (at 52,700 tons) by the London treaty of 1930—exemplifies an inherent, and hence inescapable, problem with formal processes of arms regulation. Specifically, a government may have no difficulty living with some facts of real or apparent military inferiority, but few policymakers are willing publicly and formally to bind their country to such inferiority. In short, 5 : 5 : 3 mattered in Japanese domestic politics very much because that painfully explicit legal ratio enshrined both Tokyo's acceptance of a smaller navy and the Anglo-American judgment that Tokyo should have a smaller navy.

Because the 1991 START regime should require reductions in the U.S. strategic offensive arsenal down to a *mere* 9000 or 10,000 warheads (though Bush and Yeltsin agreed in June 1992 to START II limits that translate as 3,044 weapons for Russia and 3,492 for the United States), it is difficult to argue that an absence of genuinely strategic reasoning behind such a generous range could be of much consequence for international security. But if the subjects of negotiation—as in the 1920s and 1930s, and just possibly again in the 1990s—are classes of (naval) platforms with numbers of units counted only in the very low tens, or even the teens (the London treaty of 1930 allowed Britain, for example, only fifteen capital ships and fifteen heavy cruisers), a politically expedient "optical parity" could be anything but fault-tolerant in the unforgiving real world of military action.

A process of negotiated arms regulation is certain to discover

[42] See Raymond G. O'Connor, "The Yardstick and Naval Disarmament in the 1920s," *Mississippi Valley Historical Review*, 45 (December 1958), 441–63.

that apparent parity is politically inescapable. The 5 : 5 : 3 of the Washington system thus does not stand out as being at all unique in its astrategic absurdity. Given the obvious geostrategic differences between the policy-support burdens placed upon their navies by Britain and the United States, and the widely acknowledged contemporary attitude that an Anglo-American war was an impossibility, it is a strain to find persuasive excuses for the 5 : 5 dimension to the 5 : 5 : 3 ratio. A reasonable person might ask what the two great maritime democracies were about in negotiating arms limitation *between themselves*. The 5 : 3 ratio at least made some political sense, if only in the Japanese-American case; there was little of significance dividing London and Tokyo. Unfortunately for international security, the 5 : 5 : 3 ratio and the accompanying prohibition upon new fortifications on islands in the western Pacific, legislated away the more obvious solution to a problem the treaty neglected to address. The ratios in the Washington-London systems translated into at least near-term naval impotence for the United States in the China Sea and the western Pacific and potentially a fatal danger to Britain's empire in the Far East.

Ironically, the 5 : 5 : 3 disparity, which was to Japan's real military advantage once strategic geography was appreciated, actually helped undermine the security system it was established to support. The formal, if unreal, inferiority of 5 : 5 : 3 fueled bitter domestic resentment in Japan, as did the apparently undeserved British betrayal of the old alliance in 1921 under blunt American pressure. After all, Japan had been an effective and faithful ally of Britain. Moreover, purposeful Japanese evasion of some of the terms of the Washington-London regime fueled a stream of half-hearted and ineffective, but politically irritating, Western queries and complaints.

LESSONS OF HISTORY

Writing two years before the signing of SALT I in 1972, Hedley Bull offered the apparently reasonable advice that "the political and strategic context of SALT is so radically different from that of the interwar naval limitations that it would be foolish to derive 'lessons' from the latter directly to the former."[43] More than two decades later, his advice looks overcautious. Provided one is sensible about just how rigorously one thinks of a lesson and how direct "directly derived" is required to be, it is persuasive to argue that the interwar experience with the formal negotiated regulation of naval arms offers close to a blueprint for its strategic (nuclear) arms successor. Notwithstanding the ever present fact of nuclear weapons and the much greater simplicity of the structure of the superpower arms competition over the multilateral context of naval arms negotiation in the 1920s and 1930s, there is little that has been learned about arms control of recent decades that was not learned by a previous generation of would-be Western peacemakers or competition "managers."

As readers may surmise, the Washington-London system has been treated here at some length precisely because it is almost infinitely remote to an ahistorical contemporary U.S defense community yet massively relevant in its illustration of general arguments. The case of the Washington-London system adds depth of evidence to the argument of this book, while at the same time it evades the problems of live controversy. Furthermore, because of the final verdict of history on the 1920s and 1930s, otherwise known as World War II, and the radical changes in weapons technology that separate that period from the present, the Washington-London system is a closed one. The topics treated in the next chapter, though (contemporary) historical, are to a greater or lesser degree still open-ended. Opinions vary among scholars about the merit in naval arms limitation between the wars, but at least no one can claim that the best is yet to come (e.g., you may not like START I or CFE I but wait until you see START II or CFE II—arms control by promissory note, redeemed fortuitously by the outbreak of peace in the 1990s). Whatever one's overall verdict on the Washington-London regime of naval arms regulation, candidate lessons for the present day include the following:

[43] Bull, "Strategic Arms Limitation," p. 46.

- Arms control is negotiable in unusually politically permissive contexts (e.g., 1921–22 and 1930) and collapses, or at least goes into remission, when the political context becomes much more antagonistic.
- Arms control cannot achieve its widely advertised objectives (e.g., to terminate the arms race or to guarantee peace) or even assist significantly in their achievement. Indeed, arms control is as likely to fuel antagonism as it is to alleviate or prevent it (e.g., as in the case of Japan in the late 1920s and the early 1930s).
- If arms control is negotiable at all, it will be negotiated to suit a political agenda and very much in political terms to the probable exclusion of strategic rationales. The magnetic pull of nominal parity and similar astrategic notions will render treaty regimes net problems, rather than solutions, to potentially serious military challenges (e.g., the 5 : 5 : 3 ratio and the Anglo-American problem of operating in the western Pacific without an adequate fortified base structure).
- Arms control constraints will help (mis)shape overall military posture, including the design of particular weapon systems (e.g., treaty cruisers and pocket-battleships). Treaty-compliant or even treaty-evasive weapon systems will make sense for arms control but not necessarily in tactical or operational terms.
- When arms control agreements are pending, the legislators in democracies are reluctant to fund weapons that may have to be abandoned. Both Britain and the United States were reluctant to build up to treaty limits, lest the next treaty should reduce those limits.
- Authoritarian countries cheat, while democracies are unable to design and implement a timely and effective compliance or safeguards policy.
- The severe regulation of some armaments motivates countries to focus their attention upon unregulated, or less regulated, weapon categories (e.g., from battleships and battle cruisers to heavy cruisers and aircraft carriers).

There is nothing itemized immediately above which the student of SALT and START cannot discover from the record of the 1970s, 1980s, and early 1990s. When one appreciates that these candidate lessons would seem to be common to the prenuclear and nuclear eras of arms control experience, confidence in the argument advanced here should be enhanced. The arms control record of the 1970s, 1980s, and early 1990s is entirely consistent with the lessons of the interwar period. The pattern of disappointment with arms control experience is too marked, over too many years, and covering too many different state players and weapon technologies to be dismissed plausibly as mere coincidence.

[5]

Mystery Tour:
From SALT to START

I've come to learn there are no new mistakes in arms control.
We usually just keep on making the same old ones.
                                    —Kenneth L. Adelman, 1988

THE PAST IS NOT EVEN A FOOTNOTE

Not to reinforce failure is a military maxim. A United States that negotiated fairly determinedly for nine years to achieve START and has conducted speculative analyses of a START II regime is denying the force of this venerable maxim. This chapter examines the SALT era to see if there is hope that START may perform in ways useful for peace and security.

Policymakers have returned again and again to the poisoned well of the negotiated limitation of armaments. My contention is that the protracted arms control experience of the interwar years serves as a valid paradigm for SALT and START. Both enterprises began with an apparent rough approximation to a freeze—"Stop Now," for the slogan of 1921—on the military balance in major combatant platforms (the capital ship or the ICBM and SLBM forces), and both were sanctified and viewed as expressing a dominant theory of arms race termination (or major control). The point has already been made that the founding fathers of nuclear-age arms control theory gave every appearance of having learned nothing of note from the history of the 1920s and 1930s. Indeed, the veritable torrent of arms control literature which has flowed since 1960 is all but silent on the prenuclear experience. The framers of SALT I recognized no debts to a prior generation of statesmen who had negotiated for the control of "strategic" armaments.

The U.S. negotiators of SALT II allowed themselves to learn relatively little even from SALT I, with the result that a treaty (and protocol) of trivial or negative merit was oversold in what transpired to be a politically nonpermissive environment.[1] Ironically, however, a Reagan administration publicly committed to the proposition that the SALT II treaty was "fatally flawed," nonetheless agreed until June 1986 to adhere de facto to the regime's constraints. The explanation lay in the residual grip upon the public mind of the vague association of arms control with peace and in the liberality of the provisions of the unratified treaty. More interesting than what the negotiators of SALT I inherited, or neglected to inherit, from the interwar years, or what SALT II owed to the SALT I experience, is the question of what START reveals about the practicable accomplishments of arms control.

The START treaty stands upon the better part of four decades of twentieth-century experience with the negotiated regulation of (strategic) armament. START [I] poses few demands for radical strategic decision in Moscow or Washington, large though the reductions in treaty-accountable force levels will be.[2] But, the

---

[1] People in search of the overselling of SALT II need look no further than to the classic in the genre, U.S. Department of State, Bureau of Public Affairs, *SALT II: The Reasons Why* (Washington, D.C.: Government Printing Office, May 1979). There are probably more fallacies in this two-page document than in any other document on the subject. For example, eschewing the risk of understatement, the document claims flatly that "SALT II will reduce the risk of war." If one were seeking to draft a parody of bad arguments in praise of arms control, one would be tested severely to improve on *SALT II: The Reasons Why*. For a vigorously worded contemporary complaint about the official retailing of SALT II to the American public, see Kenneth L. Adelman, "Rafshooning the Armageddon: Selling SALT," *Policy Review*, 9 (Summer 1979), 85–102. For a detailed study friendly to SALT II, see Dan Caldwell, *The Dynamics of Domestic Politics and Arms Control: The SALT II Treaty Ratification Debate* (Columbia: University of South Carolina Press, 1991). Caldwell believes that the "failure to ratify significantly set back American-Soviet relations and the effort to control strategic nuclear arms for almost a decade" (p. 199). Neither of those claims commands respect.

[2] The START treaty is structured around common ceilings of 1600 strategic nuclear delivery vehicles, 6000 total treaty-accountable warheads, a subtotal of 4900 warheads allowed to be carried on ICBMs and SLBMs, and a sublimit of 1100

START II force levels of 3000–3,500 agreed in June 1992 in the context of political peace between Russia and the United States could—as Americans and particularly Britons discovered of their fleets early in World War II—be too small a force for security comfort should the political climate deteriorate.[3] Of course, now that superpower political peace looks irreversible on all significant fronts, allocation of 3000 START-accountable warheads appears as irrelevant as do Russian-oriented U.S. nuclear strategy and

---

warheads allowed on mobile ICBMs. Bomber-carried weapons are systematically undercounted; the Soviet heavy ICBM force is to be halved (from 308 to 154); while in a side agreement *nuclear*-armed sea-launched cruise missiles are to be confined unverifiably to a *deployed* total of less than 880, a provision arguably modified in practice by President Bush's 27 September 1991 decision not to deploy nuclear-armed SLCMs to sea ordinarily in peacetime. See the bundle of fact sheets issued as *START: The Strategic Arms Reduction Treaty, US-Soviet Summit, Moscow, July 30–31, 1991,* by the U.S. Arms Control and Disarmament Agency. The scale of reduction in nuclear forces required to be effected over seven years by START may seem to be at odds with my observation that it will pose "few demands for radical strategic decision in Moscow or Washington." Paradoxically, if anything, the net effect of START is to lend greater military-*technical* (not political) credence to the war-fighting ambitions of both sides. START will oblige neither side to restructure its strategic force posture away from a triad-plus (plus nuclear-armed, long-range cruise missiles), nor to alter targeting philosophy. Bearing in mind that weapons are also targets, it follows that dramatic cuts in force levels need not be gifts for peace. The radical strategic decision that is pending in Moscow and in Washington is the sense to be made of strategic nuclear forces contingently prepared to wage world war against yesterday's foe. Compared with the political implications of the demise of the Cold War for strategy, forces, and war plans, the 1991 START treaty is very much an anticlimax. To round the picture out, one should say that START pales into the status of near-trivia when set against the future uncertainties faced by the successor states of the USSR. For an outstanding analytical history of START, see Kerry M. Kartchner, *Negotiating START: The Quest for Stability and the Making of the Strategic Arms Reduction Treaty* (New Brunswick, N.J.: Transaction Books, 1992).

[3] 3000–3,500 warheads would not be deployed as 3000–3,500 targets. If deployment platforms and delivery vehicles were not downloaded by a process of deMIRVing, or defractionation of missile payload, a single U.S. Ohio class submarine, for example, would carry an average of 192 warheads (24 × 8). The verification problem with downloading, i.e., the risk of covert "breakout," is so severe that the START treaty restrictions on this process are quite inhibiting. The treaty allows only 1250 warheads on three missile types to be downloaded. Beyond reducing the Minuteman III ICBM from three down to one or two warheads, only 500 warheads may be downloaded off one or two other missile systems. These provisions probably do not provide adequate scope for any very useful measure of downloading on the part of the U.S. SLBM force.

nuclear war plans. President Bush's success in 1992 in negotiating the elimination of all MIRVed ICBMs in order to address the stability problem as he saw it cannot have dramatic consequences for the prospects of peace. The reason why radical notions for a START II regime may be less than radical in their political implications is precisely because the extant condition of Russian-American relations already yields an "unparalleled opportunity" to change the nuclear posture of the United States and Russia.[4]

Aside from the atavistic thought that MIRVed SLBMs—a category in which the United States excels—today can do much of the hard-target counterforce job previously assigned to ICBMs, the arms control events of the present time could almost have been scripted to illustrate my thesis. George Bush spoke on 27 September 1991 of "seizing this opportunity" for bilateral and unilateral arms control created by better relations, apparently without recognizing the logical contradiction in his position. Mutual force reductions are not important for peace any more than the elimination or reduction of so-called destabilizing weapons (MIRVed ICBMs, allegedly). It is, rather, political peace that facilitates and enables further force reductions. When on 5 October Gorbachev trumped Bush's 27 September announcement and offers by promising a *unilateral* Soviet reduction in START treaty-accountable warheads to 5000—instead of the 6000 permitted—it was evident that political theater and perhaps economic desirability were firmly in the saddle of policy. If the superpowers are politically at peace, it will not matter where the level of Russian treaty-accountable warheads eventually settles.

The American experience with SALT and START can be described as a mystery tour. The tour guides have had their heads full of old wives' tales about stability and the value of arms control in general; they have proceeded often expediently in anticipatory fear of the demands of the tourists but have lacked maps or even a sense of desirable direction. It is amazing that on 27 September 1991 President Bush could talk about reducing the risk of nuclear war in the same breath that he advanced what then were

[4] President George Bush, "The Peace Dividend I Seek Is Not Measured in Dollars . . . ," *Washington Post*, 28 September 1991, p. A23.

the latest variants of old ideas for strategic arms reduction. The tactician's worldview was triumphant. A cut here, a limit there, a control somewhere else, and the *strategic* questions supposedly will take care of themselves.

THE SMALL MATTER OF PURPOSE

Unlike the case, say, of the nuclear Non-Proliferation Treaty (NPT) (signed 1 July 1968; entered into force 5 March 1970), it has never been clear just what SALT, and now START, should be designed to achieve. The U.S. government asserts that "the principal U.S. objective in strategic arms control is to increase stability in the U.S.-Soviet [now C.I.S., or Russian] nuclear relationship at significantly lower levels of nuclear weapons."[5] If the concepts of "stability" and "nuclear relationship" had integrity, the assertion would warrant respect. By way of contrast with SALT and START, whatever the problems with the administration of the NPT regime, there has never been any doubt that the nuclear-weapon state signatories shared an overriding vital interest in retarding the pace of nuclear proliferation. Overriding, that is, of occasional allied or other demands for nuclear assistance (albeit with the periodic turning of a convenient blind eye, as in the case of U.S. policy toward Israel's covert nuclear weapons program). Similarly, success or failure has been easy to measure in principle. The fewer the number of currently non-nuclear weapon states who acquire nuclear weapons, or the more slowly they do so, the more successful the NPT regime will have proved to be. Of course, this is an oversimplification. There are many reasons why a country may choose not to acquire nuclear weapons, few of which are traceable to costs imposed by the NPT. The case of Iraq has shown just how little the NPT regime and international inspection is worth in the face of a resolute political will, and the financial means, to evade its solemn provisions. Saddam Hussein's Iraq, a signatory to the NPT system, has regarded that

[5] U.S. Arms Control and Disarmament Agency (ACDA), *The Strategic Arms Reduction Treaty, Central Limits*, 29 July 1991.

treaty in the same spirit that Weimar Germany regarded the Versailles *diktat*.

From time to time some scholarly gadfly will argue that nuclear proliferation, *very selectively exercised*, can aid international stability.[6] Unfortunately, the countries that could be trusted implicitly to be reliably benign as nuclear-weapon states (e.g., Canada, Sweden, Australia, and Switzerland), are no longer the countries strongly motivated to join the nuclear club. Overall, however, there is a usefully high ratio of administration and management to politics in the care and maintenance of the NPT regime.[7] The contrast with SALT and START could hardly be more stark. The NPT does not work very usefully for the goals of arms control any better than did SALT, or will START, but that is a different matter.

In the NPT world, statesmen and administrators do not work directly and impractically for peace. Instead, they have the more manageable task of inhibiting nuclear proliferation—an unambiguous purpose that is assumed to serve as a practical surrogate for the first classic objective of arms control, to help prevent wars from occurring. In SALT and START, alas, there is no obvious and practical surrogate for the prevention of war;[8] the overall effective purpose is, to say the least, obscure (i.e., there is no self-evident equivalent to the retardation of the spread of nuclear weapons), and the policy motives of the high contracting parties would appear to have been far apart indeed.

Unlike the interim agreement on offensive arms of SALT I, SALT II, and now START, the ABM treaty of 1972 was at least firmly single-minded of purpose. "Each party undertakes not to

---

[6] For example, Kenneth N. Waltz, *The Spread of Nuclear Weapons: More May Be Better*, Adelphi Papers no. 171 (London: IISS, 1981).

[7] See the analysis in Lewis A. Dunn, "Four Decades of Nuclear Nonproliferation: Some Lessons from Wins, Losses, and Draws," *Washington Quarterly*, 13 (Summer 1990), 5–18; and *Containing Nuclear Proliferation*, Adelphi Papers no. 263 (London: IISS, Winter 1991). Dunn emphasizes the importance of the broad political context as well as political norms (e.g., nonproliferation as a value).

[8] But widely favored candidates include the reduction of arms, the reduction or limitation of first-strike weapons, arms race stability, crisis stability, and "strategic stability" writ large. For a thoroughly orthodox view, see the Panel on the Future of Strategic Systems, *Securing Strategic Stability* (Washington, D.C.: Center for Strategic and International Studies, December 1988).

deploy ABM systems for a defense of the territory of its country and not to provide the basis for such a defense" (Article I, paragraph 2). The interim agreement of SALT I referred in its preamble to "the relationship between strategic offensive and defensive arms," a relationship, it was claimed, which had been taken "into account." The SALT II and START treaties have made no such claim to take the offense-defense relationship "into account," whatever that obscure phrase might be held to mean.

As I have had occasion to observe already, arms control is about politics.[9] The SALT-START process has been an intermittent arm-wrestling contest with several outcomes at different dates expressing the balance of political will and interest, grand-strategic (not only military) muscle, and negotiating competence between the two sides. Being of necessity a political negotiation and not a process of cooperative arms race management, the various agreements and treaties on strategic arms registered since 1969 have not been by way of technical solutions, even partial solutions, to technical problems—though that was not for want of trying by U.S. arms control theorists. Bearing in mind that merit for stability, like deterrence, can be claimed in praise of virtually any favored position, weapon program, or strategic idea without fear of authoritative rebuttal, the superpowers have struggled through negotiation and unilateral military achievement to secure net military advantage and to preclude net military disadvantage. If the outcome at any particular point in time truly warranted description as "stability," then that was the product of accident, of the massive fault-tolerance toward expedient policymaking of arsenals as large as those of the superpowers, and possibly of the irrelevance of the details of the strategic nuclear balance to questions of war and peace.[10]

To date, only with respect to the ABM treaty have SALT and

[9] A point I made bluntly many years ago. See Colin S. Gray, "The Arms Race Is about Politics," *Foreign Policy*, 9 (Winter 1972–73), 117–29. Whatever the strengths and weaknesses of this article, the fact that it was published in *Foreign Policy* spoke volumes to the contemporary state of play in arms control understanding and debate. My title and thesis were akin to the revelation that the world is round.

[10] A thought developed in my "Nuclear Strategy: Do the Details Matter?" *Arms Control Today*, 20 (October 1990), 37–38.

START had an unambiguous purpose. Unfortunately, that purpose, to prevent deployment of meaningful BMD, has been achieved as successfully as its rationale is open to serious challenge.[11] It is not scholarly pedantry to ask of SALT and START what is their purpose. On behalf of the American people, the U.S. Senate must ratify treaties. What criteria should be applied? More often than not, the defense of a candidate arms control regime reduces to the claims that the treaty is: (1) the best that could be negotiated; (2) tolerably equitable, optically and in its probable consequences; and (3) sufficiently verifiable. None of those three points advances any claim in praise of the substance of what was negotiated. Thus far, one might add, the substance of what has been negotiated in SALT and START on strategic offensive arms has not much mattered, because the terms of the agreement (1972) and the treaties (1979 and 1991) have been so liberal. To the uncertain degree to which perceptions of the military balance play as a factor for war or peace, any substantial menace to American security would flow more from a failure to modernize forces as allowed, than from any fatal inequity in the regimes negotiated. As a matter of high theory it might be added that the possible benign political consequences of an arms control regime could persuade the signatories to relax their military competitive efforts. What to some critics would appear as a lulling effect of arms control might in reality reflect instead a changed perception of threat. This possibility translates as another statement of the basic case for arms control and, as such, is rejected here. It is always possible, even probable, that perceptions of threat will alter during the lifetime of an arms control negotiation or regime, though for a variety of reasons that owe little to the partially cooperative management of the arms competition. For just one glorious example, the START treaty, which took nine years to negotiate, was born into a strategic context in 1991 that no longer needed it.

---

[11] As Donald G. Brennan said in 1972, "The proposed ABM Treaty does the wrong thing well and the Interim Agreement does the right things badly." Testimony in U.S. Congress, Senate Committee on Foreign Relations, *Strategic Arms Limitation Agreements, Hearings*, 92d Cong., 2d sess. (Washington, D.C.: Government Printing Office, 1972), p. 186.

[127]

A genuine confusion lies beneath, indeed, helps explain, the plethora of rationales advanced in praise of SALT and START from the beginning of the formal negotiating process in November 1969 to the present day. The U.S. government has never really known what it was about in SALT or START. That enduring and painfully discernible fact has had a democratizing effect upon public explanations. All rationales for SALT and START are created equal, with their relative importance determined by the shifting political context. Priorities among rationales are determined tactically rather than strategically. Almost existentially, SALT and START have been about what is possible to negotiate, and they are explained with reference to the ideas and symbols that resonate most favorably with particular audiences. For the restricted purposes of this analysis, the workings of the arms control paradox are temporarily set aside as a factor. Let it be assumed that there is no such paradox and that an arms control process, in principle at least, can accomplish many positive things, great and small. On what criteria should citizens judge the venture with SALT and START which already is more than two decades in duration?

One criterion would be arms reduction. To date, SALT and START have licensed, or perhaps tolerated if not actively condoned or encouraged, an increase in strategic offensive arsenals by a factor of between 2 1/2 (the United States) and six (the Soviet Union). START was advertised as requiring massive cuts in deployed forces—roughly 50 percent—but the reality of START I will be less dramatic. START I will lead only to cuts, overall, in the 20–35 percent range.[12] This prognosis led the superpowers to promise truly radical cuts *next time*, in a START II.[13] Russo-Ameri-

---

[12] The reduction in START-accountable, as opposed to total, forces are of course more impressive. The official U.S. estimate is that START imposes 29 and 36 percent cuts on U.S. and Russian strategic nuclear delivery vehicles, 40 and 48 percent cuts (respectively) in ICBM and SLBM warheads, and 43 and 42 percent cuts on the total of accountable warheads (ACDA, *The Strategic Arms Reduction Treaty, START Data Base*, 1 August 1991).

[13] On the lessons of the START process, see Robert Einhorn, "Revising the

can peace enables the promise of deep cuts prospectively to be realized. Classic stability theory may be all but indifferent to weapon quantities, though understandably favorably leaning toward larger rather than smaller force levels,[14] but—to have resort to the Marxist notion—quantity, or its lack, does have a quality all its own. One of the reasons why the Soviet General Staff lost some of its erstwhile (mid- to late 1970s) confidence in the military merit of preemptive counterforce attacks on a grand scale was because the number of weapons available to both sides by the 1980s, lower yields notwithstanding, had become so large that the quest for decisive military advantage would be overcome by the sheer quantity of destruction involved.

To summarize, SALT I and II permitted a huge expansion in the number of nuclear warheads. START I permits an effectively unlimited size of stockpile of air- and sea-launched cruise missiles. The treaty barely counts air-borne gravity bombs and short-range nuclear-armed missiles (ballistic and cruise), purposefully undercounts long-range air-launched cruise missiles (ALCMs), sea-launched cruise missiles (SLCMs), caps treaty-accountable warhead numbers at very high levels within a framework permitting 1600 delivery vehicles. START I has paved the way for a START II that should reduce warheads to the 3000–3,500 level by 2003. The U.S. government is not sure where it would leave its comfort zone for "stability" with reference to ever lower weapon numbers. What is abundantly clear, however, is that cuts in forces are being driven by politics and economics rather than by an arms control process.

A second criterion would be the likelihood of prohibiting or at

---

START process," *Survival*, 32 (November–December 1990), 497–505; and Colin S. Gray, "START II: Good Arms Control?" *Global Affairs*, 6 (Summer 1991), 47–57.

[14] It is worth quoting the founding fathers on the subject of arms reductions. "Whether the most promising areas of arms control involve reductions in certain kinds of military forces, *increases in certain kinds of military forces*, qualitative changes in weaponry, different modes of deployment, or arrangements superimposed on existing military systems, we prefer to treat as an open question." Thomas C. Schelling and Morton H. Halperin, *Strategy and Arms Control* (New York: Twentieth Century Fund, 1961), p. 2, emphasis added. Also see pp. 56–58.

least regulating "destabilizing" weapons.[15] On the offensive side, the "heavy" (i.e., SS-18 in its various Mods—most recently, number 5) and tolerably accurate ICBM virtually defines what American stability theorists mean by a destabilizing weapon. The record of SALT and START I is unambiguous. With the one exception of strategic defense, neither superpower has succeeded in legislating out of existence, or into impotence, those weapon programs of the other which are viewed with the greatest military alarm. SALT and START I have failed to place worthwhile limits upon the Russian heavy and medium ICBM force (i.e., respectively, the SS-18s and formerly the SS-17s and SS-19s, now SS-24s [the MX look-alike]), given U.S. unwillingness to consummate a mobile ICBM program. In Russian perspective, neither in SALT II nor in START I did they succeed in legislating militarily significant regulation for U.S. SLBMs (particularly for Trident II, D-5), advanced cruise missiles, or the stealth-technology penetrating manned air threat. Until June 1992, critics of SALT and START both in Moscow and Washington had solid grounds for the complaint that the arms control process did not lay an important glove upon those weapon programs of the adversary which caused most local worry. President Bush's offer on 27 September 1991 to negotiate the elimination of all MIRVed ICBMs elicited the predictable Russian response that major and offsetting new limits on SLBM MIRVing, on air- and sea-launched long-range cruise missiles or on "stealthy" long-range penetrating bombers, would also be necessary. The fact that MIRVed ICBMs ceased to stir competitive juices in Washington and Moscow in mid-1992 was a sure sign that the START process had become strictly political decoration.

A third criterion would be the likelihood of preventing the deployment of strategic missile defenses. To date, SALT and START have helped serve this purpose magnificently well. An important

[15] Colonel General Nikolai Chervov of the Soviet General Staff advised that "the new Stealth B-2 bomber . . . is a first-strike weapon." "We'd Like to Cut Our Forces More," *New York Times*, 29 May 1990, p. 23. A statement such as this, which is quite reasonable from a Russian point of view, places in proper perspective the true vacuity that can underline the preambular language to an arms control treaty. The preamble to the SALT II treaty, for example, intoned the apparent canonical verity that "the strengthening of strategic stability meets the interests of the Parties and the interests of international security."

caveat, however, includes the strong suspicion that neither super-power has believed it was ready to move out smartly with new BMD deployments, regardless of ABM treaty prohibitions. Furthermore, one should note the formal reversal of official strategic-philosophical preference in the United States in favor of the defense from 1983 to the present time. SALT I was a package that linked a suspiciously permanent ABM treaty to the promissory note of future strategic offensive force reductions.[16] The supposedly definitive scheme for much reduced and much less counterforce-capable offensive forces failed to materialize in the 1970s. Instead, there was a SALT II treaty that all but blessed the problem of silo vulnerability, and now there is a START I regime whose long advertised radical reductions transpire to be less than strategically very significant. The treaty-mandated reductions have long been overtaken in military significance by the qualitative modernization of the permitted weaponry, as well as by the evolving political context that should give arms control its meaning. It is not self-evident that the arms control process has achieved a severity in regulation of BMD that technology, dollar cost, and politics otherwise could not have secured. Until recently, on at least four days a week the U.S. government claimed that it did not want the process of strategic arms control to prohibit or even regulate missile defenses. But on the other three days, the U.S. government favored continuation of the ABM treaty regime (always only *pro tem*, of course) because the United States was not ready to begin deployment of a sufficiently militarily effective strategic defense system. At least until the Bush administration announced in January 1991 the reorientation of the SDI to the GPALS mission of

---

[16] Article XV, paragraph 2, of the ABM treaty specifies that each party has the right to withdraw "if it decides that extraordinary events relating to the subject matter of this Treaty have jeopardized its supreme interests." In "Unilateral Statement A" (issued on May 9, 1972), U.S. Ambassador Gerard Smith stated that "if an agreement providing for more complete strategic offensive arms limitations were not achieved within five years, United States supreme interests could be jeopardized. Should that occur, it would constitute a basis for withdrawal from the ABM Treaty." Not only was such an agreement not concluded within five years (1972–77), but even the SALT II and START treaties do not deliver the kind of limitation of offensive arms which Unilateral Statement A implied to be necessary.

protection against limited ballistic missile strikes,[17] Washington had not spoken with a clear voice on the subject of the continuing value of the ABM treaty.

A fourth criterion is whether predictability in the arms competition is improved and hence mutual confidence built. The proposition is that a treaty bounds the threat, if undeniably at a high level, and thereby modifies benignly the content of worst-case analysis. The ceilings established by treaty allegedly define the worst case. History shows that there is less merit in this candidate purpose than logic or common sense indicate should be the case. Unsurprisingly, regimes of arms limitation tend not to inconvenience defense programs. States sign on for regimes that license their intentions, or alternative means of accomplishing the object of those intentions. A SALT or START regime already expresses, or in other ways accommodates, the political purposes of the high contracting parties. Arms control agreements reflect the world, albeit sometimes in a distorting and time-lapsed way,[18] they do not change it. There is no sound basis to the notion that in contrast to a treaty-unregulated context wherein threats might grow luxuriantly, a SALT or START regime can yield a useful predictability about an adversary's treaty-bounded strategic programs. Arms are limited by policy decisions that incorporate such considerations as affordability, cost-effectiveness, opportunity costs, adversary reactions, doctrinal preference, targeting require-

[17] For authoritative treatment of GPALS and ABM treaty issues one need look no further than to Keith B. Payne, *Missile Defense in the 21st Century: Protection against Limited Threats, Including Lessons from the Gulf War* (Boulder, Colo.: Westview, 1991). The anti-BMD ranks have been very slow to assimilate the seriousness and scope of the SDI's redirection and metamorphosis into GPALS.

[18] Michael Howard provides food for thought when he writes that "as we all know, strategic arms control is driven by a logic of its own that bears little relation to political circumstances. It is a closed world inhabited by experts whose task it is, like that of insurance brokers and lawyers, to guard against every conceivable risk, however remote the possibilities may be. It is for political leaders, in the light of political circumstances to decide what risks they are prepared to take. As the political climate changes, the calculations of strategic analysts, however logical, become increasingly remote from real probabilities. Eventually a point is reached when the calculus of military capabilities is overtaken by that of perceived intentions" ("The remaking of Europe, *Survival*, 32 [March–April 1990], p. 101). Howard's claim that "arms control is driven by a logic of its own" is a half-truth at best, but he is very much on target with respect to the master role of politics and policy.

ments, and so forth. Those policy decisions on national military effort then may be blessed by arms control arrangements which, more or less imperfectly, express some variant of what the politicians intended.

The history of the past two decades does not suggest that the SALT-START process should be marked high for its benefits to a benign predictability of threat. Whether or not such predictability and the fencing-in of worst-case threat projections really matter very much for the great questions of national and international security is much more debatable than widely assumed. Nonetheless, if this candidate important purpose of SALT and START is granted the prominence that successive U.S. administrations have insisted upon, what does the record show?

Unremarkably, SALT has demonstrated what already was crystal clear from the history of the Washington-London and Anglo-German Naval Agreement (AGNA) regimes of the 1920s and 1930s. Specifically, legal systems of arms regulation do not provide the kinds of regulation that really matter for international security. Weapons and policy proclivities toward general advantage-seeking and a willingness to wage war for gain, are related but not synonymous. In the 1970s, as in the 1920s and 1930s, American (and British) politicians and high officials misread the policy intentions, and hence the strategy preferences, of some of their arms control adversary-partners. In 1935, duly encouraged by unsubtle German hints, London believed sincerely, and wrongly, that the *Kriegsmarine* was to be a Baltic-oriented, anti-Soviet force for "stability." In 1972, many important Americans believed that the SALT I package of offensive constraint and defensive all-but-prohibition, would enable the USSR to relax its competitive drive in strategic offensive arms. Those optimistic Americans of 1972 were wrong about the subsequent, indeed enduring, Soviet incentives to modernize their strategic offensive forces, notwithstanding the new fact of the ABM treaty.[19] The

---

[19] The Soviet Union responded in an anticipatory mode to threats to her strategic offensive forces. The rail-mobile SS-24 and the road-mobile SS-25 (not to mention the unsuccessful SS-X-16 of the 1970s—which, in a two-rocket–stage version became the very successful land-mobile SS-20 IRBM) provide powerful testimony

quality of Soviet offensive forces, and particularly of the Soviet ICBM force, improved far more rapidly in the SALT era than predicted. None of the supposed constraints of the SALT I interim agreement, or of the unratified but politically long-effective SALT II, imposed a useful predictability upon the future course of the competition. The combination of porous treaty terms, momentum in Soviet modernization, and weak will in Washington to respond robbed the predictability purpose of much merit. The predictability of military-technical threat that does matter is completely unaddressed in the START I treaty. Specifically, new Russian competence in anti-submarine warfare (ASW) and in air defense could have earth-moving implications for standard American notions of strategic stability. The 42 percent (plus) cuts in Russian treaty-accountable warheads are monumentally irrelevant to narrowly defined threat prognoses. Of course, as a lapsed superpower the new Russia—let alone the notional C.I.S.—is not at all likely to pose high-technology challenges to American ideas of stability. That judgment does not vindicate START, however; rather it condemns it as irrelevant.

Finally, the fifth criterion would be the likelihood of taking "a step toward U.S.-Soviet cooperation to lessen the arms race—and a step away from the threat of nuclear annihilation."[20] *Time* magazine perpetrated this worthy but appallingly erroneous complex statement of purpose vis-à-vis the then-pending START treaty. One is reminded of George Santayana's immortal thought that those who forget the past are condemned to repeat it. If arms competition expresses political competition based upon an antagonism of interests, the limited cooperation of a START regime must be a consequence of a politically permissive environment. When a senator or an ordinary citizen asks whether a START

---

on this point. However, what the 1970s and 1980s showed was not that there was no predictable Soviet competitive reaction to U.S. threats to their ICBM force but rather that the anxieties which American stability theorists claimed U.S. BMD must fuel were far from providing the sole motivation for Soviet action. The Soviet Union sought maximum military effectiveness from its strategic rocket forces, not merely a secure retaliatory capability. Confusion on this point marred a large fraction of the advice tendered the U.S. government and public from liberal arms control circles during the years of the SALT I negotiations (1969–72).

[20] George J. Church, "Oh, One More Thing . . . ," *Time*, 28 May 1990, p. 32.

treaty will "lessen the arms race" and help prevent nuclear annihilation, the answer has to be that arms control in general, and
START in particular, can neither direct the traffic of competitive
armament nor serve as a sturdy barrier against war. The evidence
for such an uncompromising response is logical, commonsensical,
and a matter of rich historical record. If the Washington-London
and AGNA regimes, as well as SALT I and II, did not themselves
function quasi-independently as fences for peace, why will the
START regime be radically different in its consequences? U.S.-
Japanese antagonism in the 1930s was about China, not about the
naval balance; hence, naval arms control itself could not reduce
that antagonism. It is no less true to argue that the Soviet-American antagonism has not been *about* the balance in strategic nuclear
forces. The advocates for SALT and START have been mightily
uncertain as to just what it was that the regime at issue should
achieve.

SALT ADDICTION

In a short burst of acuity, the *Time* magazine article quoted already observed that "START in some ways seems designed to
curb the arms race of the 1980s rather than the one that might
occur in the '90s."[21] It may be recalled that the centerpiece, the
jewel in the crown, of the Washington-London system of naval
arms limitation was the 5 : 5 : 3 ratio in capital-ship standard
displacement, significant ceilings for such displacement (525,000
tons for Britain and the United States, 315,000 tons for Japan),
and a fifteen-year building holiday. The arms limitation regime
focused upon "yesterday's weapon." Inevitably, the regime helped
contribute to the slow loss of capital-ship status by battleships
and battlecruisers, but of course, it is easy to be wise long after
the event. Nonetheless, there is a pattern to arms control regimes
assaulting the military-technical problems of yesteryear rather
than tomorrow. SALT I "capped," or froze, if none too equitably
(thinking of the sixty-two Soviet missile-carrying submarines al-

[21] Ibid.

legedly then under construction), nuclear-weapon launcher numbers when the superpowers had accumulated all of those that they could profitably use, and then some (2173 for the United States, 2209 for the Soviet Union).

The U.S. problem in 1972 was the prospective modernization of the Soviet strategic arsenal, not its further growth in number of launch vehicles. Moscow needed more accurate and more reliable ballistic missiles with perfected MIRV technology on the business end. SALT I placed no barriers of any kind in the way of such Soviet weapon improvements. In fact, neither SALT I nor SALT II, nor even today's START treaty, placed meaningful constraints on the war-fighting prowess of superpower strategic forces. Stephen J. Flanagan is generally correct when he writes that "SALT II largely codified existing defense plans, with some marginal constraints and redirection. Soviet MIRVing may have been somewhat restrained, but the treaty did not require either the United States or the USSR to terminate any ongoing strategic program."[22] True to the pattern of arms control history, the START regime presses most heavily upon ballistic-missile deployment, although air-breathing weapons, and particularly "stealthy" air-breathers, appear to be the cutting edge of future strategic competition, should there be such competition in Russian-American relations. START I is designed to help channel competition in paths relatively permissive for air-breathing launch and strike vehicles.

The story of the SALT process is a simple sad tale which lends itself readily to terse summation. SALT I (1972–77), on the offensive side (recall that "SALT I" embraced an "interim" [five-year] offensive-forces agreement and a permanent ABM treaty), froze ICBM and SLBM "launchers" (*not* missiles or warheads) extant or under construction.

A SALT II treaty was completed and signed in 1979, two years late, not to mention its self-evidently interim aspects. SALT II limited the superpowers to: (1) a common ceiling for strategic nuclear delivery vehicles (SNDVs) of 2400 (to decline to 2250 by the end of 1981)—a composite concept embracing ICBMs, SLBMs, *and* heavy

---

[22] Stephen J. Flanagan, "SALT II," in Albert Carnesale and Richard N. Haass, eds., *Superpower Arms Control: Setting the Record Straight* (Cambridge, Mass.: Ballinger, 1987), p. 133.

bombers; to (2) a ceiling of 1320 for MIRVed SNDVs (with each air-launched cruise missile [ALCM] carrying bomber counting only one against the total); (3) a limit of 1200 for MIRVed ICBMs and SLBMs; (4) 820 launchers for MIRVed ICBMs; (5) the number already extant of heavy ICBMs (this applied only to the USSR with its 308 "heavies"); (6) a license to MIRV missiles only to the degree of fractionation already test-demonstrated; and (7) one "new type" of ICBM (which would be constrained, if that is the correct term, to ten MIRV warheads, to accommodate the U.S. MX and what was to emerge as the Soviet SS-24).

These few details comprise but the major pillars of the enterprise. As a painfully close student of the history of strategic arms control, I have been appalled by the exponential growth in the length and detail of the SALT and START milestones. SALT I was short and ambiguous (not by accident, on the *Soviet* part). The SALT II treaty and accompanying documentation betrayed a virulent case of growing legalism,[23] while the START treaty and its protective packaging is of a length and specificity of detail which will gladden the hearts of the legal-minded. Perhaps American consumers have come to expect the provision of excruciating detail on the packages that they buy.

Mislearning from history, each new generation of U.S. arms control negotiators has been determined to solve its problems by defining and measuring every plant in the garden of arms control. Alas, the process of strategic arms control can be rescued for real security value neither by a blessed brevity and convenient ambiguity in documentation, nor by the drafting of ever more detailed treaties. The proclivity of Russians to evade and avoid what Washington believes it has settled as the plain intent of a regime cannot be written out by cunning treaty drafting. That fallacy is akin to the notion that the United States can resolve problems of compliance policy through the design and purchase of truly won-

---

[23] The SALT I Interim Agreement, including ancillary explanations on the public record, occupies but eight pages; the SALT II treaty and related matters, thirty-two pages; see ACDA, *Arms Control and Disarmament Agreements: Texts and Histories of Negotiations* (Washington, D.C.: Government Printing Office, 1990), pp. 169–76, 267–300, respectively. Comparable treatment of START will require a second volume of approximately 700 pages.

[137]

derful national technical means of verification. Law settles legal matters, just as technology can solve technical problems. Neither copiously well-drafted treaty terms nor high-resolution imagery from sensor platforms in orbit could prevent yesterday's Soviet Union from deploying or stockpiling illegal missiles. Also, they cannot substitute for a U.S. sanctions or safeguards policy. The successor states of the old Soviet Union may prove to be effectively self-policing democratic polities, not at all needful of the dotted *i*'s and crossed *t*'s of verification or inspection protocols. In that improbable event, arms control would yet again overperform what is not difficult to achieve—in this case, compliance by a systemically politically reformed adversary-partner.

SALT II died when President Carter requested of the U.S. Senate on 3 January 1980 that a floor debate and vote on the treaty be delayed on account of the Soviet invasion of Afghanistan. The treaty was a victim of the cumulatively severe deterioration in Soviet-American political relations in the second half of the 1970s and the early 1980s. Informally, if arguably illegally in the U.S. case, however, the superpowers elected to abide by the terms of SALT II as if it had entered legally into force by ratification. This strange phenomenon assumes less strange a visage when one recognizes that neither side was noticeably inconvenienced by the treaty's terms and that even a newly elected President Reagan—with true working majorities in both houses of Congress (though nominally only in the Senate)—could pour scorn on arms control symbolism only for a six- to nine-month period in 1981. Public SALT addiction was addiction not to any particular treaty but rather to the psychological reassurance that evidence of official commitment to an arms control process apparently provides. On balance, it was politically expedient for the Reagan administration not to pour gratuitous scorn upon the concept of arms control. Nonetheless, it was somewhat embarrassing for senior officials to have to acknowledge the tacit authority of a treaty that had been condemned by candidate Reagan in the roundest of terms. No less to the point, it was militarily expedient to decline to fracture the SALT II ceilings. If truth be told, many of the Reagan administration's presidential appointees were not by any means hostile to the concept of arms control. They subscribed to the plausible fallacy that *real* arms control could be accomplished by an approach very different from that pursued in the 1970s. Achievement in 1987 of the "double-zero" INF regime appeared to lend support to that belief.

COMING TO GRIPS WITH THE SALT RECORD

Bearing in mind the general purposes of arms control—with particular reference to reducing the risks of war—and the interwar record on naval arms limitation analyzed in Chapter 4, what judgments or observations on the SALT experience should command respect?

Politics. The history of SALT proves yet again that arms control is a political subject, as contrasted to a technical subject with minor political complications. Writing in 1934 about the failure of the World Disarmament Conference, John W. Wheeler-Bennett noted that "the Conference came about as the result of twelve years of preparation by one organ or another of the League of Nations, dating from that day in November, 1920, when the First Assembly of the League had made *the momentous discovery that the problem of disarmament was a political and not a technical one,* and had issued instruction for it to be studied accordingly."[24] SALT I of 1972 was the initial consummation of an on-off superpower arms control process that can be traced without difficulty to 1958.[25] Recognition of the thoroughly political nature of arms control should

[24] John W. Wheeler-Bennett, *The Pipe Dream of Peace: The Story of the Collapse of Disarmament* (New York: William Morrow, 1935), p. 1, emphasis added.

[25] Particularly to the Soviet-American "Surprise Attack Conference" of 1958. The best treatment of this episode remains Johan J. Holst, "Strategic Arms Control and Stability: A Retrospective Look," in Holst and William Schneider, Jr., eds., *Why ABM? Policy Issues in the Missile Defense Controversy* (New York: Pergamon, 1969), pp. 245–84. See also Robin Ranger, *Arms and Politics, 1958–1978: Arms Control in a Changing Political Context* (Toronto: Macmillan, 1979), chap. 4; Colin S. Gray, *Strategic Studies and Public Policy: The American Experience* (Lexington: University Press of Kentucky, 1982), pp. 72–79; and Lawrence Freedman, *The Evolution of Nuclear Strategy,* 2d ed. (New York: St. Martin's, 1989), chap. 13. But also see Jennifer E. Sims, *Icarus Restrained: An Intellectual History of Nuclear Arms Control, 1945–1960* (Boulder, Colo.: Westview, 1990).

have been a commonplace working premise in the 1920s, and the 1960s and 1970s, but the historical record shows that it was not. Some of the would-be disarmers of the League of Nations were bent upon abolishing "aggressive armament" rather than disciplining the aggressive acquirers and potential users of armament in the great forum, *twelve years* in the preparation, of the World Disarmament Conference in Geneva in 1932.[26] Three and four decades later, many American officials and strategic experts sought through SALT to legislate a more stable strategic balance.[27] Even today, as the Bush administration irrelevantly crafts an arms control posture, post-START I, for an essentially friendly Russian-American strategic relationship, the engineers of stability are still at work. The current ploy would seem to be a bid to use strategic arms control as a political lever to effect the nuclear disarmament of the non-Russian successor states of the former USSR. This is just the latest example of the commission of the old sin of believing that inherently political matters can be reduced to the status of technical and administrative issues.

Although everybody signs on for the proposition that arms control is a political subject, few people demonstrate accurate comprehension of what that truism means. Recognition of the political character of a negotiating process, in which who gets what, when, and how is decided, is so obvious that it can serve as a barrier to deeper understanding. The view of arms control as politics just presented is fully compatible with technicist fallacies about the causes of war and conditions for peace, even with "weaponitis."[28] One may believe that the admittedly heavily polit-

---

[26] An outstanding personal memoir which speaks the disturbing truth about arms control is J. H. Morgan, *Assize of Arms: The Disarmament of Germany and Her Rearmament (1919–1939)* (New York: Oxford University Press, 1946). What is important about Morgan's story is not the fact that Germany failed to disarm as she was obliged to do under the terms of the Versailles treaty but rather that the Western democracies chose to close their official eyes to the evidence of cheating.

[27] For two period-piece classics, see John Newhouse, *Cold Dawn: The Story of SALT* (New York: Holt, Rinehart and Winston, 1973), particularly chap. 1; and Jerome H. Kahan, *Security in the Nuclear Age: Developing U.S. Strategic Arms Policy* (Washington, D.C.: Brookings, 1975), passim.

[28] William A. Schwartz, Charles Derber, et al., *The Nuclear Seduction: Why the Arms Race Doesn't Matter—and What Does* (Berkeley: University of California Press,

ical process of arms control nonetheless yields technical outcomes of enormous significance for war and peace. Those outcomes include weapon balances and imbalances, allegedly more or less perilous military operating procedures, the encouragement or discouragement of "stabilizing" trends in weapon acquisition and military doctrine, and so forth.

The SALT process demonstrated yet again just how political is the subject of competitive armament. To clarify the confusion, arms control is political in that its immediate subject—arms—and its underlying subject—war or peace—have meaning only in political terms. Whether or not arms are a problem for peace depends overwhelmingly upon who owns them or fails to own them. Covenants without swords are dangerous for international security if contemporary would-be revisionist, or rogue, states are becoming well armed.

The arms control process, like the policymaking process more generally, attracts much myth and legend at the level of well-meaning civics texts. In practice, real live politicians, who at the very highest of levels neither know nor care about the fifty-seven or more varieties of stability, aided and abetted by similarly politically-minded officials, negotiate what they can negotiate. The process of negotiation is influenced by a host of factors that have nothing of note to do with technical arguments about strategic stability. More accurately, perhaps, as the case of U.S. efforts in START to reduce the military value of the Russian heavy ICBM force attests, it is precisely the alleged *destabilizing* qualities of the SS-18 Mod. 5 which has rendered that ICBM so politically attractive in Russian perspective.[29] The terms of a SALT I, SALT II, or

---

1990), pp. 13–15. The policy prescriptions in this book are shot through with populist fallacies, but the central premise is substantially correct. The authors have stumbled upon the great truth that weapons do not make war. The healthy overlap between my distinctly nonliberal views and those of the authors of *The Nuclear Seduction* is both interesting and encouraging.

[29] In START I Washington has succeeded in securing a 50 percent reduction in the Russian SS-18, heavy ICBM force. But the current upgrade (at least) of that missile in its 10-MIRV (plus) Mod effectively nullifies the value of a 50 percent cut. The United States failed to constrain the test program for the SS-18 force to a level so low (perhaps two to seven tests per annum) that confidence in the system would erode cumulatively and severely. Washington secured Soviet agreement

START I agreement typically owe as little to stability theory as the outbreak of the great wars of history have owed to technical instabilities in the strategic balance. MIRVed ICBMs were negotiable in 1992 not because people believed they were destabilizing, but because the Russians ceased to care about their military value and the Americans ceased to worry about paying a price in MIRVed SLBMs.

Admittedly, SALT I appears to be an ambivalent case in that American stability theory, even ideology, helped drive the U.S. negotiating position and was employed to explain the outcome of all but zero defense and a supposedly capped offense. The truth is a little more complicated. The other high contracting party in 1972 most emphatically did not endorse American ideas on stability. It was quite evident at the time that the U.S. Congress would not fund the proposed Safeguard ABM deployment.

SALT illustrated the political character of arms control in that negotiated outcomes, particularly those congressionally approved, have been feasible when superpower relations were generally good and improving and infeasible when relations were deteriorating. It is obvious that 1972 (like 1922 and 1930) and 1991–92 were strategic arms control–friendly years, whereas 1979–80 (or 1927, 1932, or 1934–35) was not. It would not be correct to claim that the 1922 Washington treaty and the SALT I package of 1972 were negotiable in large part because of a fortuitous and fortunate military-technical window of opportunity. The windows of opportunity have been political, not military-technical. If the politics behind competitive armament argue strongly for agreement, mere military-technical difficulties will not be permitted to abort the politically directed course of history. For example, policymakers usually can obscure inconvenient facts of military-technical disagreement with that Orwellian device the "agreement in principle" (i.e., the disagreement). Agreements in principle typically

---

that no "new type" of heavy ICBM shall be deployed, but the experience of SALT I and II demonstrated that such a provision is worthless. START defines a "new type" of ICBM or SLBM as one which changes its number of stages, changes its type of propellant, has a 5 percent change in diameter, and/or has a 21 percent increase in throwweight. The United States finally succeeded in negotiating the elimination of all MIRVed ICBMs in June 1992—with Boris Yeltsin's new Russia.

are necessary precisely because the negotiating parties disagree on key details.

There is a season both for the negotiability of arms control and for the political impracticability of the same. In words which sadly lend themselves to application to the protracted negotiations on the SALT II treaty (1972–79), Wheeler-Bennett wrote in 1935 that "whatever other reproaches—and there are many—which can be laid at the door of the General Disarmament Conference, that of lack of preparation is not among them. It resembled nothing so much as an overtrained athlete, who, having passed the zenith of fitness, is prone alike to nervous disorder and muscle-binding."[30]

Extravagant Expectations and Faulty Theory. As best one can tell, the strategic arms control process since 1969 has contributed either not at all or, on balance, even modestly to negative effect with respect to the prevention of war. Admittedly, this is a difficult subject upon which to offer thoroughly persuasive judgment. Among the many reasons why World War III did not occur in the 1970s and 1980s, it is difficult to find a very plausible place for any important cause or condition of peace attributable to the strategic arms control process. In practice, that judgment has far short of "killer" implications for the general regard in which arms control is held. The purposes allegedly advanced via SALT have been so elusive, ambiguous, and changeable that a rigorous audit of accomplishment is all but impossible to effect.

With the minor and somewhat obscure exception of the U.S. DefCon 3 nuclear alert in October 1973,[31] the entire SALT-START era has witnessed a political stability in superpower relations which translated into a robust condition of general deterrence. Not since October 1973 has either superpower sought to rattle its central nuclear systems for the purpose of immediate deterrence

---

[30] Wheeler-Bennett, *Pipe Dream of Peace*, p. 1.

[31] See Barry M. Blechman and Douglas M. Hart, "The Political Utility of Nuclear Weapons: The 1973 Middle East Crisis," *International Security*, 7 (Summer 1982), 132–56; Kurt Gottfried and Bruce G. Blair, eds., *Crisis Stability and Nuclear War* (New York: Oxford University Press, 1988), pp. 198–206; and Bruce G. Blair, "Alerting in Crisis and Conventional War," in Ashton B. Carter, John D. Steinbruner, and Charles A. Zraket, eds., *Managing Nuclear Operations* (Washington, D.C.: Brookings, 1987), pp. 75–120.

in an acute regional crisis. The so-called Carter doctrine of 23 January 1980 was advertised as including a U.S. nuclear commitment to protect the Persian Gulf region from Soviet aggression in the immediate wake of the Soviet invasion of Afghanistan on Christmas Eve 1979. But there was no rhetorical brandishing of the U.S. central nuclear sword. That omission was significant because an important Nuclear Targeting Policy Review (NTPR) had been completed early in 1979, to be revealed to the public (and the USSR) as Presidential Directive (PD) 59 on 25 July 1980.[32]

There has been no visible and obvious occasion since the beginning of the SALT process when the military-technical details of superpower strategic forces even could have played a role in decisions for peace or war. The strategic nuclear balance contributed to general deterrence in the context of what Russian analysts understand by the correlation of forces and what Western analysts, at least those who eschew undue technicity, mean by the balance of power. That balance, however, was not called upon to service a policy for immediate deterrence. By analogy, the arms control track of SALT and START has been redecorating the façade, and possibly remodeling the lobby and other prominent if superficial physical features, of the theater of statecraft. But the choice of dramatic productions and the conduct on stage have proceeded quite unaffected by such light remodeling.

It is almost too easy to be critical of the SALT record. However, I would not wish to merit the accusation that I have scored easy successes against positions that few people of any sophistication have sought to defend. Unlike the arms control experience of the interwar years, the history of SALT and START is a history I witnessed and followed as it unfolded, and in which I played some minor part from time to time in public debate and as a privileged advisor to government. Few people today will admit to having harbored absurdly optimistic expectations of the SALT process. Moreover, a few carefully selected quotations from this or that prominent SALT hopeful, or later, SALT addict, certainly would

---

[32] See Desmond Ball and Robert C. Toth, "Revising the SIOP: Taking War-Fighting to Dangerous Extremes," *International Security*, 14 (Spring 1990), 65–92.

not prove a thesis. Any number of overblown claims pro *and con* have been leveled by a wide variety of would-be opinion leaders.[33]

Otherwise generally tough-minded and reasonable people often lay common sense aside when they contemplate the magic kingdom of arms control. By way of illustration, General Richard Ellis, then the Commander in Chief of the Strategic Air Command, a position that usually does not encourage flights of arms control fantasy, said in 1978, "I suggest to you that the best hope for the future is through SALT—a negotiated arms limitation agreement and a subsequent mutual reduction of forces. To me, the alternatives to a SALT agreement are unacceptable: appeasement, economic exhaustion resulting from an arms race, or a nuclear holocaust."[34] This was the most arrant nonsense. Of Ellis's false alternatives—a standard, if sometimes innocent, debating trick (e.g., vote for *me* and peace and prosperity, or vote for *him* and war and economic collapse)—economic exhaustion has functioned healthily to bring about the terminal political crisis for the Soviet empire.[35] Few people have been quite as imprudent as was General Ellis in his claims for the value of SALT II, but it would be wrong to endorse a rewriting of history to the effect that little of benefit was expected from strategic arms control.

Soviet strategic behavior and misbehavior in the 1970s and 1980s falsified the predictions of many of the bold arms control theorists of the mid to late 1960s. Unimpeded in serious ways by

[33] My late colleague, Donald G. Brennan, once wrote trenchantly in a review essay (of Anatol Rapoport, *Strategy and Conscience* [New York: Harper and Row, 1964]) that "it is probably difficult to criticize this book as roundly as it should be criticized without seeming to be in a position of defending every witless statement or unfeeling policy promulgated by every establishment-oriented writer on political or military affairs." "Strategy and Conscience," *Bulletin of the Atomic Scientists*, 21 (December 1965), p. 30. Brennan's observation is one for the ages. À la Brennan, I do not endorse "every witless statement" issued in criticism of SALT and START.

[34] Quoted in Center for Defense Information (CDI), *Nuclear War Quotations* (Washington, D.C.: CDI, no date [probably 1986]), p. 77.

[35] With respect to the former Soviet Union, at least, there is much to recommend the argument in Paul M. Kennedy, *The Rise and Fall of the Great Powers: Economic Change and Military Conflict from 1500 to 2000* (New York: Random House, 1987), pp. 488–514.

SALT I and SALT II, the Soviet Union translated its superior ICBM launcher numbers and throwweight into the kind of military capability that American stability theory condemned axiomatically. Moreover, Soviet officials probably misled their U.S. counterparts over key provisions of the Soviet ICBM modernization program. The point, however, is not so much whether Moscow purposefully was deceitful during the SALT I negotiations over its fourth-generation ICBMs (what was to become the SS-X-16, SS-17, SS-18, and SS-19), though the case for that is a strong one. Rather, Moscow negotiated and signed a SALT agreement while it was developing new ICBMs and delaying their test pending U.S. congressional action endorsing SALT I, whose critical dimensions would contradict what Moscow knew to be the U.S. understanding of the provisions of the arms control regime. The kind of strategic stability the Soviet Union sought under, or around, the aegis of SALT I and SALT II had little in common with the terms of U.S. canon law on the subject. The relentless Soviet modernization of its heavy and light ICBM force was not compatible with the SALT process as a joint quest after U.S. notions of a more stable balance. In the contemporary words of an American chronicler friendly to the SALT I achievement: "What then is unstable, or least stable? A stable strategic weapon should be capable of delayed response; it should be invulnerable; and it should be unambiguously deprived of what is called a first-strike, or damage-limiting, capability. Put differently, it should not be able to disarm some portions of the other side's forces, or diminish them appreciably."[36]

The fundamental architecture of SALT, and now of START, rests upon a false theory of arms race dynamics and exceedingly doubtful, certainly incomplete, theories of arms race stability and crisis stability—all of which reflects that distinctly imperfect understanding of the causes of war discussed in Chapter 2. The distinguished strategic theorist, Johan J. Holst—later to be Norway's minister of defense—wrote in 1970 that "we just do not have an

---

[36] Newhouse, *Cold Dawn*, p. 20. On U.S. SALT diplomacy and Soviet ICBM modernization in the early stages of the SALT II negotiations, see the analysis in Richard C. Thornton, *The Nixon-Kissinger Years: Reshaping America's Foreign Policy* (New York: Paragon House, 1989), pp. 299–308.

adequate explanatory model for the Soviet-American arms race."[37] The negotiators of the ABM treaty were not so humble. The pre-amble to the treaty asserts as follows: "Considering that effective measures to limit anti-ballistic missile systems would be a sub-stantial factor in curbing the race in strategic offensive arms and would lead to a decrease in the risk of outbreak of war involving nuclear weapons . . ." There was no logically or historically im-pressive body of evidence available in 1972 in support of either of the two plausible fallacies in that quotation. Moreover, the strate-gic history of subsequent years has lent them no additional support. Expectations for the SALT process varied from the extravagant to the very modest on both the positive and negative sides.

Two levels of argument need to be distinguished. At one level, there is the question of whether SALT and START in noteworthy part have been launched and sustained because of the attractions of a false theory of strategic stability. At the other level, one can enquire whether, even if the operative theory is assumed to be true, an arms control process possibly can be used to help estab-lish strategic conditions held by the theory to be benign for peace with security. The entire SALT-START process, from 1969 to the present time, has witnessed its enthusiastic proponents endeavor-ing to explain away the political compromises that proved nego-tiable, with more or less explicit reference to the glories of the stability theory purportedly reflected, albeit imperfectly, in the done deals. Ironically, the stability theory that lends dignity to arms control actually is the shakiest edifice of all. Whatever the merits in orthodox stability theory, strategic arms control has failed thus far to perform usefully in its pursuit. In support of classic stability theses, the SALT-START process has not con-strained prompt war-fighting prowess *usefully*. START II should curb war-fighting ability, but only in the context of a prior politi-cal peace between the signatories!

The near universal recognition that the peril of global nuclear war has diminished markedly over the past several years owes nothing to the vast expenditure of ever scarce official time and

---

[37] Johan J. Holst, "Comparative U.S. and Soviet Deployments, Doctrines, and Arms Limitation," in Morton A. Kaplan, ed., *SALT: Problems and Prospects* (Morris-town, N.J.: General Learning Press, 1973), p. 68.

effort that has been devoted to strategic arms control. By way of sharp contrast, decline in the danger of war would appear to owe something of note to the robust defense programs of the very late Carter years and Reagan's first term.[38] Cause and effect are difficult to establish beyond a reasonable doubt in the realm of defense programs and security. For reason of the security dilemma, the former does not invariably enhance the latter. The course of events in the 1980s, however, offers powerful support for the claim that former U.S. ambassador to the Soviet Union Thomas J. Watson was thoroughly in error when he wrote in January 1981 that "the theory that the U.S. can build enough weapons so that the Soviets go broke keeping up is not only unworkable, it would put the world in a very, very dangerous state and accomplish nothing."[39] In fact, what U.S. military-competitive effort played a significant role in achieving was nothing less than the political defeat of the USSR. Former ACDA director Kenneth Adelman penetrates to the kernel of the matter when he claims that "START's main objective, enhancing strategic stability, had already been done—not by a recondite treatise but by a geopolitical revolution throughout the Soviet empire."[40]

Permissive Terms. The SALT-START process has yet really to control arms. Prior to START II the superpowers agreed to terms of restraint that were very user-friendly. That is not necessarily a criticism, simply a statement of fact. The military problems of the superpowers in the 1970s and 1980s in the strategic forces realm were neither significantly caused, nor sustained, by the arms control process. In theory, the ABM treaty precluded a promising solution to the problem of nominal ICBM silo vulnerability. But in practice, the USSR never showed interest in developing hardpoint missile defenses, while through the ABM treaty the United States made a legalistic, and even strategic, virtue of the political necessity of BMD nondeployment. To the uncertain degree to

---

[38] For the opposite opinion see Daniel Wirls, *Buildup: The Politics of Defense in the Reagan Era* (Ithaca: Cornell University Press, 1992).

[39] Quoted in CDI, *Nuclear War Quotations*, p. 72.

[40] Ken Adelman, "START when needed least," *Washington Times*, 19 July 1991, p. F1.

which the technical details of strategic posture might matter for decisions on crisis, war or peace, the SALT-START process has not prevented the superpowers from fielding what commonly would be regarded as crisis-stable forces. Utterly without benefit of formal arms control clergy, in the 1960s the superpowers adopted a triadic (plus) structure for their strategic forces and worked hard to deny even the theoretical possibility of the other side developing the kind of "victory is possible or probable" briefing which just might seduce a desperate chief executive.

Both liberal and conservative critics of SALT, and START I, level the charge that real arms control, which in common usage is to say large-scale reductions in forces, fell victim to expediency in negotiation. Such critics betray ignorance of the working of the arms control paradox. The terms of agreement have been permissive because of the political conflict that gives meaning to arms control. Those permissive SALT-START terms which are an affront to the chimera of real arms control, happen also to be very tolerant of error in the negotiations. At least, that is true of contemporary strategic nuclear forces, where the weapon launcher value under START is to be distributed among 1600 delivery vehicles carrying up to 6000 treaty-accountable warheads, while several thousand additional, non–treaty-accountable warheads will be tolerated for good measure. The point about the tolerance of error which accrues from a wide distribution of military value can encourage the plausible fallacy that strategic arms control is a harmless indulgence. By way of contrast, such an indulgent view cannot even be considered for naval arms control, where major military value is concentrated in relatively few hulls.[41]

---

[41] "Among all the branches of the armed forces, navies have the highest per unit combat value." Roger W. Barnett, "The New Imperatives of Naval Arms Control," in Eric H. Arnett, ed., *New Technologies for Security and Arms Control: Threats and Promise* (Washington, D.C.: American Association for the Advancement of Science, 1989), p. 183. It is the Navy's position—and to date, at least, also the position of the U.S. government as a whole—that the world's greatest naval power does not favor arms control inhibition upon its freedom of fleet design, deployment, or action. The regulation of naval power is a trend that the United States does not and should not endorse. Naval arms control is either impracticable or undesirable. As a general principle, U.S. maritime preponderance is as necessary for the support of the foreign policy of *the* superpower (*pro tem*) as it is beneficial

Strategy. The synergism between strategy-guided defense planning and arms control policy is as unarguable in theory as it has been all but absent from American practice. From constituting the acceptable face of military policy toward strategic nuclear forces, SALT and START have had a troubling ability to function independent of that policy. This is not to claim that the arms limitation process has subsumed military policy and strategy, only that the SALT-START (and INF) record does not reveal at all clearly the footprints of U.S. nuclear strategy. In fact, both the interwar and the postwar protracted experiences with arms limitation show that there is a deep-rooted tension, even antithesis, between strategy and Western democratic practice with arms control negotiations. For a geopolitically distinctive United States with unique geostrategic requirements, the dynamics of negotiation and the magnetic pull of the parity concept mock the means-ends relationships of strategy.

SALT and START per se have not been fatal to intelligent strategy. As noted, the terms of agreement have been sufficiently permissive to accommodate a wide range of doctrinal, war planning, and postural preferences. But an ongoing arms control process helps erode official, and certainly public, interest in strategy and attracts adherence to the fallacy that an inherently benign cooperative alternative to the effectiveness generated by strategic forces exists. There is no necessary reason why a variant of Gresham's law should apply in this case, specifically, of arms control considerations (bearing upon counterfeit security) driving out genuinely strategic choices and strategic planning (a sound currency for se-

---

for international order. Unfortunately, the one area of potential naval arms limitation that theoretically would serve U.S. interests very well, which is to say the denuclearization of the maritime environment, lacks military-technical integrity— notwithstanding President Bush's 27 September 1991 announcement that "under normal circumstances, our ships will not carry tactical nuclear weapons." The most potent nuclear threats to ships at sea are posed by land-based systems, whose reach and general flexibility, as well as the interest of foes of the United States in posing nuclear threats at sea, render nuclear arms control for naval forces a topic of less-than-great promise.

curity). But the near universal historical experience of democracies suggests strongly that this is, even has to be, so. These remarks recognize that, ideally, security is political in character and reposes in the benign hearts and minds of those who could pose threats. The point here is that arms control menaces the integrity of strategy, not that military power is more reliable than politics.

There are many powerful and persisting reasons why American society, and those whom it elects and pays to manage its security, tend to function poorly in the realm of strategy.[42] A traditionally resource-rich country, habituated to military success, does not need to develop a tradition of excellence in the means-ends analysis that is the essence of strategy. Notwithstanding some noteworthy endeavors to reform operational U.S. nuclear doctrine and the nuclear war plans—as reflected in the SIOP-5 and SIOP-6 series from 1976 to the present[43]—too little strategy is provided for the guidance of strategic-force acquisition and contingent threat and employment. SALT and START have not been the villain, but they:

- have provided excuses for poor performance in strategy;
- often have been substantially disjoined from weapon acquisition programs, just as those programs (and support systems for them) often have been disjoined from the requirements specified or implied in the defense guidance for the SIOP;
- tempt politicians, officials, and other would-be American opinion leaders further to neglect that which they are already inclined to neglect—the design or redesign of nuclear strategy and the melding of that strategy with national military strategy overall;

[42] Colin S. Gray, "Strategy in the Nuclear Age: The United States, 1945–1991," in Williamson Murray and Alvin Bernstein, eds., *The Making of Strategy* (New York: Free Press, forthcoming).

[43] See Scott D. Sagan, *Moving Targets: Nuclear Strategy and National Security* (Princeton: Princeton University Press, 1989), chap. 1; Janne E. Nolan, *Guardians of the Arsenal: The Politics of Nuclear Strategy* (New York: Basic Books, 1989), chap. 6; Ball and Toth, "Revising the SIOP"; Melissa Healy, "U.S. Speeds Review of Nuclear-War Plan," *Los Angeles Times*, October 4, 1991, p. 10; and the report of an advisory panel to the Joint Strategic Target Planning Staff, Thomas Reed and Michael O. Wheeler, "The Role of Nuclear Weapons in the New World Order," December 1991.

- distract scarce talent from the serious business of defense planning; and
- function very much as a wild card.

SALT-START [I] restrictions have been so permissive that any competent strategic logician could explain how the terms of agreement serve the design of U.S. strategy. The truth of the SALT-START matter is that whatever the strategic ideas authoritative for Americans early in the negotiating process, before 1992 the end results were astrategic compromises at high weapon levels. Any comfortable fit between legal regime and U.S. strategy purpose overwhelmingly has been fortuitous. Even though the right things can be done for the wrong reasons, the relationship between U.S. defense planning and arms control behavior does not show a pattern to that happy effect.

Choice of Weapons—Course of Competition. There were many good reasons for fractionating missile payload by MIRVing: for example, to increase target coverage, cost-effectiveness, and to discourage or overwhelm BMD deployments. But a SALT process that crudely, if ambiguously and even incompetently, placed a ceiling upon missile launchers and silo dimensions (which?)[44] but not upon missiles or warheads (i.e., the Interim Agreement of SALT I) actually encouraged fractionation. Hypothetically, if one hundred ICBM launchers were permitted, with no other restrictions of much note, it would be difficult to resist the military logic which would argue for: (1) the production of many spare missiles (for a generous test, training, and operational evaluation program); (2) deployment of the largest missiles (i.e., with the maxi-

---

[44] Common Understanding A of the Interim Agreement, dated 26 May 1972, specified that the language in Agreed Statement C, which prohibited a significant increase in ICBM silo-launcher dimensions, meant no more than 10–15 percent of the present dimensions. Some high U.S. officials mistakenly believed that it was only a 10–15 percent increase in diameter which was licensed—they forgot that silos have depth (or length) as well as width! As a consequence the Soviet Union was able to stuff SS-19 light ICBMs into converted SS-11 silos. The SS-19 was the first Soviet ICBM to be tested with MIRVs (×6), in April 1973, and was deployed (Mod 1) beginning in December 1974. Eventually, 360 of the much improved Mod 3 (×6 MIRVs) were to be deployed in the 1980s. See Thomas B. Cochran et al., *Nuclear Weapons Databook,* vol. 4: *Soviet Nuclear Weapons* (New York: Harper and Row, 1989), chap. 5.

mum throwweight) that the rather casually negotiated restrictions on launcher dimensions could be held to allow; (3) deployment of the largest number of warheads that each missile type could carry, consistent with the yield-accuracy needed to provide tolerable damage expectancies against the targets of interest; and (4) in some political cultures, though not the American, the stockpiling of covert ICBMs.

There is much to be said in praise both of the MX Peacekeeper ICBM and the Trident II D-5 SLBM, but both are very much treaty (actually "Interim-Agreement") missiles (recall the treaty cruisers, treaty battleships, treaty carriers, and even treaty destroyers of the interwar period). In similar vein, the families of cruise missiles now being deployed in large numbers may be judged a weapon type whose technological time has come again. But the abrupt renewal of high official interest in cruise missile technology *in the immediate wake* of the SALT I signing of 1972, was no coincidence. SALT I placed restrictions, albeit not many and not competently, upon long-range ballistic missiles but not upon cruise missiles. Cruise missiles have been boosted in their attractiveness by SALT and START in the same way and for the same reasons that generally is claimed falsely for the relationship between the Washington-London system and carrier aviation.

If another class of example is useful, the SS-20 and the U.S. Pershing II were both treaty missiles. The SS-20 case is particularly blatant,[45] but the Pershing II is more interesting. The Pershing was a treaty missile in that, first, it exploited a legally unconstrained path in the arms competition. But second, the Pershing II (and ground-launched cruise missiles [GLCMs]) was required for the reassurance of nervous NATO Europeans whose confidence in U.S. strategic guardianship was shaken by the era of strategic parity blessed and encouraged by SALT. Both treaty-accountable

---

[45] A thorough analysis is Jonathan Haslam, *The Soviet Union and the Politics of Nuclear Weapons in Europe, 1969–1987* (Ithaca: Cornell University Press, 1990), particularly chap. 4. Haslam argues that the SS-20 IRBM constituted necessary modernization for aging theater systems and provided compensation for U.S. forward-based systems and British and French strategic nuclear forces not captured in SALT I or even prospectively in SALT II, but which would be serious targets for Soviet diplomacy in a SALT III.

and non–treaty-accountable weapons (e.g., respectively in START, the MX ICBM and air-launched cruise missiles of less than 600 km range) provided leverage in negotiation, whether or not they were defined as bargaining chips. The SALT-START process has encouraged extra-regime weapon development and the securing of leverage for the arm wrestling of the negotiation with the coin of the realm—credible weapon programs.

A consequence of SALT and START (as of the Washington-London system) is a strategic forces (or naval) posture that makes obvious sense for a specific, evolving arms control context but much less sense for putative operations, for strategy, or for foreign policy. The qualification "evolving" is important because a START I regime with both warhead and delivery vehicle limits catches the United States with principal modernization programs for two legs of its triad (MX and Trident D-5) designed for a previous era of no direct warhead constraints.

Arguments as to the "lulling" or "stimulating" effect of SALT and START upon U.S. strategic force modernization can be answered with a definite maybe. For example, the ABM treaty as amended (in 1974) allows only a single site with one hundred ground-based interceptors. The treaty has been an important political, legal, and psychological barrier to intelligent thought and planning on the subject of a well-integrated strategic offense-defense posture. But the treaty reflects and reinforces the political context more than it shapes it. Even in the absence of the ABM treaty the United States would not have deployed BMD in the 1970s or 1980s.

Cheating. The United States discovered that the Soviet Union cheated persistently and quite systematically on SALT matters great and small. Embarrassingly, the United States was unable to decide what to do about the verified facts of Soviet noncompliance. It is true that many scholars judged Moscow unambiguously guilty only with reference to the construction of the large phased-array radar at Krasnoyarsk, but my close study of the violations field over many years leads me to a less charitable conclusion. The Soviet Union is by no means the only polity in history—ancient, medieval, or modern—to lie, cheat, avoid, and

[154]

evade on matters pertaining to supposedly solemn legal undertakings. The Soviet Union, however, ranks high among modern history's worst offenders. So long as the parties to strategic arms control maintain healthily structurally diverse and large strategic arsenals, it is difficult to argue even that systematic treaty noncompliance makes much military difference. There are powerful reasons for not tolerating cheating, some of which are outlined in the next chapter, but they need not detain the discussion here. If, however, the true SALT-START recidivist designs models of future START regimes, he or she should be required to confront the cheating problem directly.

It may be objected that the process of domestic revolution, married to presumptively ever improving superpower political relations, plainly is yielding a Russian (or a Ukrainian and so forth) polity totally different from the suspicious, secretive, and noncomplying Soviet Union of yore. In response one must cite, yet again, the arms control paradox. A wholly open, trustworthy, and effective, even self-policing, Russian START-regime partner would not be needed as a partner in arms control. Why would Americans care about the missiles of such a Russia? The fashionable answer is that through formal arms control arrangements the risk can be minimized of those missiles falling into the wrong hands and being usable thereafter. This is a example of the fallacy of political engineering. The menu of political possibilities for the future of the former USSR is too rich to be fireproofed against nuclear peril by the technicians of arms control. There is only one certainty about the current ex-Soviet domestic scene and that is the transience of its political arrangements. Americans should not be reduced into crafting arms control proposals that make sense only for the conditions of today. A proper control by strategy over arms control would minimize this danger.

With respect to the INF treaty in particular, though not exclusively, the director of ACDA, Ronald F. Lehman II, could speak persuasively about the superpower experience "in expanding the envelope of verification."[46] He could not speak very persuasively

---

[46] Ronald F. Lehman II, "Intelligence and Policy Formulation," in Catherine M. Kelleher and Joseph E. Naftzinger, eds., *Intelligence in the Arms Control Process:*

about either an expanding envelope of compliance or a noteworthy expansion in U.S. policy for coping with verified cheating. Notwithstanding all of the new thinking that has so shaken the former Soviet system, the scope and scale of Moscow's misbehavior—both legal, if improper, as well as illegal—toward compliance with the terms of the CFE treaty of 1990, are wholly in the Russian tradition of *caveat emptor*.

DÉJÀ VU ALL OVER AGAIN

The judgments offered above on the SALT-START record were framed to suit the historical circumstances of the late 1960s to the early 1990s. I avoided applying the lessons from the interwar years specified at the close of Chapter 4 as a template over the SALT experience. This chapter has not purported to tell the full story of SALT and START in a fashion even-handed between truth and error. The discussion has unashamedly excluded some counterarguments and most of the inessential detail. Nonetheless, I do claim that the interpretation offered here of the SALT-START record is more true than any rival view.

The bad news about arms control is not that it leads to a fatal unpreparedness on the part of democracies but rather that it cannot work as advertised. The experience with strategic arms limitation over the past two decades shows some quite unremarkable parallels with the interwar years. One must say unremarkable because an enterprise like arms control, in common with collective security,[47] which offends the equivalent of the law of gravity for

---

Lessons from "INF" (College Park, Md.: Center for International Security Studies at Maryland, School of Public Affairs, University of Maryland, 1990), p. 9.

[47] Neoliberal arguments for the net efficacy of collective security arrangements commit logical and historical errors virtually identical to those that lurk in the halls of arms control advocacy. For example, in an article on "Concerts, Collective Security, and the Future of Europe" (*International Security*, 16 [Summer 1991], 114–61), Charles A. Kupchan and Clifford A. Kupchan inadvertently do their best to demonstrate why political scientists should not be entrusted with the serious business of national security. The authors' arguments in praise of collective security came close to mirroring the standard wisdom in praise of arms control. Just about every faulty judgment that could be made of allegedly collective security practice in

international political relations, is no more likely to succeed in one era than in any other. The optimists who discern in START the SALT III that was brutally aborted by the international unpleasantness which denied dignity and full legality, though not all authority, to SALT II in 1980, should take heed of the maxim that impossible missions remain impossible, even as contexts change.[48] START in the 1990s is no more capable of helping to shape peace-friendly strategic force postures, than would a hypothetical SALT III in the 1980s. Those force postures, managed or not by the political bargains of a SALT III and now a START regime, do not provide fuel critical for decisions to fight.

---

modern history is perpetrated in this lengthy article. The Kupchans' subject is that fashionable political science entity, albeit often only a "notional" entity, the international regime. In praise of the regime of collective security, *or arms control,* they assert: (1) an increase in information to all parties, (2) an increase in the costs of defection from the norms which are the ethos of the regime, (3) the promotion of cooperation by issue linkage, and (4) the promotion of interstate socialization. Not to mince matters, this constitutes a stew of liberal fallacies. The first point is simply refuted by the historical evidence of the workings of the arms control and collective security paradox. No one very familiar with the international history of the twentieth century would cite the Kupchans' first point as their lead blocker. The three remaining points all reflect misunderstanding of cause and effect in international relations. In practice, what tends to happen in so-called collective security and arms control is that the rogue revisionist "partner" uses, in jujitsu fashion, the normative value that we attach to the international regime to deter our calling him to account. The fourth point on the claimed promotion of interstate socialization is so egregious an error as to risk becoming a self-parody. The still thin literature on political and strategic culture advises caution on aspirations for benign convergence. The Kupchans give the game away when they write, "we contend that the ability of institutions to promote cooperation increases substantially as consensual beliefs among the major powers dampen the rivalries and insecurities of a Hobbesian setting. When inter-state cooperation already begins to emerge because of shifts in elite beliefs, and the Realist assumptions of a competitive self-help world are thus relaxed, a fertile ground exists for institutions to play a much more prominent role in shaping state behavior" (p. 131). These pretentiously worded sentences actually destroy the heart of the argument and, lightly translated, comprise the basis of the logic behind the arms control paradox. I and the Kupchans are saying that statesmen who want to agree find it relatively easy to agree. But for collective security, or arms control, to fulfill its promise, it should be capable of addressing the difficult issues as well as the gimmes.

[48] See the "Joint Statement of Principles and Basic Guidelines for Subsequent Negotiations on the Limitation of Strategic Arms," which accompanied the SALT II treaty. Reprinted in ACDA, *Arms Control and Disarmament Agreements,* pp. 298–99.

To appreciate the weight of historical support across the nuclear divide for my general argument, it is appropriate to remind readers of the lessons of the 1920s and 1930s. It was found that formal arms limitation agreements: (1) are negotiable and sustainable only when the political context is unusually friendly (i.e., when war is nowhere near in sight); (2) cannot achieve their objectives (help prevent war, promote stability, and so forth); (3) are so thoroughly political that their terms typically make no strategic sense; (4) lead to the development and deployment of treaty-compatible, treaty-evasive, or treaty-avoiding weapon systems which make sense primarily for arms control and not for military utility for national geostrategic needs; (5) help discourage legislators from funding weapon programs which either are constrained or might be eliminated (why waste money?); (6) provide irresistible incentives for nondemocratic countries to cheat; and (7) partially rechannel the flow of arms competitive traffic.

One can argue just how close a fit there is between those seven lessons from the interwar years and the events of the 1970s and 1980s, but there is no reasonable doubt that the fit lies somewhere between close and very close. There is a great deal more to arms control than the cases selected for examination in this chapter and the previous one. But the historically protracted cases of naval arms limitation between the wars and of the SALT-START process since 1969 can serve very adequately, though not by any means perfectly, as bases of evidence for the development of a paradigm that comprehends and explains how arms control works or, strictly, fails to work. If the historically based arguments presented here point to a rather mindless pursuit of the impracticable, readers can rest assured that other realms of arms control endeavor do not tell any more pretty a tale. To cite an intensely contemporary example, what should one make of a treaty to reduce chemical weapons when the United States does not know the size of the stockpile in the former USSR (the baseline for reductions), cannot possibly verify that the chemical industry there is not secretly producing weaponable by-products, and knows that many toxic chemical–producing factories could convert to weapons production in 24 hours?

Demands for ASAT arms control and for the incorporation of

naval forces in the widening gyre of negotiation are both, in their distinctive ways, thoroughly poor ideas. Separated from their geostrategic contexts, military space systems and naval forces are mountains that the arms control lobby would very much like to climb. With only minor and generally unverifiable exceptions, it is difficult to see how naval arms control could serve the goal of peace with security, given the degree of enduring maritime dependence of the Western World.[49] As for ASAT arms control, the subject cannot be defined in a meaningful way for legal capture. It would be incompatible with most strategic missile defense options, and often it is advocated without careful reference to understanding of space as a possible, and exceedingly important, environment for war.[50]

The political context for superpower relations and the dependent details of arms control proposals have both evolved recently with what can only be described as dazzling speed. My argument in this book is with the validity of the arms control theory that underpins government practice. This argument explains the 1920s as well as the 1930s, the 1980s as well as the 1990s. Senior officials and other opinion leaders scamper to adjust to the day's headlines—a successful Soviet coup, an unsuccessful Soviet coup, and so forth—and produce ever new arms control agendas. The fundamental error in their thinking easily escapes notice, particularly when it appears to be a time of new opportunities. As of this time of writing, when political developments have all but abolished the prospect of global nuclear war (*pro tem*, at least), the hour of arms control at last would seem to have arrived. The irony in this situation should promote second thoughts as to the soundness of the arms control venture.

---

[49] See Rear Admiral J. R. Hill, *Arms Control at Sea* (Annapolis, Md.: Naval Institute Press, 1989); and Colin S. Gray and Roger W. Barnett, *An Approach to Naval Arms Control* (Fairfax, Va.: National Institute for Public Policy, July 1989).

[50] ASAT arms control finds some favor in Paul B. Stares, *Space and National Security* (Washington, D.C.: Brookings, 1987), but none in Colin S. Gray, "Space Arms Control: A Skeptical View," *Air University Review*, 37 (November–December 1985), 73–86.

[6]

Verification without Compliance

I believe that . . . arms control commitments must be scru-
pulously observed. Nothing less will do.
                         —President George Bush, 6 February 1991

The most verifiable agreement imaginable is meaningless if one
party is allowed to violate international commitments with im-
punity.
                    —Senator Malcolm Wallop, 8 December 1987

A CASE OF FRAUD

If a government lacks the political courage to impose sanctions
or implement safeguards for treaty violations, is it a good idea for
it to verify noncompliance? This question is not rhetorical. Arms
control verification and assertions of the importance of compliance amount to a fraud perpetrated against credulous members of
the U.S. Congress and general public. The record of the past
twenty years shows that many of the people who pay lip service
to the importance of verification and treaty compliance are able to
find excuses for condoning or simply ignoring, Soviet misbehavior. Some of the others who pretend to care about verification and
compliance are serious only about using those subjects to undermine interest in possible arms control regimes.

U.S. policymakers knew that even under Mikhail Gorbachev
the Soviet Union either cheated or was not careful to comply with
the fine print, or reasonable interpretation, of solemn agreements.[1]

---

[1] President George Bush informed the Congress on 6 February 1991 that "the

Neither the CFE nor START processes have yielded readily verifiable regimes, while the United States still has no policy to cope
with cheating. A worldly-wise U.S. arms control policy during the
Cold War should have begun with the assumptions that the treaty
partner cannot stand a rigorous verification audit and that misbehavior by that partner *in effect* would be ignored by Washington.

Such appears to be the enduring, deceitful character of Russian
political culture,[2] and so richly varied is the menu of ambiguous
military practices that a standard-bearer for effective verification
and full compliance can hardly help but uncover probable malfeasance. Unfortunately, there is little in the extensive history of
twentieth-century arms control which provides grounds for optimism over the political willingness of a Western democracy to
exercise negative sanctions in the event that a treaty cosignatory
is caught cheating.[3] Although reviews of then-Soviet military be-

---

United States views the violations, the instances of bad faith, the inattention to
scrupulous compliance, and the less than forthcoming responses to U.S. concern
described in this report to be matters of serious concern. These potentially undermine U.S. confidence in Soviet compliance with existing agreements and threaten
the future viability of the arms control process, a process which relies on the willingness of treaty partners to comply." "Report to the Congress on Soviet Noncompliance with Arms Control Agreements" (Washington, D.C.: Office of the Press
Secretary, White House, 6 February 1991), p. 9.

[2] The outstanding treatment of this subject is Brian D. Dailey and Patrick J.
Parker, eds., *Soviet Strategic Deception* (Lexington, Mass.: Lexington Books, 1987).
The relevant traits in Russian political culture were outlined magnificently in Mar-
quis de Custine, *Empire of the Czar: A Journey through Eternal Russia* (1839; rpt. New
York: Doubleday, 1989).

[3] In an inspired analysis, Robin Ranger has argued forcefully that President
Roosevelt—greatly aided and abetted by "Mr. Navy" in the Congress, Representative Carl Vinson—crafted and applied what today would be called a "proportional
response" safeguards policy vis-à-vis possible Japanese noncompliance with treaty
restrictions. Ranger points correctly to the enabling legislation passed in 1934 and
1938 that authorized a build-up to, and then beyond, the Washington-London
quantitative limits which expired at the close of 1936. Also he points to the escalator clauses in the second London treaty (1936) which allowed battleships' main
batteries to have a 16-inch caliber, instead of the treaty-specified 14-inch, should
Japan not accept that treaty provision by 1 April 1937. Furthermore, Roosevelt
insisted, via a second escalator clause, that should any country build capital ships
with greater than 35,000 tons displacement, treaty (second London) adherents
would be at liberty to build to a 45,000 ton limit. Robin Ranger, "Learning from

havior under arms control restraint constitute the bulk of the material in the violations and compliance debate, more often than not those reviews are scarcely of more than tangential relevance to the U.S. problem, as commentators define it. Liberals and conservatives could agree that the Soviet Union was wont to misbehave when expedient. But the former found the most egregious fault in a U.S. policy disproportionately censorious about purportedly trivial, and virtually always ambiguous, matters; the latter was less inclined to find fault with the Soviet Union for misbehaving in traditional Soviet ways and more inclined to criticize the United States for its failure to design and execute a compliance or safeguards policy.

With a START treaty now concluded and the USSR now defunct, the principal path toward policy improvement for the United States surely does not lie in the direction of ever more rigorous examination of the current Russian record on treaty compliance. More important is the sustained political will, fueled by moral courage, to develop and execute a safeguards and compliance policy. Technically and legally persuasive charges of treaty violation must be preferred to charges resting upon slight evidence and considerable imagination. But no quantity and quality of raw data on Russian behavior, and no amount of skill in the

---

the Naval Arms Control Experience," *Washington Quarterly*, 10 (Summer 1987), particularly pp. 51–53. Ranger's argument is interesting and perhaps important as a stimulus to constructive thought on a new approach to U.S. compliance policy, but ultimately it is not persuasive. The Vinson-Trammel Act of 1934 neither found money for, nor commanded a build-up of, the U.S. Navy. Moreover, the build-up that was envisaged was only, at that time, a build-up to treaty limits (in face of persisting reports of Japanese violations). In fact, there was a great deal less in practice to Roosevelt's proportional response policy from 1934 to 1938 than one might suppose. After late 1934, it should be recalled, the context for application of Roosevelt's alleged compliance policy was dominated by the fact that Imperial Japan had served formal notice of the intention not to be subject to legal arms limitation restraint after 31 December 1936. To risk understatement, Roosevelt's policy action toward a cheating, and then an unregulated, Japan was both belated and feeble. Robert Gordon Kaufman, *Arms Control during the Pre-Nuclear Era: The United States and Naval Limitation between the Two World Wars* (New York: Columbia University Press, 1990), pp. 99–107, and 151–54, is convincingly scathing on the poor quality of U.S. policy toward Japanese misbehavior, proved and suspected, in the 1930s.

complex business of treaty monitoring, can substitute for the political will and moral courage needed if the United States is to
respond.[4] Senator Malcolm Wallop was very much to the point
when he observed that President Reagan's praise of the verification provisions underpinning the INF treaty were "like arguing
that AIDS testing is the solution to the AIDS epidemic."[5]

It should be noted that even after six years of Gorbachev's re-
forming leadership, the Soviet Union was still lying—a word selected with care—about its transfer of SS-23 short-range ballistic
missiles (SRBMs) to then–Warsaw Pact allies, contrary to U.S. understanding of the situation extant when the INF treaty was
signed. Well into the Gorbachev era Soviet officials were asked if
treaty-accountable missiles had been transferred to other countries, and repeatedly they replied no.[6] That was not only a lie, it
was a stupid lie, which is to say it was a lie whose security lay
outside Soviet control to maintain. An East German report eventually broke the story. More recently, post–Cold War but still-
Soviet policy lied about its CFE-accountable equipment parks in

---

[4] This problem is recognized, but not examined, in Kerry M. Kartchner, "Soviet
Compliance with a START Agreement: Prospects under Gorbachev," *Strategic Review*, 17 (Fall 1989), 47–57.

[5] Senator Malcolm Wallop, "Verify, but Also Punish Violations," *Wall Street Journal*, 18 December 1987, p. 22.

[6] Transfer of the SRBMs in question would have been legal prior to the signing
of the INF treaty in December 1987, but politically, the United States would have
demanded that the double-zero cover those East German, Czechoslovak, and Bul-
garian, SS-23s, just as the Soviet Union demanded (successfully) that West Germany abandon its Pershing Is. Reportedly, Soviet officials were asked no less than
ten times whether or not the missile systems designated as INF treaty–accountable
(i.e., with ranges between 300–3400 miles) had been transferred to allies. See Bill
Gertz, "Discovery of Soviet Missiles Sidetracks Arms-Control Efforts," *Washington
Times*, 2 April 1990, p. A3. Arms control efforts may well be sidetracked by political events that alter the tenor of political relations, but the article just cited is alas
far too optimistic in its title. Then Soviet Foreign Minister Edward Shevardnadze
claimed, almost certainly correctly, first, that the transfer occurred before the INF
treaty was signed—which was legal but ignored the issue of repeated lies to direct
questions—and second, improbably, that neither he nor Mikhail Gorbachev knew
anything about it at the time. See "Shevardnadze Fields Questions," FPIS-
SOV-90-068, *International Affairs* (9 April 1990), p. 11; Bush, "Report to the Congress on Soviet Noncompliance . . ." (1991), pp. 11–13; and Bill Gertz, "Soviets
Cheated on Warheads, New Report Said," *Washington Times*, 23 September 1991,
p. A3.

the treaty area of the Atlantic to the Urals, transferred so much of that equipment east of the Urals as to undermine a plain purpose of the treaty, though not—in most cases—of the specific terms of CFE, and lied about the forward deployment of some chemical weapon stocks in Eastern Europe. As of this time of writing the successor states of the Soviet Union are far from constituting a polity meriting complete trust to be self-policing in habits of treaty observance.

Too much should not be made of this fact. Certainly, I do not argue that arms control is a snare and a delusion because authoritarian, or even still shakily democratic, countries are wont to lie and cheat. The arms control paradox suffices to explain why arms control must fail to meet the more demanding goals specified for it. The issue of cheating is politically important for reasons developed later in this chapter. The central purpose of this discussion is to demonstrate the fraudulent nature of the booming U.S. monitoring and verification industry. CFE and START have promoted exponential growth in the inspection business. This chapter argues, on the extensive evidence available, that U.S. policy toward treaty noncompliance is so shamefully craven that it mocks the activity of monitoring and the judgmental process called verification.

THE CRISIS OF ARMS CONTROL

Notwithstanding the hectic pace of treaty conclusion, there is a general crisis of the relevance of arms control of which the (*non*)compliance problem is an integral part. Specifically, an indeterminacy about the purposes of arms control negotiations renders basic treaty assessment, as well as compliance issues, difficult to approach strategically. Obviously, arms control, its verification, and a compliance or safeguards policy to deter or cope with potential or actual violations are not ends in themselves.[7] Therefore, critics of the Reagan administration claimed to

[7] For example, Dick Cheney (Secretary of Defense), *Annual Report to the President and the Congress* (Washington, D.C.: Government Printing Office, February 1992), p. 10.

discern an unreasonably absolutist strand in official pronounce-
ments on verification and compliance, a stand not related plausibly to a net assessment of the strategic costs and benefits of the
alleged offenses.[8]

Proponents of arms control generally adhered to the plausible,
though actually flawed, argument that because arms control
agreements were quite valuable to the Soviet Union, it was not
likely to cheat. Unfortunately, the corollary to that reasoning held
that because the agreements in question were so valuable to us,
we should not object rigorously if the Soviet Union is caught
cheating at the margins. There is a central difficulty with grand
strategy. The grand-strategic effect of a treaty, or of particular
treaty violations, cannot be assessed solely as means in the
means-ends nexus of strategy. For example, if it is not certain
what the Western strategic purposes are with the INF, CFE, or
START treaties, how can one assess the likely strategic significance of the violation of some treaty terms?

No serious attempt has been undertaken to provide grand-strategic justification for the drive to complete, ratify, and give effect
to new arms control treaties. The crisis of arms control relates to
the shaky foundations of the enterprise. This shakiness finds ample reflection in the U.S. debate over compliance issues. Without
notable exception, opinion leaders in the U.S. debate on arms
control affirm the importance of verification and compliance,
though it is not unknown for these ideas to be confused. In practice, the Reagan administration, which adopted an uncompromising rhetorical position on the necessity for compliance with treaties,
was willing to negotiate and sign new agreements even while its
negotiating partner still was found not to be in a state of grace on
compliance with old agreements.[9] What message did that convey?

---

[8] For example, Richard N. Haass, "Verification and Compliance," in Albert Carnesale and Haass, eds., *Superpower Arms Control: Setting the Record Straight* (Cambridge, Mass.: Ballinger, 1987), p. 318.

[9] Just six days before he signed the INF treaty, President Reagan reported to the
Congress that "the Soviet Union to date has not corrected its noncompliance activities. Indeed, since the last report, there has been an additional case of Soviet
violation of the ABM Treaty in the deployment of an ABM radar at Gomel, and
other violations are continuing." "Report to the Congress on Soviet Noncom-

Similarly, leading members of the extra-official Arms Control Association and the Federation of American Scientists have yielded to none in their public devotion to the cause of the sanctity of treaties. But in practice, and no doubt honorably, those members have seemed somehow always, or nearly always, to be functioning as counsel for the defense of ever-arguable then-Soviet (mis)behavior.[10] For example, the leading lights of the U.S. arms control community were almost painfully slow to come to grips with the accumulating evidence on the flagrant violation of the ABM treaty represented by the Krasnoyarsk radar.[11]

In the light of this dismal record, it is not unreasonable to ask if it is politically possible for a U.S. administration to apply a sanctions policy, or to implement national military safeguards, in the event of verification of treaty noncompliance. After all, if the Reagan administration could not do this, can any other administration? Also, one might ask if any type of treaty violation would spur the central command of the U.S. arms control community to urge a serious sanctions policy.

The compliance problem, like the more general crisis of arms control, has crept up on the U.S. body politic and evaded suitably forthright discussion. Until recently, at least, U.S. officials and

---

pliance with Arms Control Agreements" (Washington, D.C.: Office of the Press Secretary, White House, 2 December 1987), p. 1.

[10] Characteristic reports include "Arms Control Treaty Compliance," *F.A.S.* [Federation of American Scientists] *Public Interest Report*, 37 (March 1984); and Gloria Duffy et al., "Compliance and the Future of Arms Control" (The Stanford Report), reprinted in *Congressional Record—Senate*, 19 February 1987, pp. S2326–35. To be fair, the Stanford group did find one clear Soviet violation, the Krasnoyarsk (or Abalakovo) radar.

[11] The reluctance of the U.S. arms control community to concede that the Reagan administration was right about Krasnoyarsk is traced carefully in Sven F. Kraemer, "The Krasnoyarsk Saga," *Strategic Review*, 18 (Winter 1990), 25–38. In what amounts to an inadvertent parody of much of the American problem, Abram Chayes and Antonia Handler Chayes have written of Krasnoyarsk that "it is hard to fashion an appropriate response to this violation. It is of little military significance and would not justify withdrawal from the [ABM] Treaty." "Living under a Treaty Regime: Compliance, Interpretation, and Adaption," in Antonia H. Chayes and Paul Doty, eds., *Defending Deterrence: Managing the ABM Treaty Regime into the 21st Century* (Washington, D.C.: Pergamon Brassey's, 1989), pp. 200–201.

arms control theorists generally predicted, with conveniently circular logic, that compliance with arms control regimes would not be an important problem because states only sign on for agreements which serve their interests. Hence, an arms control treaty virtually by definition must be largely self-enforcing. The same coincidence of interests that renders a treaty negotiable also must work to provide adequate incentives for compliance.[12] The Western arms control literature from the later 1950s to the very early 1970s had a great deal to say on the subject of verification, but strangely, given the interwar experience with cheating,[13] the subjects of possible noncompliance and the design of a sanctions policy was not heavily traveled country. Perhaps in part because so many American arms control theorists were physical scientists, economists, and political scientists, the sad history of noncompliance problems in the 1920s and 1930s seemed almost totally to escape modern notice.[14] A noteworthy exception was Fred Charles Iklé's justly celebrated 1961 article, "After Detection—What?"[15] The passage of three decades since that question was posed so bluntly has yet to yield practical evidence of a convincing answer. The basic premise of modern arms control, that the self-interest of the high contracting parties will render treaties self-enforcing, has been shown by events to be incorrect. Recognition of that unexpected fact is reflected in the ever more detailed provisions for

[12] Henry Kissinger expressed these thoughts very directly when he briefed legislators on SALT I. See U.S. Congress, Senate Committee on Foreign Relations, *Strategic Arms Limitation Agreements Hearings*, 92d Cong., 2d Sess. (Washington, D.C.: Government Printing Office, 1972), p. 401.

[13] See Richard Dean Burns and Donald Urquidi, *Disarmament in Perspective: An Analysis of Selected Arms Control and Disarmament Agreements between the World Wars, 1919-1939*, vol. 3: *Limitation of Sea Power* (Los Angeles: California State College at Los Angeles Foundation, July 1968), chap. 20; Ranger, "Learning from the Naval Arms Control Experience"; and Kaufman, *Arms Control during the Pre-Nuclear Era*, pp. 90–108.

[14] It would be more excusable, though still wrong, were the arms control compliance record of the 1930s to be viewed in the 1990s as arcane data of antiquarian interest only. But when arms control theory was being invented and reinvented in the late 1950s and early 1960s, the older participants at conferences would have had personal memories of the 1930s.

[15] Fred Charles Iklé, "After Detection—What?" *Foreign Affairs*, 39 (January 1961), 208–20.

cooperative inspection which now accompany the texts of treaties.[16]

The prospects for timely detection of cheating were greatly enhanced by the advent in the very early 1960s of unmanned eyes and ears in space—spy satellites ("overhead assets," in the language of the defense community). Yet another paradox of arms control is that today, more than three decades on from the bold new beginnings of modern arms control theory and practice, advances in national technical means (NTM) of verification have far outrun ideas and policy on what to do if and when cheating is verified.[17] It is almost as if American officials would *talk and behave* like carnivorous deer hunters but really are vegetarians frankly embarrassed when they find, track, and kill their quarry. One should not exaggerate the achievements of NTM nor overpraise the benefits of on-site inspection,[18] but—imperfect though national information gathering is and will remain—the U.S. problem with noncompliance by a treaty partner is much more political than technical.

FIRST-ORDER VERSUS SECOND-ORDER ISSUES

It would be judged politically irrelevant to argue that the START treaty is fundamentally flawed on strategic grounds. The train already has left the station. Even if they have a sound grasp of what is meant by strategic argument, many of the active public debaters give the appearance of being more comfortable with controversy over second-order issues. Compliance is just such a second-order matter, though potentially with some first-order impli-

[16] For example, see the Inspections Protocol to the INF treaty in U.S. Arms Control and Disarmament Agency (ACDA), *Arms Control and Disarmament Agreements: Texts and Histories of Negotiations* (Washington, D.C.: Government Printing Office, 1990), pp. 431–44.

[17] On the scale of U.S. advances in information gathering from low earth orbit, see Jeffrey T. Richelson, *America's Secret Eyes in Space: The U.S. Keyhole Spy Satellite Program* (Cambridge, Mass.: Ballinger, 1990).

[18] See Lewis A. Dunn (with Amy E. Gordon), *Arms Control Verification and the New Role of On-Site Inspection* (Lexington, Mass.: Lexington Books, 1990), for a balanced treatment.

cations. A treaty might be strategically unwise for the West, whether or not the former Soviet Union complied fully with its terms. But there could be important cases where U.S. attitudes toward a treaty should rest upon confidence either that the other side would comply in all significant respects, or that noncompliance would meet promptly with a suitably offsetting U.S. response. If that confidence is not felt, then there should be no treaty. Unequal compliance with a nominally equal treaty translates into an unequal treaty.

It has long been nearly axiomatic among dedicated arms controllers to affirm the functional equivalent of the Athanasian Creed. The true believer affirms faith in the dedication with which states pursue their interests, the robust basis in mutual self-interest of arms control agreements, a presumption of intent to comply, and the self-enforcing nature of treaties. This creed is not wholly ill-founded. But events have proved it to be sufficiently, and persistently, in error, so there is no excuse for further evasion of frank consideration of Fred Iklé's question, "After Detection—What?"

Political and strategic-cultural analysis tells us two important and embarrassingly inconvenient things. First, a cultural proclivity to try to deceive is very much the Russian way in statecraft. Cheating for advantage or simply for convenience is probably inalienably, though certainly far from uniquely, Russian. The Russian tradition in statecraft is very different from the American. Moreover, Moscow will cheat in matters small as well as great.[19] Lenin's disdain for bourgeois values in statecraft—after all, the young Bolshevik republic was a revolution masquerading as a country—was planted in the fertile soil of a distinctly Oriental tradition (Asian and Byzantine). Deception is integral to Russian

[19] Until historical experience proved them wrong, it was an article of commonsense belief in the West that the Soviet Union would not imperil a great enterprise of arms control, let alone the political relationship associated intimately with that enterprise, for the sake of trivial military advantage or convenience, illegally pursued. That commonsense belief was simply wrong, unless one credited the Soviet Union with the no less commonsense belief that the very disproportion between the likely gain and the total military-political stakes effectively discouraged Western countermeasures.

[169]

strategic culture.[20] Western societies can deceive systematically, though as a matter of policy, not culture, only in conditions of dire strategic necessity. The triumphs of British intelligence in World War II illustrate this point.[21] Second, to date in the twentieth century no Western democracy has been able to design *and implement* an adequate compliance policy to deter or a safeguards policy adequate for responding to arms control violations. This judgment is written against the backcloth of recognition of Roosevelt's attempts at a proportional response policy in the mid-1930s and of the so-called safeguards attached politically both to the 1963 Limited Test Ban Treaty as well as to SALT I in 1972. If history is a guide, the student of arms control should not hinge support for an arms control treaty upon the presumption of a U.S. sanctions policy for verified violations. The presumption should be neither that Russia will be deterred from cheating nor that suitably offsetting measures would be adopted in response.

The Soviet Union could be trusted never to provide a gun so obviously and offensively smoking that even a very reluctant U.S. body politic would be obliged to implement a sanctions policy out of self-respect and concern for reputation. Similarly, the United States could be trusted to provide a body of influential arms control sophisticates determined that whole woods of arms control

[20] See David M. Glantz, "The Red Mask: The Nature and Legacy of Soviet Military Deception in the Second World War," in Michael I. Handel, ed., *Strategic and Operational Deception in the Second World War* (London: Frank Cass, 1987), pp. 175–259. On Soviet strategic culture, see Yitzhak Klein, "The Sources of Soviet Strategic Culture," *Journal of Soviet Military Studies*, 2 (December 1989), 453–90. Also useful are the essays in Carl G. Jacobsen, ed., *Strategic Power: USA/USSR* (New York: St. Martin's Press, 1990), part 1: "Strategic Culture in Theory and Practice"; and Yitzhak Klein, "A Theory of Strategic Culture," *Comparative Strategy*, 10 (January–March 1991), 3–23. Michael Vlahos, "Culture and Foreign Policy," *Foreign Policy*, 82 (Spring 1991), 59–78, is overly ambitious but interesting and insightful. The degree of commonality between Russian and Soviet strategic culture awaits authoritative analysis.

[21] "There is nothing more stimulating for intelligence work than a feeling of weakness and vulnerability, from which comes the impetus to learn as much as possible about the enemy." Michael I. Handel, "Technological Surprise in War," *Intelligence and National Security*, 2 (January 1987), p. 13. For authoritative, if distinctly incomplete, treatment of the British uses of strategic deception in World War II, see Michael Howard, *British Intelligence in the Second World War*, vol. 5: *Strategic Deception* (London: H.M.S.O., 1990).

value not be destroyed in the interest of taking out single rotten trees of arguable malpractice. The political consequence was that Soviet misbehavior (*inter alia*) generally was denied, or de facto condoned. By way of an unconscious self-parody of this attitude, some Senate witnesses in favor of the INF treaty testified that there had been no *general pattern* of Soviet treaty noncompliance; by and large, so it was asserted, Moscow complied. Selective compliance is noncompliance, simpleminded and unsophisticated though that may seem as a position. President Bush recognized this point: "In one sense all Soviet violations are equally important. As violations of legal obligations or political commitments, they cause concern regarding Soviet commitment to arms control."[22]

COMPLIANCE

The literature on compliance questions, both liberal- and conservative-authored, has yet to come to terms with the true scope of the policy problem. Both poles of the debate seriously understate the difficulty of finding solutions to the problem, as they define it. The principal liberal approach is to affirm rhetorically the importance of verification *and* compliance but then in virtually every instance to find more fault with the ever-flawed U.S. case than with the adversary-partner for possibly or probably misbehaving. This functional tolerance of noncompliance could have adverse military-technical and political implications for U.S. security. For example, the technical-tactical interface and overlap between air and missile defenses and between early-warning and battle-management radars could result in an unwary United States monitoring the undramatic arrival of a Russian nationwide BMD system. The principal conservative approach, which is to insist that behavior incompatible with the plain meaning of the terms, or the U.S. purposes, of an agreement must not be tolerated, has yet to cope with the apparent fact that American politicians do not really care very much about arms control violations

[22] Bush, "Report to the Congress on Soviet Noncompliance . . ." (1991), p. 9.

or technically legal avoidance measures. Somewhat ironically, all schools of American opinion on arms control favor more rigorous monitoring regimes for verification, even though none of them have anything very impressive to say on the subject addressed in this chapter: the policy problem of coping with verified noncompliance.

Through their strategically ill-considered and extravagant praise of the theoretical benefits of the arms control process, Western governments thus find themselves riding the tiger with no domestically politically safe means of dismounting. The only respectable positions for politicians to adopt in public are, first, affirmation of the importance of arms control for the preservation of peace—even though there is no historical evidence linking the two—and, second, affirmation of the importance of verification—even though experience has shown that effective verification of noncompliance cannot readily, if ever, be followed by corrective or punitive sanctions.

The more the process of arms control is praised as a bearer of the decent opinions and hopes of humanity, the more intractable becomes the problem of responding prudently in strategic terms to evidence of arms control noncompliance. How can one imperil progress in a field which, allegedly, can make the difference between peace and war, over issues which are always both to a degree ambiguous, and hence excusable, and substantively typically minor? It can be difficult to arouse military-technical excitement on issues of possible noncompliance, when a START I treaty leaves the United States with a residual nuclear arsenal allowance in the 9000–10,000 warhead range. On an alternative logic track to the same conclusion, issues of noncompliance may seem to be trivial footnotes to an arms control process that itself is perceived as more and more trivial in its implications for the quality of international security. Such an appearance is indeed an accurate reflection of reality. The purpose here is not to contradict the argument threading throughout the rest of the book that military-technical details are not very important but rather to show that although there can be an all but mind-numbing detailed technicality to questions of verification and compliance, the aspect of this subject that matters most is deeply political.

Systematic apologists for Soviet noncompliance practices, when pressed for supporting arguments, were wont to assert that the strategic balance was massively stable and insensitive to damage by postural change at the margin. In part, belief in this assertion was shared also on the conservative side of the argument. A conviction or strong suspicion that nothing of real military significance is at stake cannot help but incline people to treat noncompliance as being in the category of condonable misdemeanors, rather than felonies. It is ironic that although military capability at the margin of a large and diverse arsenal becomes trivial when considered as grounds for policy change in face of verified cheating, similar marginal changes are allegedly destabilizing when the case is made for arms control.

To avoid a plausible charge of inconsistency or even hypocrisy, the U.S. government should think through the problems both of just how serious it means to be and of just how serious it could be about a noncompliance problem. In the 1980s the Soviet Union was found not to be in compliance on a wide range of arms control provisions, yet Washington proceeded to conclude a new arms control treaty (INF) and to advance the prospects for others (the future CFE treaty and START). Given the cultural proclivity of Russia to be none too careful on compliance, more elaborate arrangements for the monitoring of treaties carry the promise of sharpening the U.S. policy dilemma, not of easing it. Moreover, as the Russia of the 1990s becomes more "politically correct" (rather like Weimar Germany after 1925), so the incentive to ignore noncompliant practices assuredly will grow.

Notwithstanding all the pontificating and moralizing, the United States as a practical matter assigns little policy weight to the persisting facts of treaty violation. Rhetoric aside, the U.S. government has chosen to live with verified Soviet noncompliance with the ABM treaty (for but one example), presumably on the grounds that it judges continuance of that regime to be in the U.S. interest, noncompliance and all. The truth of the matter is that U.S. policy has been caught without an endgame. Both Western and Soviet observers of the tough U.S. language after 1984 on the subject of noncompliance had a right to be puzzled over the policy ends which that language was designed to serve.

[173]

The U.S. administrations of the 1970s warranted and probably re-
ceived some Soviet disrespect for their unwillingness to call cheating what it was. But what could be made of a Reagan administration, and now a Bush administration, which had the political
courage publicly to find the Soviet Union in noncompliance but
did not permit that finding to influence its willingness to negotiate new agreements?

TREATY MONITORING AND THE VERIFICATION PROCESS

What is the purpose of careful treaty monitoring and of a political process of verification? In principle, verification should help
deter illegal or arguable activity. But if verification of noncompliance *never*, or only very rarely, has consequences harmful to
Russian security, how much incentive is Moscow (et al.) likely to
have to overcome its cultural attraction toward the securing of
illicit military advantage?

Of course, there is merit in the monitoring of ambiguous or
even plainly illegal activity, whether or not the U.S. government
is politically able or motivated to take corrective or punitive measures in response. Knowledge is important. It is tempting to argue
that the U.S. policy problem with Soviet noncompliance was the
absence of that smoking gun which surely must sweep aside political objections to the application of sanctions. That temptation
were best resisted, particularly in light of the Krasnoyarsk experience. Opinion poll data show consistently that the American public believes that Russians cheat on treaty obligations. Outside the
hard core of the arms control community and its constituency in
the Congress, the U.S. policy problem has not been the credibility
of findings of noncompliance. Why then has presidential report
after presidential report on Soviet noncompliance had so few consequences for broad arms control policy? The answer appears to
be that high administration officials have not sufficiently agreed
on the purposes they wished to have served by the publicized
findings.

Few people who recognize the practical force of Russian strategic culture expect the successor states of the Soviet Union to be-

have very much better in the future,[23] at least not unless it can be demonstrated to their leaders that U.S. anger or irritation with noncompliance has painful consequences. The collapse of the Soviet Union, potentially a cultural-social-political *revolution* though in 1992 more a condition of anarchy, may produce a Russian polity whose society would police effectively the defense and arms control behavior of its elected government and permanent bureaucracy. However, the arms control paradox intrudes yet again. A genuinely trustworthy Russia would be of little interest to Western arms control policy. The United States, for all its irritation and occasional anger with the arrogance in the pattern of Soviet misbehavior, never determined to punish the Soviet Union for its offenses. The Soviet *mea culpa* over the Krasnoyarsk radar was the product of the calculation that to continue lying would pose insuperable difficulties for START ratification by the U.S. Senate.

The root of the problem has been that both the U.S. government and the American public came to attach such unreasonable importance to the so-called arms control process that they were caught in a trap of their own devising. The Soviet Union continued to violate agreements when and where it was administratively convenient, militarily advantageous, and economically efficient to do so. All the while a real U.S. sanctions policy for noncompliance was held hostage to Western hopes for the benefits of arms control. This is not to suggest that future violations generally are likely to be insultingly blatant on the Krasnoyarsk model. The current hand at the policy tiller in Moscow has been advised that verification and compliance issues potentially are killer political hurdles for arms control treaties to jump.

The political demotion of the superpower arms control process by the ending of the Cold War and the demise of one superpower

---

[23] There is much of value in Joseph Whelan, *Soviet Diplomacy and Negotiating Behavior: Emerging New Context for U.S. Diplomacy*, vol. 1: *Special Studies Series on Foreign Affairs Issues, Committee on Foreign Affairs, House of Representatives, U.S. Congress* (Washington, D.C.: Government Printing Office, 1979); Leon Sloss and M. Scott Davis, eds., *A Game for High Stakes: Lessons Learned in Negotiating with the Soviet Union* (Cambridge, Mass.: Ballinger, 1986); and Raymond F. Smith, *Negotiating with the Soviets* (Bloomington: Indiana University Press, 1989).

has not achieved the better balance in U.S. policy toward non-compliance that might have been predicted. It should be the case that a U.S. government and public less interested in arms control outcomes in the context of a burgeoning political peace could afford to be less tolerant of arms control misdemeanors and felonies by the adversary-partner. To date, however, the evidence suggests that the decline in policy significance of arms control endeavors is more than matched by a parallel decline of serious interest in compliance topics.

No Solution in Sight

Six conclusions emerge from the argument developed here. Unfortunately, none of them suggests some magical method by means of which the base metal of past and present Western performance in face of treaty noncompliance can be transformed into the gold of an effective policy.

First, there needs to be full and explicit recognition of the depth and origins of the policy problem. The villain really is the arms control paradox of which so much is made in this text. When a Western democracy signs an arms control treaty with a putative enemy who attaches no normative value to the observance of law, incentives for, and habits favoring, noncompliance should be recognized. Indeed, it is important to recognize that virtually all arms control agreements invite efforts at evasion by military organizations, regardless of the political complexion of the state.[24] Avoidance is not illegal. Through prudent and perhaps imagina-

---

[24] Reasoning that offense can be the best defense, Moscow has charged periodically that the U.S. record on arms control compliance is none too pristine. There have even been some American commentators willing to endorse this canard. Two leading charges over the years pertained to the USAF's practice of temporarily placing environmental covers over ICBM silos that were in the process of being upgraded with additional cement. That practice was no more genuine an affront to the SALT principle forbidding "deliberate concealment measures which impede verification by national technical means" (Interim Agreement of SALT I, Article V, para. 3) than modernization of the Ballistic Missile Early Warning System (BMEWS) radars allowed for an illegal BMD battle-management role. The political reality of U.S. compliance practice was all but self-parodied in the "broad versus narrow" debate of the late 1980s over the ABM treaty and SDI development.

tive treaty avoidance one attempts, responsibly, to ensure that a particular regime of arms regulation has the least harmfully constraining effect upon the home team. With variable success, arms control negotiators seek through various noncircumvention clauses to limit the possibilities for avoidance, particularly avoidance of a kind that would subvert the explicit purposes of a regime.

For a case in point, Western and Eastern European governments prefer to see heavy items of Russian military equipment destroyed rather than simply moved beyond the treaty area (the Atlantic to the Urals). For entirely understandable reasons, the effective authority in Russia on this subject has preferred to move and reassign equipment rather than destroy it. By moving the items at issue out of Europe prior to the signing of the CFE treaty, Moscow was indulging in treaty-avoidance behavior. By continuing to move that equipment after the treaty signing as well as by redesignating some ground force units as "naval infantry" and by transferring heavy ground equipment to the Strategic Rocket Forces, Moscow challenged its fellow signatories with illegal treaty-evasive behavior.

Second, the general public, and perhaps some senior officials and politicians, needs to contemplate the history and promise of arms control stripped of its mythology. Casual, or calculated politically expedient, remarks by American political leaders to the effect that the formal process of arms control negotiations is critical for the prospects of peace is a nail in the coffin of a compliance policy worthy of the name. Readers might recall a venerable maxim about negotiations: do not sit down unless you are prepared to stand up.

Third, both the executive and the legislative branches of government should consider committing themselves in a binding public manner to the principle that noncompliance with solemn treaty obligations would justify a punitive, *disproportionate* response. No administration could, or should want to, commit itself to execute specific sanctions or invoke particular safeguards in the event of hypothetical treaty violations. But a formal statement of compliance policy, really of the intention to effect a healthy overcorrection for noncompliance, should be required of any administration submitting an arms control treaty for the advice and consent of the Senate.

Fourth, the complex subject of verification and compliance needs to be considered with reference to what history teaches about the real fuel of crisis instability. Compliance policy does not impact the danger of war very much, if at all, through the small likelihood that a state might secure a covert, or even overt but arguably legal and condoned, military advantage. The problem is not that covertly secured advantage at the margin might incline political leaders to lend credence to promises of victory from their military experts. Rather, policy failure on compliance issues may encourage a putative enemy to disrespect the political determination of an American president. Compliance policy should be seen as a *character check*. Perceived military advantage at the margin, such as might be secured by a pattern of arms control noncompliance, is not the stuff of which decisions to fight are made. Perception of weakness in political leaders, as with those who proclaim that treaty noncompliance is intolerable, and then tolerate it, is exactly the perceptual material which can fuel the courage to undertake military adventure. Crisis instability does not reside so much in the technical detail of rival military postures as rather in the miscalculation by foreign leaders that the United States would not do what its leaders have pledged to do.

Fifth, since it is always a poor idea to attempt the truly impossible, one should never sign on for an arms control regime that plausibly could endanger military security in the predictable event of noncompliance. Because of its inherent limitations, as argued in this book, the so-called arms control process cannot achieve major benefits for international security. But that process might wreak real damage were it ever to mandate force-level reductions that could be sound *only* if the adversary-partner complied meticulously.

Sixth and finally, the somber judgment must be registered that the achievement of some approximation of success in the quest for an intelligent and politically practicable U.S. policy on arms control compliance is unlikely. It is no accident that in the course of the twentieth century thus far no Western democracy has crafted and demonstrated an ability to execute a timely and effective sanctions or safeguards policy for arms control noncompliance.

[7]

To Bury Arms Control,
Not to Praise It

If arms control should die, it would have to be speedily resur-
rected. Arms control has become an essential mechanism or currency for management of international relations in the nuclear
age.

—Johan Jorgen Holst, 1983

GIVE THE DEVIL HIS DUE

The directing staff of the International Institute for Strategic
Studies (IISS) has lent its collective authority to the view that "in a
world in turmoil where massive armaments still exist, arms control can continue to play a useful role in equalizing capabilities at
lower levels, easing tensions and reducing uncertainty, and make
it legally and politically difficult to revert to former force levels
and postures."[1] Similarly, echoing Johan Holst's proposition quoted
above, Joseph S. Nye, Jr., of Harvard has written that "if an arms
control process did not exist, we would assuredly have to invent
it."[2] The critical words are "have to." This book is an extended
critique of the contention that we "have to" proceed with an arms
control process. More narrowly focused, this chapter explores the
reasons why governments and people as sophisticated as Joseph
Nye, Johan Holst, and the staff of the IISS, believe that arms control is important.

[1] International Institute for Strategic Studies (IISS), *Strategic Survey, 1989–1990*
(London: IISS, May 1990), p. 194.
[2] Joseph S. Nye, Jr., "Arms Control After the Cold War," *Foreign Affairs*, 68
(Winter 1989–90), p. 64.

[179]

The central problem with arms control is that it rests upon a principle that is fatally flawed; as a consequence arms control cannot work in practice as advertised. Arms control theory, the ideas that help inspire policy, are attractive but, alas, untrue. By way of analogy, Edward N. Luttwak's brilliant exposition of *The Grand Strategy of the Roman Empire* has everything to recommend it except probable historical accuracy.[3] As with arms control theory, Luttwak's theory of Roman grand strategy refers to a universe which ought to have been but which the weight of available evidence suggests strongly just was not so. Nonetheless, in the course of being wrong "in the large" (vis-à-vis reduction in the risk of war occurring, or truly grand strategic design), a theory still may provide useful and plausibly accurate insights.

There is some merit in arms control theory and practice. This is not a world wherein reigns a mutually exclusive either-or. The purpose of this chapter is to select and discuss fairly, though critically, the better among the arguments and claims advanced in praise of arms control. It is important that like not be compared irrelevantly with unlike. The debate here is not only between two distinctive rival *philosophies*: the one in praise of arms control, the other in criticism. Instead, the debate, dialogue perhaps, also is between arguments for arms control and the actual accomplishments of such activity. The test is not of attractiveness of theory but rather of reality and feasibility of achievement. There is no case for treating arms control as though it were a religion whose

---

[3] Edward N. Luttwak, *The Grand Strategy of the Roman Empire: From the First Century A.D. to the Third* (Baltimore: Johns Hopkins University Press, 1976). For a devastating critique, see Benjamin Isaac, *The Limits of Empire: The Roman Army in the East* (Oxford: Clarendon Press, 1990), particularly pp. 416, 419. Scholars today can neither prove nor disprove the existence, character, and detail of a Roman grand strategy. However, Isaac argues most carefully and persuasively from archaeological, epigraphic, and literary sources that Romans did not approach questions of foreign policy and military opportunity/peril in ways conducive to development of a grand strategy. Civil and military architecture has been confused, construction and troop deployment for internal rather than external security has been misidentified and, generally, inappropriately modern strategic ideas have been superimposed upon Roman minds. Above all else perhaps, Luttwak, inter alia, insists upon a very territorial idea of empire and imperial security, whereas the original sources suggest that Romans did not conceive of their imperium as being in essence territorial; rather, it was an imperium over peoples.

truth has to be taken on faith. Arms control has an extensive history readily accessible if not always easy to interpret. I advance a theory that explains why arms control must fail. This theory has in its support the historical evidence of the protracted interwar and postwar experiences with arms limitation regimes. The superiority of the theory critical of arms control advanced here is such that there is a massive asymmetry possible in the terms of engagement for debate. Although two rival theories are in contention, the theory critical of arms control is compatible with the course of history, while arms control theory is not. The merit in arms control as a branch of strategic theory pertains to practical activity in the world, not to strictly intellectual values.

POINT-COUNTERPOINT

Much of the case developed in this book thus far against the theory and practice of arms control has been rather narrow. The focus generally has been upon the relationship between arms control and the prevention of war, upon great powers and superpowers, and upon *structural* arms control or arms limitation rather than more broadly upon *operational* and other forms of arms control. This narrow focus has been chosen in order to concentrate attention upon the most important questions of the arms race, crisis, war, and peace among the principal actors in international security, with particular reference to their "strategic" armament (capital ships or long-range and nuclear-armed weapons). Insofar as there is a diffuse collection of rationales for arms control activity, it would be inappropriate to neglect to address at least an approximation to the full breadth of the positive case. What follows, therefore, is discussion of a selection of the more interesting arguments advanced in praise of arms control. Notwithstanding the critical thrust of this book, the arguments selected here have been chosen because of their relative strength, inherent interest, or plausibility (though admittedly one or two owe their selection simply to their popularity). I have not knowingly picked a second-string team for easy dismissal.

No fewer than eleven more or less distinctive claims for the benefit to be derived from arms control are examined below. The overriding, central claim that "arms control can reduce the risk of war"[4] is not debated here directly. This claim already has been examined at length in Chapter 2. This chapter treats peace like happiness, as a condition whose existence (arms control) policy can help bring about but which cannot be advanced directly. The discussion, therefore, generally eschews explicit attempts to answer the question, "can or does arms control *cause* peace?" Instead, the terms of reference are somewhat skewed in favor of arms controllers' arguments: their points are discussed without formal connection to the outcomes of either war or peace.

My intention is not so much to structure a dialogue between approving and disapproving views of arms control as rather to broaden the discussion so that a wide range of positive claims is recognized, introduced, and considered. The distinctions between arms control that can be formal or informal, structural (arms limitation) or operational, and bilateral or multilateral may matter greatly for some purposes. Those distinctions have not been ignored, even when they are not cited directly. Some of the issues and arguments presented below have been introduced already in previous chapters. Such limited repetition of arguments as cannot be avoided here is warranted by the broad purpose of this chapter. So uncompromising is the thesis that this book advances that I am unusually obligated to demonstrate to readers that I have taken account of rival arguments.

Threat Control. Arms control agreements can slow the pace of growth of military threats. This applies when participation in an arms control regime limits the quantity and quality of military capability which can be acquired, when a state is in an active breakout mode from an arms control regime and is seeking to recover momentum in military modernization or weapon accumulation, and when a nonsignatory state is limited in its ability to surge toward the securing of certain kinds of military power because the activities of other (supplier) states are inhibited by treaty.

[4] President's Commission on Strategic Forces, *Report* (henceforth, the "Scowcroft Commission Report") (Washington, D.C.: White House, April 1983), p. 3.

There is a commonsense appeal about this general claim. Given the near universal "pull to parity" inseparable from arms control—except when states club together to help deny military options to other states—it is apparent that this first point is thoroughly apolitical. Threats are a subjective matter, which arms control or disarmament can rarely handle directly.[5] Instead, arms control treats a part of the "threat mix," which is to say, military capabilities, and of necessity treats all weapons of like type even-handedly. Just as the political meaning of weaponry is a value added by its owner, so the strategic meaning of weaponry is a value added by the distinctive details of geopolitics.[6] An aircraft carrier has different strategic implications for a Eurasian continental power than it does for a continentally insular United States.[7]

The blanket claim that arms control can limit the growth of military threats should not obscure the fact that arms control can limit the provision of military counters to those military threats whose growth cannot be inhibited by an international regime. Moreover, the historical record suggests that would-be aggressor polities, if they can be corralled at all by arms control, are less inhibited by

[5] The very occasional apparent exception serves to prove, not cast doubt upon, the rule. The disarmament provisions of the 1919 Versailles treaty were just such an exception. They were flouted extensively in German malpractice long before Hitler came to power in 1933; see J. H. Morgan, *Assize of Arms: The Disarmament of Germany and Her Rearmament (1919–1939)* (1945; rpt. New York: Oxford University Press, 1946), and Hans W. Gatzke, *Stresemann and the Rearmament of Germany* (Baltimore: Johns Hopkins University Press, 1954). Nonetheless, the draconian disarmament provisions of the Versailles settlement unquestionably denied any German government the option to pose a serious military threat to anybody until the mid-1930s. However, the very substantial disarmament of Germany in the 1920s and early 1930s was not a triumph for arms control; rather, it attested to what could be imposed through victory in war.

[6] See Colin S. Gray, *The Geopolitics of Super Power* (Lexington: University Press of Kentucky, 1988).

[7] Among the many reasons why the United States is less than friendly toward the idea of negotiations upon naval arms is the fact that Russia does not require or ask a strategic performance of its naval power at all comparable to the burdens placed by Washington upon the U.S. Navy. See Roger W. Barnett, *Naval Arms Control: Faith, Hope, and Parity* (Fairfax, Va.: National Security Research, 1990); and Douglas M. Johnston, "Naval Arms Control—Not in the Nation's Best Interest," U.S. Naval Institute *Proceedings*, 116 (August 1990), 36–38. For a less negative, but still cautious, view, see John Borawski, "Oceanic Overtures: Building Confidence at Sea," *Arms Control Today*, 20 (July–August 1990), 18–21.

treaty accountability than are would-be defenders of the status quo.

The claim that arms control can help slow the pace of growth of military threats functions as a generic defense of arms control. As such, it invites generic criticism leveled in the form of the arms control paradox. An arms control process can institutionalize and multilateralize policy trends to which countries already subscribe—to inhibit the spread of nuclear weapons, for a leading example. But the proposition that an arms control process itself can be distinctively useful in retarding the growth of military threats lacks persuasive empirical support. In practice, military threats are controlled by many factors, including scale of policy ambitions, available and politically defense-allocable national resources, and military doctrine. Even when an arms control regime cuts into net national military prowess, one should enquire whether that is desirable for national and international security. For example, a Russian-American naval arms control regime easily could have negative consequences vis-à-vis the U.S. ability to project military power into the Persian Gulf region. For a further case, would it be desirable if the ABM treaty indirectly denied the United States and Russia the ability to provide effective missile defenses against regional rogue polities? One has to recognize the ambiguities of military power. A U.S. Navy capable of projecting power into the Persian Gulf against a major regional state has to be a navy of a kind able to menace some Russian littoral values. Undue U.S. empathy with understandable Russian concerns about the latter could promote a tolerance for structural and operational naval arms control seriously inhibiting the former.

Overall, arms control cannot help control threats very usefully because it is political intention that yields meaning to military power. Also, the military capabilities that arms control constrain may be needed to support policy toward third parties. When arms control is not permissive of both sides' favorite programs (unlike SALT II and START I), it tends to operate like a disease, striking without prejudice at the worthy and the unworthy alike. Threats do not reside in weapons and hence cannot be expunged neatly by their removal.

Vulnerability and Crisis Instability. Arms control can restructure military forces so as to reduce their vulnerability to surprise attack. Particular weapon qualities (e.g., agility, reach, lethality, and speed in execution), or the lack thereof, are critical for military incentives to strike first. Arms control can help reshape military development so that considerations of vulnerability do not figure significantly in crisis-time decision making.[8]

This claim is promoted in praise of both the START and CFE regimes. Yet again, the argument founders on the reefs of politics. On the one hand, if the political environment truly is exceedingly friendly for arms control negotiators, their technical accomplishments will be as irrelevant as they are relatively easy to achieve. On the other hand, the restructuring of force posture via arms control will be impracticable if political hostility endures.

Compare and contrast MBFR and CFE.[9] MBFR sought formal goals that vastly overreached what the political traffic would bear. What the West thought it had negotiated in CFE, however, overreached what international security requires. CFE poses difficulties for international security not dissimilar in kind from those of START. Specifically, political life-support for the arms control process in both cases is very high indeed *in general terms*. Unfortunately, a large political and strategic indeterminacy threatens to render both START and CFE ventures of thoroughly unknown significance. The problem is that the user-friendliness of the political context for these exercises leaves the forces permitted with uncertain strategic missions. Even in the militarily relatively simple world of START, questions of post–Cold War targeting policy intrude to trouble thoughtful observers.[10] With respect to CFE,

---

[8] For this familiar and important claim, see "Scowcroft Commission Report," p. 3, and Walter B. Slocombe, "Strategic Stability in a Restructured World," *Survival*, 32 (July–August 1990), p. 306.

[9] By way of a mercy killing, the sixteen-year long MBFR exercise was concluded formally on 2 February 1990. CFE talks began on 6 March 1989, leading to treaty signing on 19 November 1990.

[10] Will the U.S. SIOP come to be viewed in the mid- to late 1990s much as British and American naval officers in the 1920s regarded their plans for war with each other? As the premier historian of the subject of U.S. war plans in the interwar

even the fundamentals—let alone the details—of the future political framework for security in Europe currently are unknown. People who should know better are aspiring to use CFE as a vital means to help define a new political structure for regional security. The basic problem has been identified well by Lawrence Freedman: "Not only does the current approach [to CFE] assume the political *status quo*—it helps to reinforce it. An arms control regime deliberately introduces rigidities. It is regulated and bureaucratic, based on negotiated norms rather than the free-play of the decisions of individual states, and is more or less guided by sensitivity to the concerns of allies and adversaries.[11] A problem for CFE, seen by some as an opportunity, is that at present there is no status quo in Europe. It is difficult to design, let alone assess, an arms control regime when it is not clear what it is that needs doing, or by whom.

The primary fallibility of this popular second claim lies in a historical record that shows no correlation between the kinds of military vulnerabilities to surprise attack, which arms control might help correct, and demonstrated crisis instabilities, which is to say, the onset of war. The secondary weakness is the fact that arms control regimes have not accomplished this vulnerability-reduction mission, whether or not that mission is judged important. Theoretical explanation of why this has to be so was advanced in Chapter 2. Already it is apparent that START I bears some small promise of having a net negative impact upon force structure with respect to technically viewed crisis instabilities. The fluid state of European security arrangements renders the CFE regime a politically unanchored technical instrument with thoroughly unpredictable implications. Given that the former Soviet Army was able to save much of the heavy equipment that Western negotiators believed they had corralled for destruction under the treaty, even

---

years has noted, "The possibility of a contest with Britain was extremely remote, for there was no sentiment for war on either side of the Atlantic." Louis Morton, "Germany First: The Basic Concept of Allied Strategy in World War II," in Kent Roberts Greenfield, ed., *Command Decisions* (1959; rpt. London: Methuen, 1960), p. 4.

[11] Lawrence Freedman, "The Politics of Conventional Arms Control," *Survival*, 31 (September–October 1989), p. 394.

the narrowly military-technical consequences of CFE are highly debatable.

Window of Opportunity. "Because the institutional effects of arms control tend to continue, an important goal now for the United States is to *lock in the benefits* of the Gorbachev era."[12]

Both liberal and conservative commentators on arms control policy, as well as Secretary of State James Baker, have come to identify the current phase of Russian-American relations with a window of diplomatic opportunity which could evaporate rapidly.[13] It is argued that the United States should hasten to secure arms control agreements with Moscow, take those negotiated regimes to the bank, as it were, and lock them in place before the political climate alters for the worse.

This claim has some limited merit, but that merit is greatly overshadowed by fallacies. On the merit side, it is true that there are historic windows of political opportunity for arms control agreements through which states are able to jump; 1921–22, 1930, 1972, and now 1990–92 spring to mind. It is worth noting that some of the advocates for near-term arms control "lock-in" also subscribe to variants of the contradictory notion that irreversibly benign changes are underway in the East. The fact of change is not controversial; rather, the idea of irreversibly benign change should give pause. Some Western optimists on the subject of the transformation of the Russian political culture have noticed that START and CFE would seem to risk locking in licenses for forces and ways of thinking that already have been overtaken by events.

On the skeptical side, this claim transpires to be a lightly disguised version of a familiar, characteristically American fallacy. The lock-in claim amounts to a bid to defeat, or at least offset, possible adverse political developments through the agency of the military-technical fix of arms control. The lock-in theory, if it is more than a briefly fashionable phrase, posits a less arms control–

---

[12] Nye, "Arms Control after the Cold War," p. 63, emphasis added.

[13] "Lock-in" thinking is presented by former U.S. chief negotiator at START, Richard Burt, in "Is START Obsolete?" *Washington Post*, 13 November 1990, p. A23, and by the editor of *Arms Control Today*, Matthew Bunn, in "Arms Control's Enduring Worth," *Foreign Policy*, 79 (Summer 1990), p. 154.

friendly future, else why hasten to lock in arrangements now? The history of the twentieth century to date should suggest to the arms control community that there is something badly wrong with the lock-in theory. After all, the early 1990s are not exactly the first opportunity that statesmen have had to lock in a benign military-strategic environment. The soon-to-be-rogue states of Imperial Japan and Nazi Germany were both, as of 1933, locked into arms limitation regimes which, in the German case at least, were profoundly inhibiting of adventure.

Sovereign polities simply cannot be locked into arms control structures that express yesterday's political assumptions and power relations. History, theory, and common sense suggest that an arms control regime negotiable only under ephemeral conditions of great good will is unlikely to have the features that would enable it to survive, let alone help accomplish anything useful for international security, in stormy political weather. Indeed, the arms control regime that supposedly locks into place military relationships which are, or are believed to be, asymmetrically disadvantageous to a Japan and Germany in the early 1930s or a Russia in the mid 1990s itself will fuel political tensions. An arms control structure itself can become a part of the problem rather than a part of the solution.[14]

Wherever one looks, the claim that there are windows of opportunity for the locking in of advantageous arms control agreements falters under critical scrutiny. A fundamentally implausible proposition is that states can be locked into adherence to agreements that they come strongly to resent. But another disturbing possibility, which has some empirical basis in the 1930s, is that when the locked-in polity in question elects to break out, the consequences may be more troubling for peace than if there had been no period of formal arms control restraint at all.

---

[14] Slocombe cautions that "it is important for stability that the arms-control regime is not in itself a source of tension." "Strategic Stability in a Restructured World," p. 307. Much more boldly and accurately, John Tirman has written that "arms control agreements themselves are often sources of friction." *Sovereign Acts: American Unilateralism and Global Security* (New York: Ballinger, 1989), p. 10. This claim is particularly significant, given that Tirman has been senior editor at the Union of Concerned Scientists, a charter barony in arms control country.

Arms control advocates should contemplate the analysis of great-power arms relationships in the 1930s provided by Charles H. Fairbanks, Jr., and Abram N. Shulsky.[15] Should the United States succeed in locking in truly radical follow-on CFE and START agreements, the *relatively* low levels of forces permitted would all but guarantee that a break out, if and when it occurs, must have maximum consequences for instability, on any definition, as the level of forces changes rapidly. A Russian break out from a START II regime would promote security alarm precisely because it would constitute rapid expansion from a relatively low base. The German transformation of European security politics in the mid-1930s was the product not only of the rising absolute— though still rather modest—level of its armaments but also of the gigantic leap represented by that rising level relative to its military condition in, say, 1932–33.

One can craft this lock-in claim in terms that point to arms control more as an obstacle to rather than as a jail cell against rapid military modernization or build-up. However, the idea that one can negotiate arms control terms that would lock an adversary into a legal structure which would deny it the ability to change military relations rapidly is really naïve. It is not possible to engineer the future in this way, save via the *diktat* of an imposed peace settlement following victory in war, particularly since experience advises that even military behavior in a treaty-accountable mode is not all that reliably predictable.

Yesterday's arms control regimes would be unlikely to help protect the United States and others against many of the worst effects of a Russian policy reversal away from cooperation. Instead, arms control most probably would impose rigidities on the Western ability to adjust to adverse changes in a timely manner. Those rigidities would have an inhibiting effect far more burdensome in the West than in the East. It may be recalled that the United States and Britain harbored unreasonable aspirations for

[15] Charles H. Fairbanks, Jr., and Abram N. Shulsky, "From 'Arms Control' to Arms Reductions: The Historical Experience," *Washington Quarterly*, 10 (Summer 1987), 59–73. The pending delights of a START II world wherein force levels are in the 3000–3,500 range—as agreed in June 1992—might be reviewed usefully in the light of the Fairbanks-Shulsky argument.

arms control even as late as 1937–38. The reluctance of democratic polities to face unwelcome facts about yesterday's cooperative arms control partner is an enduring condition for policy making.

Political Process. Arms control often is more important as a political process than as a medium for the military-technical regulation of relations.[16] An arms control process provides important political reassurance for the domestic public as well as for adversaries.

This claim constitutes an important half-truth, or perhaps quarter-truth. But in recognizing fully the salience of politics, it advances an argument with greater potential to mislead than the view it criticizes. Proponents of variants of this claim are entirely correct in pointing to politics rather than to technical details for a treaty's significance to international security. This view can come perilously close to the assertion that treaty details do not matter, a stance that could provide an excuse for some poor negotiating outcomes. There is merit in Jervis's judgment that "because having a larger nuclear arsenal or more nuclear options than the adversary cannot keep the interaction [nuclear escalation] under control, the outcomes of confrontations are not strongly influenced by the details of the nuclear balance."[17]

With narrow reference to the outbreak of war, as opposed to the control of war once underway, Jervis is persuasive. It is not that the details of military posture and plans do not matter, but that other factors matter more. Unless one holds as a canonical verity to a belief in the uncontrollability of nuclear war, the military-technical details must matter greatly once one enters the realm of policy and strategy application in the tactical and operational action that is war.

The great fallacy in this fourth claim is the implied reversal of the horse-and-cart nexus. Somehow, one is asked to believe, the arms control process preeminently is important as a political and not a military-technical process. Apart from saying do not bother

---

[16] Nye, "Arms Control after the Cold War," pp. 44–45.

[17] Robert Jervis, *The Meaning of the Nuclear Revolution: Statecraft and the Prospect of Armageddon* (Ithaca: Cornell University Press, 1989), p. 22.

us with the military details, what can this claim mean? It would appear to be a sophisticated version of the old idea that an arms control process itself could function to benign political effect. But in this new variant the argument is the quasi-theological one that arms control *is*, not is about, politics. This convenient fusion, actually confusion, of categories, could serve as a powerful idea in the hands of the unscrupulous or the uncritical. Appealing and ingenious though it is, the notion that the arms control process works as a political process should be resisted.

The merit that lurks in this claim is overwhelmed by the scale of the fallacy it advances. Namely, the political health of an arms control process, and the meaning of that process, is provided by a political process about "high policy" antecedent to, and distinctive from, itself. For example, the relationship between genuinely political and arms control processes could hardly be delineated more clearly than with reference to the CFE and START treaties. Neither arms control venture is, or could be, responsive to the still rapidly changing political structure of international security.

The limited truth that an arms control process acts upon, expresses, and in some sense is a part of its political environment is prone to mislead because it threatens to confuse carts with horses, tails with dogs, or tactics with strategy. If an arms control process is invested with inherent value as a political process, wherein lies its meaning and what is the source of policy guidance?[18]

It seems to be true that arms control is politically necessary in a democracy as a distinctive track in national security policy. In the early 1980s the American public was willing to support a military build-up for deterrence and national respect. But that public also insisted that its government work the other, prospectively cooperative, side of the aisle. The public appeared to require reassurance against the risks of war, in the form of proof positive that the president was on the job vis-à-vis nuclear peace. President Rea-

---

[18] An unprincipled arms control opportunism could be almost as unfortunate in its consequences as the more familiar phenomenon of military opportunism. Military opportunism sees states in wartime drive from one adventure to another as operational opportunity would appear to beckon, without benefit of prior strategic, let alone grand-strategic, calculation.

gan was obliged to tick the box of arms control activity in order to satisfy that public demand for reassurance.

The allegedly real arms control of large-scale force reductions in the INF treaty and in START and CFE, whatever else might be said about it, had its roots in official U.S. policy positions designed to appease, or reassure, Western publics. With the double-zero focus in its INF stance, the Reagan administration sought belatedly to outbid the left as a champion of peace. When people are apprehensive about their survival, they are prone to attach talismanic significance to an arms control process. Jervis is almost correct when he claims that "arms control matters because people take the agreements to symbolize the state of Soviet-American relations."[19] People monitor visible activity and a positive or negative mood rather than agreements, let alone the detailed content of agreements. The ground-zero and nuclear-freeze mass movements of the early 1980s were neutralized by a combination of President Reagan's announcement on 23 March 1983 of what became the SDI and by sheer public boredom with rhetoric about alleged nuclear peril. Eventually, the salience of arms control as a vehicle for East-West strategic discourse was overwhelmed by the political rumblings, then upheaval, in the East.

By the early 1990s there was no noticeable public demand for, or even much interest in, arms control. Whatever the pressures for a START treaty, they did not include public demands for reassurance against the danger of nuclear war. This is not to say that such demands would not reemerge with a vengeance, should Russian-American relations relapse into acute hostility.

Nye claims that an arms control process provides reassurance to adversaries, as well as to domestic and allied publics. He argues also that "in a sense, all of arms control is a confidence—and security—building measure. By increasing transparency and communication among adversaries, worst case analyses are limited and security dilemmas are alleviated."[20] There are difficulties with this attractive word picture of the blessings of arms control. First, it is precisely because some state-adversary pairs or groups lack

---

[19] Ibid., p. 224.
[20] Nye, "Arms Control after the Cold War," p. 45.

confidence in their security vis-à-vis each other that they need what arms control theory *claims* arms control practice can provide. If confidence and security is high, then arms control is irrelevant or even harmful. Political judgment determines what an arms control process will be permitted to attempt to achieve. That process is not an independent agent promoting confidence and security. Second, it is simply not true that arms control, as an agent purportedly distinctive from a high political process, has promoted a useful measure of transparency and communication among adversaries. Worst-case analyses and classic security dilemmas should be impacted benignly by treaty regimes that place specific boundaries upon particular classes of weapons. But appealing though this claim certainly is, it flies in the face both of the historical record and of logic.

Worst-case analyses generally are tempered by a host of modifying considerations, for example, affordability, plausibility, and unwelcome implications for policy. When worst-case or very-bad-case analyses acquire political authority, no measure of arms control is going to be able to limit them. Advocates of this claim for arms control tend to have in mind the less than plausible analyses that various policy players advanced in defense of a SALT process which would restrict ballistic missile defenses and offensive missiles and, later, warhead inventories. Suffice it to say that the more heroic of the SALT-unconstrained threat projections of the early and late 1970s were plausible neither at the time nor in retrospect as might-have-beens.

Arguments for the political benefits of an arms control process read well until examined closely. To adapt the familiar adage, arms control cannot put in what politics has left out. When the superordinate political process of interacting high policies favors limited cooperation, then arms control offers a convenient vehicle to express that political desire. The further one advances from that core reality, the more dubious the claims for arms control become.

Robert Jervis has presented far and away the most plausible variant upon this category of claim praising arms control as a political process. Stripped to its essentials, Jervis's argument is that arms control treaties have as their main purpose the "control [of] our expectations and beliefs, not our arms."[21] He finds that arms control as "a psychological endeavor" usefully can help discourage people from entering a dangerous state of mental resignation toward the likelihood of war. This argument is wrong but warrants respect. The slim evidence in its support is interesting but thoroughly inconclusive. Can an arms control process usefully help fireproof a strategic relationship against psychological conditioning for acceptance of the inevitability of war? This argument reveals itself on close examination to be a sophisticated version of the standard dominant argument for arms control as a quasi-autonomous factor for peace.

Jervis's theory does not, indeed cannot, refute the arms control paradox that organizes the argument in this book, while it lacks explanatory power over the historical record. The political antagonism that dooms familiar arms control theory and practice to futility also serves to sink Jervis's thesis. The absence or failure of an arms control process in the years immediately preceding 1914 and 1939 rather makes the point advanced here. It would be very farfetched indeed to argue that the likelihood of war in the early to mid-1980s was influenced by the presence or absence of arms control activity. Jervis may have stumbled into the same confusion that beset the interwar theorists of strategic airpower. Those theorists assumed that a weakening of the morale of the enemy's civilian population must translate promptly into recognition of defeat by the enemy's government. So what if an arms control process helps to build fences against conditioning for the acceptance of war in the minds of many people? High policy is not made by an all but autonomous public mood; at least it was not in 1914, 1939, or the early 1980s. Things were different in the direct democracy of ancient Athens and the First French Republic, but such exceptions to the rule should not guide theory and practice today.

Defense Planning. "Arms control and defense plans tend to reinforce each other."[22]

This fifth claim is a hardy perennial which is as false in practice for the 1990s as it was for the 1930s. The Washington treaty of

---

[21] Jervis, *Meaning of the Nuclear Revolution*, p. 225.
[22] Nye, "Arms Control after the Cold War," p. 45.

1922 mandated capital-ship standard displacement ratios that denied the feasibility of the U.S. Navy's plans for operating in the western Pacific in defense of China against Japanese aggression; while the cruiser allocations of the 1930 London treaty equally made little strategic sense beyond the logic of a fair-weather arms limitation regime.[23] The cases of INF in the 1980s and of CFE and START in the 1990s, merit the same criticism. The INF treaty of 1987, far from tending to reinforce NATO's then-extant defense plans, actually contradicted those plans in a manner guaranteed to generate maximum irritation and embarrassment in West Germany. The CFE treaty may or may not make sense for (whose?) defense plans. But as observed already, the future security structure for Europe is so much in flux that it has been impracticable for the negotiators to craft a strategically rational grand CFE design.

START is an egregiously astrategic exercise in arms limitation for its own sake. Politicians and strategic analysts, like moths around a light bulb, have a distressing habit of fixing their attention upon, and dignifying, some magic number or range. Such a magic range for START II regime is 3000–3,500. As noted earlier, embarrassment over the modesty of today's arms control achievement is a frequent reason for a fast-forward focus upon some weapons state radically different from a current or pending one. The origin of the 3000 warhead figure for a START II is wholly political, at least insofar as the U.S. government is concerned. It was a prominent, if arbitrary, solution to the problem of what to attempt next after a START I scheduled to permit 6000 treaty-accountable warheads.[24] If readers suspect that 3000 was picked for no better reason than because it was half of 6000, I would not venture to dissent. Applying the same logic, one could anticipate a START III regime that would specify 1500 warheads, and so on, with equal strategic authority.

Close analysis reveals that the 3000–3,500–warhead START II lacks persuasive rationales in strategy and weapon-platform

---

[23] See Correlli Barnett, *Engage the Enemy More Closely: The Royal Navy in the Second World War* (New York: W. W. Norton, 1991), pp. 42–43.

[24] On why and how prominent, or "conspicuous," solutions are arrived at in a process of tacit bargaining, see Thomas C. Schelling, *The Strategy of Conflict* (Cambridge: Harvard University Press, 1960), chap. 3.

survivability. If one chooses to worry about putative military-technical crisis instabilities between countries that no longer regard each other as foes, the United States would be well advised not to proceed to a 3000-plus–warhead START II, at least not until the ratio of warheads to delivery vehicles, and even delivery vehicles to deployment platforms, is lowered dramatically. START II fails leading tests of attractiveness, notwithstanding its capture of MIRVed ICBMs. If peace has broken out and the details of Russian and American strategic nuclear arsenals are irrelevant to their mutual deterrence because such deterrence is not required, then why bother to limit arms formally?[25] If peace has broken out, but not in a form which a prudent government should assume to be irreversible, then the U.S. government ought to be concerned about the structure, scale, and quality of its militarily, if not strategically, most powerful weapons. The details of the strategic force posture may not matter for crisis stability, but they could be crucial for U.S. ability to conduct and terminate a war in a way supportive of high policy.

I may well be prejudiced by my occupation as a strategic thinker in favor of approaching military problems in an unduly strategic manner. Nonetheless, regardless of one's views of nuclear strategy—oxymoron or not—the claim that arms control and defense plans tend to reinforce each other is wrong as a historical generalization. The pull toward parity, considerations of negotiability, the tendency for foreign policy in action to reduce vacuously to diplomacy (and "treatyism"),[26] and the enduring cultural disinclination of Western democracies to think and function strategically, all translate into a yawning chasm dividing defense plans from arms control policy.

One may believe that an INF or a START treaty has significance

---

[25] In Jervis's words: "Mutual vulnerability exists and casts an enormous shadow. This condition is not subtle nor does it depend on the details of the strategic balance or targeting that may loom large to academics or war planners; such details are dwarfed in the eyes of decision makers by the danger of overwhelming destruction." *Meaning of the Nuclear Revolution*, p. 98. But see Colin S. Gray, "Nuclear Strategy: What Is True, What Is False, What Is Arguable," *Comparative Strategy*, 9 (1990), 1–32, for a cautionary discussion.

[26] For "treatyism" I am indebted to Arnold Beichman, *The Long Pretense: Soviet Treaty Diplomacy from Lenin to Gorbachev* (New Brunswick, N.J.: Transaction Publishers, 1991), p. 15.

as an expression of a political process of arms control. Be that as it may, the proponents of arms control should not be permitted to claim that their favored activity often, let alone typically, is supportive of trends in defense planning.

Rogue Behavior. Arms control can help establish or reinforce norms of behavior beneficial for international security, and it can add to the burdens of the rogue, or would-be rogue, state which is tempted to break taboos.

Some tasks are so important that they are even worth performing poorly. Automobile speed limits routinely are broken by most people, but they are still essential. Law does not have to be universally enforced or enforceable in order to be of great benefit to the community. It should not be presumed that I hold arms control uniquely to an unreasonably absolutist standard of performance. I am not deeply skeptical of the value of arms control because the Soviet Union (inter alia) cheated on its treaty obligations or because the NPT regime has failed to arrest completely the proliferation of nuclear weapons. The various instruments of grand strategy and tracks of policy record both successes and failures. Even arms control, like astrology in its faulty assertion of relationships, occasionally will coincide with policy success. One just has to be careful on the subject of cause and effect.

It is quite plausible to claim that arms control can help discourage what the norms of international life identify as rogue behavior. Indeed, arms control agreements, be they structural or operational, can function as legal markers which express dominant political and even moral opinion. For example, the 1925 Geneva Protocol prohibiting the *use* (not the manufacture and stockpiling) of poison gas, the 1968 NPT which obliges signatories neither to acquire nor help others to acquire nuclear weapons, and the 1987 Missile Technology Control Regime (MTCR), which seeks to inhibit the diffusion of missile systems capable of delivering 500 kg payloads more than 300 km, all both express and reinforce emerging norms of state behavior.[27] Arms control regimes can help insti-

---

[27] On the MTCR see Martin Navias: *Ballistic Missile Proliferation in the Third World*, Adelphi Papers no. 252 (London: IISS, Summer 1990), pp. 47–69; W. Seth Carus, *Ballistic Missiles in the Third World: Threat and Response*, Washington Papers

tutionalize broad international preferences, just as they symbolize and advertise norms and can assist in the registration of useful taboos. They can also help promote taboos that may prove harmful for international security.

It is no criticism of the Geneva Protocol, the NPT, or the MTCR to note that although they are on the side of the angels, they themselves did not create the norms which they express, even though they have played useful reinforcing roles. The fact that the principal combatant powers in World War II did not employ poison gas against each other had everything to do with considerations of deterrence and expected net military benefit, and very little to do with respect for the decent opinion of humanity. A rogue Third Reich committed to the Final Solution (using poison gas domestically, let it be noted) was hardly a state respectful of international law. Speaking to his generals on 30 March 1941, with reference to his subsequently infamous (license to murder) "commissar order," Hitler said that "the commissars are the bearers of ideologies directly opposed to National Socialism. Therefore the commissars will be liquidated. German soldiers guilty of breaking international law . . . will be excused. Russia has not participated in the Hague Convention and therefore has no rights under it."[28]

The NPT and its associated controls on the diffusion of nuclear technology and materials is one of the lesser factors working to slow the dissemination of nuclear arsenals. After all, the NPT exists precisely because none of the 1968-extant nuclear-weapon states perceived an interest in adding to their number, while rela-

---

no. 146 (New York: Praeger; with the Center for Strategic and International Studies [Washington, D.C.], 1990), chap. 5; and Kathleen C. Bailey, "Reversing Missile Proliferation," *Orbis*, 35 (Winter 1991), 5–14. Nye is correct in observing that the effectiveness of the MTCR is limited (inter alia) by the fact that "unlike nuclear or chemical weaponry, there is no taboo against ballistic missiles. . . . There is no moral stigma attached to ballistic missiles." "Arms Control after the Cold War," p. 60.

[28] Quoted in John Keegan, *The Second World War* (London: Hutchinson, 1989), p. 186. Technically speaking, Hitler was correct about the lack of legal protection enjoyed by Soviet prisoners of war. The grim statistics of Germany's Soviet POWs show that out of a total of 5,700,000 taken, no fewer than 3,300,000 died in captivity (p. 187).

tively very few non-nuclear states at the time discerned a strong net security benefit from acquiring nuclear status. The NPT reflected but did not create a new reality. That is not a criticism, but it is a mild corrective to those who point to the NPT as an important reason for the slow course of nuclear proliferation over the past twenty years.

That arms control can help mildly to discourage rogue behavior, can strengthen taboos against strongly undesirable international behavior, and can increase the political price paid by rogues for their antisocial activities is not really worth debating. Unfortunately, the scale of the positive contributions to international order which arms control can make, as just conceded, are very modest. It is only the really hard cases that are of concern here. It is a Nazi Germany, a terrorist-supporting Libya, and a great-power–intending Iraq which need strong discouragement from committing offenses against international norms of civility and tolerable neighborliness.

The case of the Iraqi nuclear-weapon program, details of which are still emerging, illustrates yet again the central thesis of this book: arms control fails to be very useful in the clutch. The apparent fact that Iraq, a signatory to the NPT, covertly could come plausibly within eighteen to twenty-four months of acquiring nuclear weapons,[29] is vastly more impressive a datum than is the general opinion that the NPT helped forge a useful taboo. Again, arms control could not handle the really tough challenge. Iraq is *not* the exception that proves the rule of the overwhelming utility of the NPT. Rather, Iraq is precisely the kind of rogue polity whose potential to be a nuclear-weapon state has fueled the international effort to inhibit proliferation.

By and large, it is a convenience for states to abide by international law and by accepted norms of behavior, whether or not those norms are framed in legal terms. The issue flagged here is how useful can arms control regimes be vis-à-vis polities that have decided it is inconvenient to respect norms and taboos. Again, the problem is inescapably one of politics. Saddam Hus-

[29] The estimate of the inspection team sent to Iraq by the U.N.'s International Atomic Energy Agency in late September 1991.

sein's Iraq came to be overarmed not because the world was un-
derregulated by arms control regimes that worked but because
the political and economic self-interest of all most concerned so
determined matters.

Misunderstanding. "Arms control can . . . remove or reduce the
risk of misunderstanding of particular events or accidents" and
"reduce misunderstanding about the purpose of weapons developments."[30]

This claim, alas, is a plausible fallacy. Robert Jervis understates
the facts when he notes that "strategic weapons are usually easy
to count, although the vital associated apparatus, like military doctrine and command and control arrangements, are more opaque."[31]
For example, the more than twenty years of SALT-START experience has yielded *no* authoritative information on intended strategy for the conduct of nuclear war by the former Soviet Union.
The Western literature on Soviet, now Russian, style in nuclear
strategy is as prolific as it remains thoroughly inconclusive.[32] The
U.S. defense community had somewhat better information about
Soviet strategic command facilities, channels, and procedures. For
political as well as practical military reasons, doctrine, strategy,
and strategic command arrangements are not fit topics for discussion between adversaries. Adversaries wish to avoid being seen
to discuss modes for nuclear combat, and they dare not take the
risk of sharing information that might grant a critical military advantage.

Of course it is important that states should not send false mes-
sages to each other in time of crisis in the form of military activities likely to be misinterpreted as evidence of intention to attack.
However, there can be tension between the need to reassure an
adversary that peace is still possible and the need to flag intent to
stand firm, that is, to threaten. Also, operational arms control regimes inadvertently could contribute to crisis-time tension by in-

[30] "Scowcroft Commission Report," p. 3.

[31] Jervis, *Meaning of the Nuclear Revolution,* p. 60.

[32] See Edward L. Warner III, *Soviet Concepts and Capabilities for Limited Nuclear
War: What We Know and How We Know It,* N-2769-AF (Santa Monica, Calif.: Rand
Corporation, February 1989).

vesting prudential military maneuvering of an unusual, typically prohibited, kind with a political meaning it may not warrant. Moreover, civilian policymakers probably will have a very imperfect understanding of the details of the military process of how their own state approaches war readiness, let alone the details of another state's march toward ever-fuller mobilization. An arms control process cannot usefully fireproof crises against the small possibility that events might escape central control. The stand-down from alert status of some U.S. strategic forces announced by President Bush on 27 September 1991 made good political theater and certainly reflected the tenor in political relations.[33] Bush's irenic measures and gesture came with a price tag for future U.S. statecraft, however. Restoration to a higher alert status of those forces stood-down by Bush must be invested with a quite extraordinary political symbolism. In theory, it is useful for a president to have such powerful signals in his flag locker, but in practice, it would be difficult for a president to reverse Bush's nuclear non-alert course on a prudential timetable.

The myriad reasons why wars occur do not lend themselves very obviously to arms control treatment. But the factors that render arms control practicable, if unimportant, are the same factors that make for nonbellicose international relations. Indeed, the latter fuels the former. In their own eyes, statesmen do not plan to wage aggressive war or otherwise to offend Nuremberg standards of proper behavior. The idea that an arms control process can help remove misunderstanding is not a powerful one. Generally speaking, for arms control to be a potentially significant instrument of policy, there has to be a presumption of some important measure of interstate antagonism. Given that a condition of military competition expresses high-policy antipathy, how could an arms control process reduce misunderstanding in ways helpful for peace? The weapons relevant to a process of arms control have to be assumed to be pointed at the adversary; so much is politically prejudged. Political perception, strategic culture, and narrow

---

[33] President George Bush, "The Peace Divided I Seek Is Not Measured in Dollars . . ." *Washington Post*, 28 September 1991, p. A23.

military analysis will all yield meaning about a rival state's armaments which arms control can only reinforce, not alter.

Dangerous Weapon Developments. "Arms control can . . . seal off wasteful, dangerous, or unhelpful lines of technical development before either side gets too committed to them."[34]

The popularity of the proposition that arms control is a suitable instrument for the discouragement or prohibition of "wasteful, dangerous, or unhelpful" weaponry, is matched amply by its vacuity and impracticality. Whether or not a line of weapon development is "wasteful, dangerous, or unhelpful" is not a judgment susceptible to omniscient, transcultural arms control determination. Many American strategists and most U.S. administrations since the early 1960s have believed that the British and French national nuclear "deterrents" fitted into this undesirable weapon category.[35] After all, four British nuclear-powered ballistic missile submarines, with *every missile* targeted on the Moscow area,[36] might not mesh any too constructively with U.S. plans for carefully controlled escalation.

A further example would be the understandably unfriendly view taken by some developed countries of the proliferation of ballistic missiles to the Third World. Writing about the utility of the MTCR of 1987, Janne E. Nolan and Albert D. Wheelon are surely correct when they argue: "Had this agreement come earlier, it might have been more effective. But now that developing states are themselves exporting missile technology, it seems difficult to put this genie back in the bottle. In any case, arms control cannot be imposed by a few countries on all the rest—such great-power prerogatives are no longer sustainable."[37] Armed with the Great Truths of arms control, the Western cognoscenti would like

[34] "Scowcroft Commission Report," p. 3.

[35] A classic statement of superpower disapproval was Albert Wohlstetter, "Nuclear Sharing: NATO and the N + 1 Country," *Foreign Affairs*, 39 (April 1961), 355–87.

[36] See Eric Grove, *The Future of Sea Power* (Annapolis, Md.: Naval Institute Press, 1990), pp. 200, 263.

[37] Janne E. Nolan and Albert D. Wheelon, "Third World Ballistic Missiles," *Scientific American*, August 1990, p. 34. The same point was made in Colin S. Gray, "Traffic Control for The Arms Trade?" *Foreign Policy*, 6 (Spring 1972), 153–69.

to translate theory into practice for the purpose of engineering a more stable world security environment. The problems are two-fold. First, the truths of stability are redefined locally and tend to have everything to do with identity of weapon ownership, rather than character of weapon. Second, the stability theory that under-pins most Western approaches to arms control (and deterrence— "the core of Western doctrine has been 'stability' ")[38] meets too much local resistance to be applied. Virtually by definition, weap-ons worth some effort to ban or restrict are going to be very at-tractive in the eyes of many people abroad.

Above all else, this claim fails not on grounds of defense philos-ophy but for reasons of impracticality. When in doubt, look at the evidence as well as consult the theory. As far as reasonably can be determined, is it the case that arms control processes have sealed off "wasteful, dangerous, or unhelpful lines of technical develop-ment"? The answer is a resounding no, with the substantial, not total, exception of ballistic missile defenses after 1972—an excep-tion that lends itself to debate. It is just possible, but not proba-ble, that in the absence of the ABM treaty the United States would have deployed some ballistic missile defenses and that the USSR would have moved toward a geographically more extensive system than what had been legally licensed. Thinking back over the whole course of the twentieth century, it is difficult to find even arguable cases in support of this claim. Putting aside appro-priate skepticism about the validity of the assumption upon which the claim rests, has the claim any noteworthy basis in fact on its own terms? Have "rogue" weapons been arrested and banished from the security scene, or otherwise markedly inhibited from de-veloping in ways that are "wasteful, dangerous, or unhelpful"?

In different decades of this century there have been quite ener-getic campaigns, often steering an uneasy path between structural and operational arms control (for example, a case wherein posses-sion of a weapon is permitted but perhaps not its use in particular ways) for the control of bombing aircraft, submarines, chemical weapons, heavy mobile artillery, tanks (and even all armored fighting vehicles), nuclear weapons, ballistic missiles, "heavy"

---

[38] Slocombe, "Strategic Stability in a Restructured World," p. 304.

ICBMs, MIRVed ICBMs, ASAT weapons, naval forces generally, and so on and so forth. In addition, one could cite the off-re-peated bid to secure international controls upon, even just a register of, the global trade in armaments.

The point of importance is not that the Western arms control community has pursued the chimera of some allegedly objectively true vision of stability but rather that the effort has been futile or worse.[39] History records that international relations cannot be much assisted by arms control viewed as safety engineering. War and peace are political phenomena.

Predictability and Uncertainty. Arms control can increase the predictability of interadversary behavior and hence can help reduce the uncertainties that feed anxiety. Also, formal arms control agreements can serve as tripwires, which when snagged by a state in a break-out mode, will serve as a wake-up call for the guardians of order.

This argument was addressed in Chapter 5 with regard to the SALT-START record and was found to have only very modest merit. However, the logic of the predictability claim for *structural*—not operational because behavior can alter overnight—arms control is impressive, indeed. On the positive side, even allowing for some cheating at the margin, the principal arms limitation agreements discussed here did place actual, or potentially,

---

[39] Narrowly viewed, the Washington treaty can be claimed to have spared Britain and the United States both some wasteful naval competition and a potentially politically dangerous trend in relations that could have accompanied such rivalry. It was argued in Chapter 4 that these points are not very persuasive. Financial constraints, war weariness, and the absence of deep political antipathies would have served to dampen the course of Anglo-American naval competition, with or without negotiated arms limitation. However, the Washington-London arms limitation system did affect the quantity and quality of the Royal Navy at the margin and for the worst. The margin of a sufficient British naval strength was slimmer than it should have been, was certainly much slimmer than prudence required, in the spring and summer of 1941. It is true that 1941 was a British defense planner's worst nightmare, with the Royal Navy vastly overstretched to oppose to help deter three major opponents in different parts of the world (Germany in the Atlantic, Italy in the Mediterranean, and Japan in the Far East). Naval arms limitation did not create this problem of British overstretch—though it contributed to it politically in the case of Japan (see Chapter 4)—but it helped make a bad situation worse.

major formal constraints on freedom of national choice over the growth of treaty-accountable forces. So long as, for instance, the Washington-London treaties (1922, 1930), the Anglo-German Naval Agreement (1935), and SALT I (1972) and SALT II (signed 1979 but not ratified), had legal or political (SALT II) authority, each high contracting party knew with some confidence the scale of military threat *which legally could be posed* by its treaty adversary-partners *in treaty-accountable categories of military power.* The qualifications are important to that judgment.

Also on the positive side, and to reprise the lock-in point raised earlier, although arms limitation as predictor cannot guarantee the durability of a treaty regime, or indeed of anything else, it can guarantee that treaty break-out to much higher levels of armament, or with some new kinds of armament, will take years to accomplish. This point has been the essence of the military rationale for the CFE treaty. The CFE treaty cannot guarantee Europe against major war, but it ought to be able to ensure that any would-be rogue polity must be desperately short of the ready military wherewithal for aggression in the near term. Such at least was the belief prior to realization of the full scale of Soviet, now Russian, treaty-avoidance misbehavior.

The argument is completed with the logically attractive corollary that arms control treaties, though admittedly prone to political obsolescence, nonetheless lay down clear markers or serve as tripwires for the awaking of status quo powers. If a very dissatisfied state serves notice to leave a treaty regime (as did Japan on 31 December 1934) or behaves in a manner flagrantly incompatible with legal obligations, that unmistakable fact should serve as a wake-up call to other powers. Arms control regimes, thus, can function as an alarm system for sometimes sleepy democracies. Also, de jure or blatant de facto disdain for an arms control treaty itself should make it easier for the governments in democracies to mobilize domestic political support for a prudent response.

The nominal merit in this claim is fairly obvious. The problem lies in the attempt to answer the question, so what? Four principal sources of skepticism are worth noting about the importance of the claim that arms control can increase predictability in military competition and, hence, reduce important uncertainties.

First, although numbers, or lack of numbers, matter, arms control tends to be unable to capture the more operationally relevant qualities of treaty-accountable forces. START, and particularly a rigorous 3000–3,500–warhead START II, would remove some uncertainties about future superpower arsenals. The value such predictability might have for typical arms control aspirations, however, would be grossly overshadowed on the negative side by the fact that a move to much smaller numbers of warheads, effected in a shotgun marriage to existing weapon platforms, would pose new qualities of potential vulnerability to surprise attack.

One should beware of the claim that Europe can be fumigated by CFE, or other measures of arms limitation, against even the possibility of successful aggression. The proposition is that so much of the military hardware necessary to seize ground rapidly will be scrapped that it must take a would-be aggressor many years to rebuild a Europe-menacing scale of mechanized landpower. Everything is wrong with this idea. In effect, the idea is a practical translation of one of the age-old commonsense prescriptions for peace: remove the weapons and people cannot fight. It should suffice to say that much of Europe has been conquered time and again by thoroughly unmechanized armies. The military potential of a much smaller Russian inventory of armored fighting vehicles and heavy artillery will depend, inter alia, upon the quantity and quality of the arms-limited opposition it must face. What is more, crisis outcomes have rarely been attributable to the analytical conclusion of careful evaluation by all concerned with the military balance. The proposition that the CFE treaty regime makes aggression in Europe much less likely, is not a powerful one. Neither the political context for CFE nor the military context of the treaty-avoiding heavy-weapon inventory in the East is as envisaged by CFE negotiators. There are many reasons—political, economic, and sociocultural—why aggression on the grand scale may be unlikely in Europe for years to come. The CFE treaty, however, does not figure significantly as one of those "causes" of peace.

Second, the salience of the predictability of the future course of military competition for the likelihood of crisis and war is less than overwhelming. Even if arms control regimes could perform as advertised, if they were able to assist predictability and reduce uncertainties, still one has to answer the so what question. Some future unpredictability and uncertainty is healthy for peace and security. History records that in the face of uncertainty defense planners and their political masters are by no means prone inexorably to postulate worst-case assumptions. There is no obvious merit for peace with security in bounding formally, aiding predictability concerning, the future military power of status quo states. If it is true that democracies are structurally disadvantaged when they compete with authoritarian states in an arms control framework, the exploitable predictability of that fact should be a source of concern.

Third, the historical record of arms limitation regimes in the 1920s and 1930s, and the 1970s and 1980s, has not yielded evidence supportive of the ideas behind this popular claim for the merit of arms control. The Washington-London system crafted a naval security framework which was predictably unfriendly to American and British endeavors to maintain a balance of power in the western Pacific. SALT and START I have not touched directly the military qualities of most concern to defense planners and policymakers. Such predictability as the enterprise facilitated has been either irrelevant or, in effect, a blessing of emerging military-technical dangers.

Fourth, far from serving as potential wake-up calls for sometimes sleepy democracies, arms control regimes instead generally have functioned as sources of illusory reassurance or, at least, hope. For a related case, one might recall the 1925 instance where Germany's adherence to the Locarno regime inoculated many foreign observers against serious worry about Berlin's flagrant disregard for some of the disarmament provisions of the Versailles treaty.[40] Or even when Japan served formal notice in 1934 of its intention to leave the Washington-London system, Britain and the United States were purposefully dilatory in their response. Germany in the 1920s and early 1930s, Japan in the 1930s, and the

---

[40] A balanced treatment is Jon Jacobson, *Locarno Diplomacy: Germany and the West, 1925–1929* (Princeton: Princeton University Press, 1972).

Soviet Union in the 1970s, all took advantage of what amounted to arms control "cover" (admittedly, unwillingly in the German case) to press for unilateral military improvements.

The limited evidence available suggests that a would-be rogue state need not be very fearful of an alleged tripwire or a wake-up call. If the would-be rogue does serve notice and leaves an arms control regime, it is more likely than not that the forces of the status quo will aspire for months or even years to bring the nation back into the fold of civilized practice and will delay for a long time any very focused muscular reactions. By and large, the would-be rogue state will be able to proceed satisfactorily, if not optimally, under the protective political cover provided by formal adherence to an international security regime of arms control.

Reduce Potential Damage, Reduce Costs. "Arms control can . . . help make arsenals less destructive and costly."[41] This composite claim approximates the second and third of the classic purposes of arms control: to reduce the damage that otherwise might be suffered in war and to reduce the cost of peacetime defense preparation.

The potential destructiveness of nuclear arsenals is more a matter of prevailing targeting doctrine than of number or character of weapons. That judgment assumes reasonably that the superpowers are exceedingly unlikely to return to nuclear inventories containing only hundreds of weapons (because of relations with third parties as well as discomfort over possible vulnerabilities). Dramatic reductions in nuclear arsenals, particularly if coupled with greater barriers to counterforce success (i.e., BMD deployments and greater agility or hardness in deployment), could incline the makers of policy and shapers of doctrine to reverse the trend of thirty years and favor instead the targeting of non-nuclear forces or the civilian values of society.[42]

Even if an arms control process were able to reduce noticeably the prospective destructiveness of weapons, it is not obvious that international peace and security must benefit. For example, if

[41] "Scowcroft Commission Report," p. 3.
[42] See Michael J. Mazarr, "Beyond Counterforce," *Comparative Strategy*, 9 (1990), 147–62, for advocacy of a "counterpower" strategy.

complete nuclear disarmament were feasible, which it is not, would it be desirable? "The long peace" between the superpowers since 1945 is unlikely to have persisted to the point of the political collapse of one protagonist in the absence of a general nuclear dread.[43] The unprecedentedly destructive military machines of the super and great powers after 1945 (and particularly after 1954–55 with the operational arrival of the hydrogen bomb) have carried the credible promise of removing the profit from war, even from great military success in war.

The raw destructiveness of superpower arsenals has decreased hugely since 1960 for the United States and the early 1970s for the USSR. However, that reduction is attributable scarcely at all to well-designed measures of arms control. Improvements in weapon accuracy in the context of better target-location intelligence for im- mobile targets, meshed with a powerful determination to mini- mize unwanted collateral damage and with the ability to design efficient nuclear weapons. The result was the sharp decline in total megatonnage which superpower arsenals revealed for the past 2½ decades.

The idea of rendering military power less destructive through arms control discipline, while noble, is rife with significant peril. One can imagine how arms control "triumphs" might deprive would-be combatants of the legal-political right to acquire some of the more lethal military capabilities which, otherwise uncon- trolled, should have been achievable. What arms control might secure would not be peace but rather the war whose outbreak it could not arrest, a war waged at the outset without the most ef- fective weapons that could have been perfected.

Unsurprisingly, the military history of the twentieth century re- veals that arms control has no independent value for the putative reduction in the destructiveness of war. As noted above, Adolf

---

[43] For contrasting opinions, see John Mueller, *Retreat from Doomsday: The Obsoles- cence of Major War* (New York: Basic Books, 1989); and Jervis, *Meaning of the Nuclear Revolution.* "The long peace" is borrowed from a newspaper article published by Winston Churchill on 26 May 1932. "The cause of disarmament will not be at- tained by mush, slush and gush. It will be advanced steadily by the harassing expense of fleets and armies, and by the growth of confidence in a long peace." Quoted in Martin Gilbert, *Winston S. Churchill,* vol. 5: *1922–1939* (London: Hei- nemann, 1976), p. 445.

Hitler declined to employ poison gas because he anticipated no net benefit from doing so. Saddam Hussein's Iraq, in its eight-year war with Iran in the 1980s, correctly anticipated exactly the reverse. There is no escaping the fact that if disaster threatens, "a country will do what a country has to do." Arms control regimes, which have the moral and political effect of vilifying nuclear and chemical weapon employment, do indeed increase the broadly determinable costs of such employment. But those regimes would function more as redundant inhibitors in cases of lesser temptation than as effective retarders when national survival was believed to be on the line.

The formal arms control registry of transnational horror at the prospect of chemical or nuclear warfare is appropriate and may have some minor value as an inhibitor of such conduct. But one must not be confused between easy and difficult cases. The most important test of the merit in an arms control regime is whether or not it can serve usefully to help constrain the behavior of a state strongly motivated to flout it. As Britain's Royal Navy believed and behaved in the nineteenth century, "international law was not to be observed beyond the point of serious strategic disadvantage."[44]

The claim that arms control can save money has a weak theoretical basis. When adversary states formally control some of their armaments, they compensate by seeking advantage in weaponry that is unconstrained as well as by the improvement of treaty-accountable forces. If the political motivation is as it should be if arms control is to be important, which is to say, if war is deemed possible, then it is virtually foreordained that arms control success will not generate a financial dividend. The argument as to why money is not saved points to the more basic reasons why arms control is a house of cards. The point is not, or not only, that cunning and self-interested munition manufacturers and defense officials will spend an arms control dividend on compensating safeguards, not to mention on the monitoring of treaty-accountable activity. Rather, recalling the laws of thermodynamics, the

---

[44] Geoffrey Best, *Humanity in Warfare* (New York: Columbia University Press, 1980), p. 250.

energy in suspicion and antipathy that renders an arms control treaty important must find an outlet in permitted behavior elsewhere.

Arms control cannot render military competition less costly. What it does is to effect some rerouting of that competition. If an arms control regime reduces radically the burden of defense preparation, it will be because high policy already has demoted the perceived threat. It will not be arms control, acting autonomously, which scales back the economic burdens of security but rather political judgment acting through an arms control instrument. If anything, that instrument will serve to delay and malform the reduction in defense effort that otherwise would be achieved.

Arms Control's Best Shot, and the Cynic's View

In an important article, long-time American arms control negotiator James E. Goodby advanced what he regarded as "the main answer to those who question why we bother with the negotiations on Conventional Forces in Europe (CFE) at this time."[45] Goodby quoted approvingly a senior Bush administration official's claim that conventional and nuclear negotiations are "part of creating a context of progress in East-West relations in which we might have to persuade Mr. Gorbachev that Germany's relationship in NATO is a sensible notion."

It may well be that *in a politically permissive context* arms control can function usefully as an integral part of a general process of international accommodation and cooperation. The first part of the view just quoted almost equally could have been said of great power relations in the 1920s and of superpower relations in the early 1970s. The point of most significance, however, is the contextual dependency of the feasibility of modestly useful arms control. The prior existence of a "context of progress in East-West relations" is precisely what enables arms control to advance. Arms control cannot create such a context, as the history of the

---

[45] James E. Goodby, "Can Arms Control Survive Peace," *Washington Quarterly*, 13 (Autumn 1990), p. 95.

mid-1930s, the late 1970s, and much of the 1980s, attests. This is not to deny arms control some small utility, but it is to recognize that that utility is provided when international security most likely could manage well enough without it.

There can be little doubt that Soviet leaders welcomed what they regarded as an advantageous arms control framework to accompany the reunification of Germany. But it should not be supposed that Russian policy toward east-central Europe in general and Germany in NATO in particular hinge upon the perilous achievements of arms control. Arms control may help legitimize whatever shakes out eventually as the new security order for Europe, but the politics of that order will owe little to arms control in any shape, manner, or form.

Russian policymakers and defense planners can be under no illusion that they will be able to craft a Russian-friendly Europe through arms control arrangements designed in the early 1990s. Arms control designs come and go as the politics of international security permit. It is plain for anybody to see that the new, or renewed, Germany, as leader of a Europe very different from a European Community–Europe or NATO-Europe, will need reliable policy access to a nuclear arsenal if its future is to be secure vis-à-vis Russia. The arms control framework extant today will not work for such a different balance of power in Europe. The point here is not to predict that a German-led Europe will decide on this or that option to satisfy its needs for a reliable nuclear dimension to its security policy. Rather is the point to remind readers of the commonsense proposition that Russian policymakers know that they cannot engineer a relatively safe future via the "locking-in"—to pick a term not wholly at random—today of a particular German security-policy future.

At some risk of seeming to be gratuitously unfriendly, I would alert readers to the fact that the quotation from the senior administration official which launched this section of the discussion and which Goodby finds so appealing is typical of a major thread in State Department thinking. In the right hands, the ideas of arms control arrangements as a supportive "sweetener" to much larger political purposes is by no means a foolish one. However, people whose focus is upon diplomatic method, and whose understanding of how military power can and should support foreign policy is often rudimentary at best, are unlikely to worry about the details of arms control designs save as grist or grit to the mill of negotiation.[46] To sound a familiar note, should CFE and START prove to be militarily, as opposed to vaguely politically, supportive of U.S. foreign policy, that fact would be as remarkable as it would lack for historical precedents.

Goodby offered a second point in praise of formal arms limitation: "Another answer [in addition to that specified in the quotation above] mentioned by the secretary-general of NATO [Manfred Wörner] is that only by securing treaty rights can we limit and verify the levels of Soviet forces in the Soviet Union."[47] Four difficulties with this formula emerge immediately. First, it offers a blanket rationale for *any* arms limitation treaty. Second, it neglects the fact that arms control limits both sides to an agreement and that the forces of stability, which is to say, the forces of the West for international order, may pay too high a price for it. Third, it propagates the old canard that, absent arms control arrangements, adversary or possible adversary forces are not limited (when in fact they are limited by resource constraints, doctrine, calculation of prospective net advantage, and so forth). Fourth, Wörner's argument cited by Goodby obscures the oft-demonstrated fact that the Western democracies face extraordinary problems in preserving strategic integrity in defense planning when confronted with the siren calls of negotiated arms limitation. It may be important to "limit and verify the levels of Soviet [or Russian] forces in the Soviet Union [or Russia]," as Wörner maintains, but it is rather more important for Americans and NATO-Europeans to determine the answer to the question of which forces the United States and NATO require. When that question is dominated by arms control considerations, diplomacy, not strategy, has a way of jumping into the driving seat.

---

[46] Borrowing again from the fecund pen of Arnold Beichman, a focus upon treaty making is the *déformation professionnelle* of diplomats. Beichman finds this weakness in "U.S. foreign policy-making elites," but that is a little too sweeping for my taste. *Long Pretense*, p. 15. *Déformation professionnelle* is a close relative to Herman Kahn's delightful concept of "trained incapacity."

[47] Goodby, "Can Arms Control Survive Peace."

Finally, there is what may be called the cynic's case for arms control, or perhaps—more accurately—the cynic's case for apparent activity of an arms control kind. The idea of arms control and expectations for its frequent and earnest pursuit, have secured a wide, if not deep, penetration and following in the American body politic. Truly, arms control has come to be a flag of convenience to be worn by any weapon program or defense lobby facing political difficulties. As noted much earlier in this discussion, so many and so accommodating are the interpretations which can be placed upon stability theory, that any defense program in search of additional rationales can identify itself as purportedly arms control–friendly (or even essential). Claims of this sort have the signal virtue to their authors of being totally beyond refutation. If, for example, Russian negotiators should reject some practical and particular application of this claim, perhaps over the SDI, one could always argue that the Russian policymakers are at fault and have yet to appreciate their own best interests.

The political necessity of an arms control rationale for a menaced defense program, almost invariably translates into a vision of the military environment wherein any system but the one of most concern is tradeable in a deal. With impeccable logic the point is made that bargaining chips bearing designer labels to that effect are promptly devalued as currency in negotiations because, of course, one is perceived as being prepared, or eager, to trade them. The preeminent challenge to the proponents of arms control rationales for a favored weapon system is the need to craft arguments that both point to the value of a system X for U.S. negotiators yet explain why that system should, and need, not be bargained away. This can prove to be no easy task.

Arms control has come to be a constant subject on the landscape of U.S. defense politics. One may be tempted to regard arms control in all its many variations as a set of problems, but really, in toto, it comprises a condition for U.S. policy making. Whatever the military capability at issue, its official proponents are obliged by political necessity to be able to discuss it in arms control terms.

[8]

Can So Many People Be Wrong?

In no other organized endeavor of the nations of mankind has so much work been expended to so little effect as in the efforts to achieve arms control. We must suppose that there has been something fundamentally wrong at the conceptual level to account for so consistent a failure on so large a scale over so long a period. . . . When such vast and sustained efforts as went into the pursuit of disarmament between the wars come to nothing [with particular reference to the League of Nations' World Disarmament Conference of 1932], we may properly suspect that the conceptual foundation on which the efforts were based was wrong.

—Louis J. Halle, 1984

"Globaloney" and a New World Order

Not without good reason, if a little prematurely, some suggest that the decade 1985–95 may prove to be a "golden decade" of arms control.[1] Strong proponents of both arms control and a defense-minded approach to national security ironically find their long-settled beliefs and prescriptions under challenge in the 1990s. This decade is yielding an unprecedentedly friendly environment for the flourishing of arms control negotiations and regimes, but who needs those negotiations and regimes when peace is break-

[1] Ambassador Ronald F. Lehman II, Director of the U.S. Arms Control and Disarmament Agency, "The U.S. and the Future of Arms Control," in *America's Role in a Changing World*, Adelphi Papers no. 256 (London: IISS, Winter 1990/91), p. 49.

ing out and politicians are waxing lyrical about the establishment of a new world order.[2]

Whether the future course of international security will be so conflict-ridden that people will think nostalgically of the order and relative safety of the Cold War era remains to be seen.[3] Nonetheless, the conditions of insecurity that have fueled bids for arms control, as for enhanced defense effort, are predictably only temporarily in abeyance—vacationing in the Persian Gulf perhaps. The argument of this book has in no sense been overtaken by events, any more than have the claims of the arms control faithful with which I disagree.

This book has buttressed its theory, that arms control must fail when most needed, with evidence from different decades when (some) different state players developed different kinds of weapon systems, from capital ships to capital missiles. The variants of globaloney, which today are proffered in politicians' speeches and by the pens of some prominent armchair statesmen, are as flawed and implausible as were their predecessors in the 1920s and 1940s. The idea of collective security, as with the idea of arms control, prospers when it is not tested by divisive issues. With the former Soviet Union temporarily all but *hors de combat* from active foreign statecraft, and with a Middle Eastern villain from central casting as the immediate focus for hostility, an apparently easy triumph was registered for the cause of collective security in 1990–91. Alas, the facts of the matter are that collective security does not work when the international community really needs it in those hard cases which matter most. Moreover, considerations of balance of power for national security will prompt states to resist establishment of an effectively unipolar (*American*) world system. The course of international security politics in this decade is by no means as likely to herald a new U.S.-led world order as some American optimists, or fantasists, have predicted. Arms control will not work in the 1990s any better than it has in the

[2] President George Bush, Remarks to the Joint Session of Congress, 11 September 1990, and *National Security Strategy of the United States* (Washington, D.C.: White House, August 1991).

[3] This thesis is advanced in John J. Mearsheimer, "Back to the Future: Instability in Europe after the Cold War," *International Security*, 15 (Summer 1990), 5–56.

past, but many of the erroneous arguments advanced in promotion of weapons limitation or military-behavioral constraint will not lose their salience because a benign new world order is emerging.[4]

Although statecraft may raise its game to meet some of the challenges of the 1990s, still there are grounds for concern that the new world order which might arise may be the kind of order meant by the Chinese curse, "may you live in interesting times." The relevance of policy debate over arms control is indicated by a brief discussion of the possible trend of events in Europe.

At present, as I noted in Chapter 7, there is no status quo in the security order for Europe. However, this should not obscure the further fact that the prolonged absence of such an order is unlikely. From being organized into two camps by competing superpowers, Europe will not settle into a new structure-free order, a kind of idyllic chaos. As a precaution against hegemonic trends or out of ambition, endeavors to find or impose a new security order will be made. There will be competing self-serving visions of a new order (even the term *new order* has a Teutonic historical chill about it), just as there will be attempts to evade the difficult questions altogether via elevation of a more institutionalized Conference on Security and Cooperation in Europe (CSCE). The CSCE structure, a Europe-oriented, though not exclusive, example of aspirations for collective security, most probably will prove to be an evasion of policy responsibility masquerading as a solution. It will be as effective as either political consensus permits, or as emerging, or *reemerging*, hegemonic power allows. A CSCE system would collapse predictably under pressure into competing blocs or associations because the basic idea of collective security confuses carts with horses. The horses of compatible interests have to pull the cart of collective security effort. If the former is lacking, the latter cannot function.

To predict future political and economic conflict in Europe and

---

[4] It was a wonderful novelty for the United States to be able to intervene in a regional conflict without having to neutralize the policy of an inevitably hostile Soviet Union. Even if the self-demotion of the other erstwhile superpower persists, the United States will rediscover the frustrations of playing regional police officer and the fragility of gratitude in international politics.

elsewhere is a great deal easier than to predict who will wish to ally with whom. Policymakers are in the business of politics, conceived at its broadest; to them arms control is one among many policy tools believed to be more or less useful to serve political goals. Those who guide statecraft do not knowingly allow grand designs of arms control to shape political structures of security and order. When visions of order are inchoate or competing, the case at present, arms control cannot play even a modestly constructive supporting role. If no agreement exists on what the political structures for order should be, compatible arms control regimes cannot be designed and implemented.

In the European case just cited, for example, who or what will provide the nuclear protection for a predictably German-dominated east-central Europe? And which measures of arms control would best serve the need for German nuclear protection? For a further example, if a new world order is to be unipolar in the U.S. favor with regard to global power projection (i.e., collective security with a U.S.-led, and largely U.S.-provided, police force), how can an unreconstructed ABM treaty possibly serve the ends of international security? Virtually by definition, the security problems of such a world should not include fears of a Russian-American arms race but rather would focus upon the weaponry available for regional conflict. In that context, the unipolar ordering power, the United States, might be in dire need of BMD cover, in addition to air cover, in order to protect its ability to project power into regions wherein late-model weaponry had proliferated.

The arms control ideas and assumptions inherited today in people's beliefs and government policies from previous decades are acutely in peril of en bloc obsolescence. Many people are left apparently advocating solutions to problems that have passed. That is one level of criticism. A higher level of criticism of principal concern here is that arms control cannot work to accomplish the more important objectives specified by its promoters. The latter level of criticism suggests that arms control will not work in the 1990s to achieve any ambitious goals allotted to it, regardless of policy adjustments for a changing political context. In other words, the challenge in this decade is not to make systemic alterations in the approach to, and content of, arms control policy. Arms control cannot work when it is needed.

Some issues will be new, or relatively so, but as long as they are framed as *arms control* issues they will escape suitable treatment. A constant from decade to decade throughout this century has been the steadiness of error in arms control reasoning. In the excitement of facing new security challenges, otherwise generally straight-thinking folk easily forget that arms control is conceptually so flawed that it simply cannot work. The focus of policy and intellectual debate will shift from East-West questions to the problems of missile proliferation in the Third World. Or policy for START and CFE follow-on negotiations may be crafted less to assault the old terrors of East-West instabilities and more to help reshape military postures in the successor states to the USSR that are safety-engineered by arms control against the perils of illegal seizure and possible use of nuclear weapons. The familiar fallacies of arms control theory keep reappearing in new guises. The arguments do not improve, but in their fresh new clothing they can disguise their nature and cause people to forget their generic weaknesses.[5]

I do not argue that arms control is always of absolutely no, or even negative, value for peace with security. Instead, I have argued that arms control theory, and the practice it variably inspires, is a house of cards that must fail when severely stressed. In theory, some arms control measures might make the difference between peace and war, but the cases are remote and utterly

[5] Publicly, at a conference in Canberra, Australia, in July 1991, I was told by a leading Soviet, actually Russian, civilian defense analyst (Alexei Arbatov) that the principal reason why the United States should move out expeditiously to negotiate new arms control agreements, was to help Soviet democrats control their military establishment. The abortive coup the following month highlighted both the salience and the folly of Arbatov's advice. Obviously, he was correct in pointing to the difficulty in controlling the Soviet military establishment. But it is no less obvious that following this logic the United States could rush into some technically very unsound agreements. So many and so deep are the problems facing the former Soviet Union that there is no certainty just who will inherit the Russian end of the Russian-American military balance a few years hence. Arbatov's sincere, interesting, yet flawed argument is of a type which has a ready political appeal in the West.

dominated by causes of war that cannot be so alleviated. For example, something can be said in favor of President Bush's policy of eliminating all ground-based short-range nuclear weapons.[6] But, that sea change in U.S. official thinking is not likely to be able to save squabbling Soviet successor states from nuclear peril in time of internal conflict. Arms control is not a factor independent of political choices. An arms control agreement to ban all ground-based short-range nuclear weapons provides useful political cover for a Russia determined to see the other successor states disarmed of nuclear weapons. But one should beware of context-free analysis. Just as arms control cannot return conflict-prone polities to a state of prenuclear innocence, so one can be sure that arms control agreements cannot function as adequate fences for peace more broadly. The only solution to the problems of nuclear-weapons security in the former Soviet empire has to be political in character. Arms control can help administer what policy has decided when policy does decide.

A MATTER OF FAITH

The enduring popularity of arms control probably owes much to the simplified terms of public debate. If discussion of arms control is locked into contrast with military expenditure, war, or some inchoate notion of arms *un*control, it is easy to understand why its political constituency endures. Also, the defense of arms control in public debate tends to focus on objectives or contingent promises, rather than upon the strategic issues of means and ends (i.e., *Can* arms control means deliver the identified ends?) or upon the historical record of outcomes to arms control processes. When a religious prophet offers personal salvation or a church functionary claims a warrant from God for the remission of sins, people *want* to believe that it is so. Similarly, arms control is an inherently attractive story. Unlike salvation, however, the truth or falsehood of arms control theory-as-practice is to an impressive degree accessible to careful audit. The kingdom of arms control is

---

[6] President George Bush, "The Peace Dividend I Seek Is Not Measured in Dollars . . .," *Washington Post*, 28 September 1991, p. A23.

a kingdom of this earth. Endeavors to build that kingdom already have marked eight decades of this century.

People want to believe that the formal control of arms procurement and military behavior can help reduce the risks of war. That control is understood to function in addition to, indeed synergistically in combination with, a well-crafted unilateral defense effort. The theory of arms control is not reliably testable in the laboratory that is a historical record inconveniently comprising but a single stream of experience. There have always been sufficiently distinctive voices pronouncing on arms control desiderata, sufficient hedges in the language used, and sufficient differences between the friction-free world of theory and the messy reality of practice so that claims for or against the merit in arms control for international security will rarely be definitively verifiable. The broad-gauged promise of arms limitation in different periods, however, is not compatible with reasonable interpretation of the outcomes of arms control processes. The hypothesis of the arms control paradox serves well to explain why that should be so.

The appeal of arms control is the appeal of a chocolate diet to chocoholics. Like chocolate, arms control is superficially attractive but really is bad for us. It is particularly likely to be bad for us because, as with chocolate, the demand for its ingestion tends to grow with consumption. In principle, arms control could be treated as a helpful adjunct to defense planning and acquisition, but in practice, that hardly ever happens in a democracy. Moreover, the unhealthy diet of arms control for often wrongly diagnosed security problems comes to assume a moral life of its own as a value. Whatever else in this book readers may feel moved to challenge, there are no good grounds for questioning the point that arms control has advanced so far as a value that people aspiring to influence in public life dare not criticize it root-and-branch as an approach to security problems. Pragmatically, there is often no real need to risk the moral opprobrium that would attach to a fundamental challenge to arms control. Apparently constructive criticism over the detail of arms control application can achieve the same goal with greater ease and with total legitimacy.

The problems with arms control, therefore, have at least two leading thrust points. The first is the fact that arms control simply

[221]

cannot work as advertised vis-à-vis its principal goals. Second, whatever one's stance on the merit in the full sense of the first point, arms control has proved to be singularly ill-suited an activity for prudent conduct by popular democracies. Those polities tend to have difficulty approaching security issues in a strategic mode and arms control proffers a made-to-order excuse for not doing so. This should not be the case. Far from demeaning the salience of strategy and strategic reasoning, the classic texts of arms control theory emphasized strongly the synergisms among arms control, strategy, and military policy.[7] This second problem is not with arms control theory but rather with the practice of arms control and defense in a democracy. From the 1920s to the 1990s, major examples abound of British and American officials pursuing arms limitation agreements which offend against strategic common sense, not to mention preferred strategy.[8] If a young child drinks himself or herself to death because he or she had access to a liquor cabinet, it is unjust to blame liquor for the tragic outcome. By analogy, it is possible to argue that the ideas of arms control are entirely commendable and that popular democracy is a wonderful genus of political system but that they really do not mix safely.

The continuing political attractiveness of arms control lends itself to description as a case of what Edward Rhodes has called "nonintelligent calculation," which is a principal form of irrationality.[9] People persist in endorsing an arms control approach to problems, even though the available evidence suggests strongly that arms control means are unlikely to secure the policy goals pursued. Incorrect ideas that have great apparent practical (spend less money, build fewer weapons, take fewer risks) and moral (strike a blow against the arms race, or war, or the "merchants of

[7] See Thomas C. Schelling and Morton H. Halperin, *Strategy and Arms Control* (New York: Twentieth Century Fund, 1961).

[8] The Washington system of the interwar years offended critically against the U.S. ability to extend sea-based deterrence over China, while the SALT, INF, and START regimes of the 1970s, 1980s, and 1990s all help to compromise the U.S. ability to extend nuclear deterrence over the periphery of Eurasia.

[9] Edward Rhodes, *Power and MADness: The Logic of Nuclear Coercion* (New York: Columbia University Press, 1989), pp. 61–63.

death") appeal are not easily deposited where they belong, in the dustbin of history.

WELCOME TO FLAT EARTH: ARMS CONTROL COUNTRY

Quantity of repetition of assertion has a quality all its own. The authority of familiarity now invests the principal claims of arms control and generally protects them from the kind of head-on theoretical challenge provided here. Whether questions tend to be banished by how questions (e.g., how to frame a follow-on to START not whether to make the attempt). U.S. political and strategic culture has been educated to take many of the pretensions of arms control theory and policy advocacy at face value. The result has been more than a quarter-century of much ado about little. Activities centrally identifiable as arms control, as contrasted with some of the sensible goals of arms control that can be pursued unilaterally as well as by formal negotiation, have contributed negligibly—if, indeed, they would register on the positive side at all—to international security. The achievements of sundry arms control processes have been very modest. As noted earlier, the arms control–friendly Harvard study led by Albert Carnesale and Richard N. Haass reached exactly that conclusion.[10] More recently, Robert Jervis, certainly no fellow traveler with strident views critical of arms control, nonetheless has registered some elements of skepticism close to those advanced here.[11]

Readers should be reminded of the claims this book is *not* advancing. First, I do not argue here that arms control must place democracies in positions of the direst peril (though this could happen through an ill-judged START regime, and came close to happening with reference to the quantity and quality of the British Royal Navy in 1940–41). Second, I do not argue here that arms control invariably has a net negative impact on international

---

[10] Albert Carnesale and Richard N. Haass, eds., *Superpower Arms Control: Setting the Record Straight* (Cambridge, Mass.: Ballinger, 1987).

[11] Robert Jervis, *The Meaning of the Nuclear Revolution: Statecraft and the Prospect of Armageddon* (Ithaca: Cornell University Press, 1989), pp. 164, 225. But Jervis does find value in arms control.

peace and security. The impact may be neutral or even marginally positive on some occasions. However, the political cultures of Western-style democracies are liable to encourage imprudently astrategic arms control policies and to find extreme difficulty responding appropriately in a timely fashion to evidence of malfeasance by arms control adversary-partners. But the hypothesis of the arms control paradox does not, *ab extensio*, predict Western defeat through the ill consequences of arms control. The centerpiece of this book, restated, simply is the claim that arms control does not and cannot work to achieve very useful things for international peace and security. As decoration to a political peace process, arms control may function innocuously, even positively. If, however, arms control is touted to play a significant role as a quasi-independent factor contributing to peace and security, the evidence is lacking and the more persuasive theory denies it.

A claim that arms control country, intellectually and practically, amounts to a flat-earth cosmology may seem extravagant. After all, every peacetime American administration from the days of Warren Harding to the present has endorsed publicly the proposition that arms control is important and more or less actively and successfully has lent some policy reality to that rhetorical claim. Could so many experienced policymakers be wrong? Similarly, arms control has comprised one of the three main pillars of modern American strategic studies. Along with deterrence theory and limited war theory, a revived arms control theory was a principal product of the golden age of modern American strategic thought in 1955–65.[12] It might be considered churlish to observe that American limited war theory did not fare well in action in Southeast Asia, while modern deterrence theory probably has never been subject to a severe test (no goal line stands of recent decades for the testing of U.S. national security performance).

The modern defense intellectual carries in his or her backpack of professional tools a small battery of notions largely attributable to the insights of arms control theory. Above all else, the several

---

[12] See Lawrence Freedman, *The Evolution of Nuclear Strategy* (1981; rpt. New York: St. Martin's, 1989), chap. 13; and Colin S. Gray, *Strategic Studies and Public Policy: The American Experience* (Lexington: University Press of Kentucky, 1982), pp. 72–79.

cans of stability that can be opened readily on demand (arms race stability, crisis stability, first-strike stability, even ceasefire stability),[13] provide fuel seemingly suitable to use for assault upon problems in national security. Many university courses in national security or strategic studies either have a noticeable arms control segment or are organized wholly according to an arms control approach. In addition, a review of university and other research institutions reveals the existence of some programs, centers, and institutes that affirm in their title and by their character that formally they are dedicated to an explicitly arms control-centered view of the security world. False religion will, of course, spawn many dedicated communities of initiates and acolytes. Again, can so many people be wrong?

Conflict, competition, war and peace among political communities are political activities, explicable and curable, if at all, by the medicine of politics or by some instrument of politics (war, for the Clausewitzian example). Arms control cannot treat serious conditions of conflict, actual or plausibly pending, because arms are not the heart of the problem. Arms express, provide public focus for, and certainly can help exacerbate deteriorating political relations, just as arms control can function positively as a tool of policy when political relations are improving. But arms control cannot work as preventive medicine against conflict and war unless it serves merely to complete a political resolution achieved already. The worldview of people who approach problems and opportunities of security from the vantage point of arms control thus rest upon a fundamental error, an error akin to the pejorative flat-earth analogy that heads this section. Arms control theory and policy advocacy, with its heavy battery of stability weapons, postulates a value—political, strategic, economic—for its ideas that powerful theory, historical evidence, and common sense condemn as unfounded.

The typically minor and mixed positive-negative outcomes and consequences of arms control processes are not widely understood. If my argument is broadly correct, why does administration

---

[13] Ceasefire stability/instability is identified in Rhodes, *Power and MADness*, p. 148.

after administration invest so heavily in arms control processes on subjects close to the core of national security?[14] Readers will have to decide the answer to this question for themselves. By way of a clue, however, before the Copernican revolution in astronomy political leaders believed that the sun revolved around the earth because that is what the experts—who should know, being experts—claimed and that it was sacrilegious to believe the reverse to be true. U.S. officials in search of policy advice can reach out for the wisdom of a bevy (or perhaps *conundrum* is the better collective noun)—of experts that will assert the value of the standard propositions of arms control. Those propositions come clothed in some moral value and themselves have assumed some such value: arms control as contrasted with arms uncontrol, stability as contrasted with instability, and so forth. Professional politicians, busy administrators, and members of the general public can be excused for taking largely on trust much of the theoretical and policy-oriented pretension of an approach to national security which happens to be fundamentally flawed.

WHY ARMS CONTROL DOES NOT WORK

The appeal of arms control, particularly of arms reduction, is almost wholly rhetorical. In practice, it has proved all but impossibly difficult to make arms control work as a partner to, or even as a component of, defense policy. Arms control tends to compound the difficulties in the already peril-prone field for a democracy of strategy design and force planning in peacetime.

The theoretical case for arms control among potential enemy polities that recognize the logic of the security dilemma is superficially so attractive as to render fundamental critiques close to politically illegitimate. Like politicians' promises, the sundry goals of arms control are beyond reproach. Just as politicians should not be judged according to the attractiveness of their platforms,

---

[14] This is not to argue that of recent decades arms control processes have had much impact upon U.S. military posture, procedures, or doctrine. Important exceptions include the decisions to deny the Patriot and the Aegis air defense systems ABM capability.

however, so approaches to national security should not be weighed according to their inherent attractiveness treated in isolation. Often quite inadvertently, efforts to stimulate public debate reduce simplemindedly to advocacy of arms control as opposed to arms and of negotiation as opposed to war.

The case against arms control is a case not against any and every endeavor to secure some negotiated or tacit grip upon the structure or operations of rival armed forces. Rather, that noble cause cannot deliver anything very useful with respect to its principal and overriding purpose, the reduction in the risk of war occurring. With plausible parallel cases drawn from different periods in this century, this book has illustrated the theoretical proposition that arms limitation cannot be an important factor for peace. The argument lends itself to overstatement and, admittedly, the causes of war and conditions for peace are very complex with cause and effect rarely evident beyond grounds for dispute. Nonetheless, the discussion here suggests strongly that any grand design for international security which relies critically upon support from an arms control process is doomed to fail. Should such a system succeed nonetheless, it will probably be despite arms control hindrance. Sometimes the right things are done for the wrong reasons. Not only is it entirely appropriate to test arms control regimes with severe pressure, but such tests are the only ones that really matter.

Eight arguments comprise the core of the critique offered in this book. These are the peaks of the rationale for claiming that arms control is a house of cards which must fail systematically and persistently when confronted with the kinds of tests it should be able to meet were it a valid and useful approach to security problems.

First, impressed by the pattern of failure of arms control, I have leaned heavily upon the concept of the arms control paradox. The paradox argues that the reasons why paired groups of states should be able to benefit from arms control is the very reason why arms control proves unobtainable for the alleviation of their security problems. Recalling the adage that for every solution there is a problem (and that no good intention goes unpunished), it transpires, paradoxically, that states cannot benefit from arms control precisely because they need such benefit. The case for arms control was presented in paradoxical form in the classic texts on the subject. Specifically, the paradoxical point was registered that the need for arms control arose because of the tensions and hostility between states. That logically correct point founders upon its own paradoxical reasoning. Rival states with antagonism in their relations at a level where war is distinctly thinkable are not likely to deliver some significant measure of their military prospects over to the brutal surgery conducted with blunt instruments that could be "real," if not necessarily wise, arms limitation.

Second, accepting some minor risk of overstatement, I have pursued the logic of the argument that governments and their policies, not their weapons, make war. It follows that the control or removal of weapons cannot make for peace. The enterprise of arms control expresses a classic confusion between directing brain and implementing muscle. The truth is not quite as clear-cut as this formula might appear to suggest. Of course, changes in weapon inventories, and military behavior in time of high political tension, can stimulate political judgments abroad which their state-owners did not intend. Nonetheless, the second point holds. States arm and counterarm for political reasons. Security policies that focus on the means of policy, to the neglect of the ends, are foredoomed to come to grief.

Third, arms control policy imposes substantial, but generally invisible, opportunity costs. By way of analogy, and acknowledging gratitude to Edward Gibbon,[15] the loss to practical statecraft was inestimable when many of the better minds of the later Roman Empire turned to the Christian religion and became theologians, administrators, mystics, or simply only partial participants in a civil society that Christianity demoted drastically in significance. Similarly, arms control ideas divert always scarce intellectual resources and official energies from valid toward invalid, or *at best*, less valid, approaches to national and international security. An American society that has devoted scant attention to

---

[15] See Edward Gibbon, *The History of the Decline and Fall of the Roman Empire*, vol. 4, ed. J. B. Bury (London: Methuen, 1909), particularly p. 175.

strategy, despite public recognition of the need, ironically has produced a library on all kinds of arms control subjects. To resort to another analogy, it is as though a political scientist enters a promising-looking bookstore and finds that it has only one case devoted to history and six or seven cases filled with tomes on mysticism and the occult.

Fourth, arms control processes bear witness to the illusion that security can be engineered. This fallacy is distinctively, though not uniquely, American. The problem-solving proclivity of American culture, which can be a virtue, inclines a machine-minded people to address political-military difficulties much as an engineer would tackle a mechanical challenge. A touching faith in the availability for application of the right answers, of a few correct principles, pervades the U.S. approach to arms control. By analogy, if a screw is tightened here, a bolt loosened there, if a counterweight is added somewhere else, the outcome should be some tolerable approximation of a workable equilibrium for stability. The principles of stability allegedly tell us which weapons and military practices should be encouraged and which discouraged. An American defense community broadly persuadable that it could learn how to wage, and promptly practice, limited war, could master crisis management, and could understand how to terminate wars offered little resistance to fashionable theories of arms control. The intellectual hubris with which U.S. policy launched the SALT process was matched fully by the shallowness of the leading ideas on how the misnamed arms race worked.

Fifth, the outstanding guiding light provided by arms control theory for arms control practice, the concept of stability, transpires to be a wreckers' lantern and not a lighthouse. The stability theory that both guides and lends intellectual respectability to arms control effort does not bear close critical examination. The popular, even authoritative, concepts of arms race stability and crisis stability represent and advance some classic confusions.

The connections between what are called arms races and war are obscure. Not only is it difficult to identify historical cases of arms races leading to war in some causal sense, but also it is no easy matter to explain why arms races would significantly help cause or trigger war. Analytical flabbiness about arms races, particularly the alleged nexi between arms races and wars, leaves the concept of arms race stability in no little trouble.

A similar point embattles the even more popular concept of crisis stability. Propositions about crisis-stable military forces and operating procedures can only be as valid as the theory of war causation to which they are applied. The causes of war compose one of those academic happy hunting grounds wherein the richness of the historical evidence threatens forever to thwart the ambitions of theory builders. The arms control literature is populated heavily with advice about which weapons, military postures, and operating practices are more or less likely to trigger hostilities—that is to say, allegedly are crisis-destabilizing. The central problem with the dominant school of arms control thought on crisis stability is that it elevates falsely the significance of weapons, military postures, and military doctrines to an all but independent role in the occurrence of war. Weapons do not make war. States have not gone and do not go to war because some of their weapons would seem to be vulnerable to surprise attack. This argument today is endorsed even by some of those who for decades have contributed most pervasively to the popularity of a flawed, apolitical approach to stability. For example, long-time Rand analyst Fred S. Hoffman writes as follows:

> The limited attention so far to the future prospects for nuclear strategy is symptomatic of how isolated that branch of our strategy has become—a kind of art for art's sake—and how divorced it now is from its primary purposes. *Stability*, in the context of nuclear strategy, has acquired a highly restricted meaning, without explicit relationship to plausible contingencies of conflict or other aspects of our military posture, much less to the political objectives that motivate our posture.[16]

Stability did not acquire "a highly restricted meaning" in the same way that a dog acquires ticks and fleas. Instead, it was be-

---

[16] Fred S. Hoffman, "Deterrence, Stability, and Reassurance: U.S. Nuclear Strategy after the Fall of the Soviet Empire," in Andrew W. Marshall, J. J. Martin, and Henry S. Rowen, eds., *On Not Confusing Ourselves: Essays on National Security Strategy in Honor of Albert and Roberta Wohlstetter* (Boulder, Colo.: Westview, 1991), p. 211.

cause people in the dominant Rand tradition of vulnerability analysis did not reason politically about strategy that the theory of arms control, and the associated stability notions, gained ascendancy. The Rand vulnerability studies of the 1950s led by military logic, to the neglect of political judgment, to the theoretical peril expressed elegantly by then-Rand consultant, Thomas C. Schelling, as "the reciprocal fear of surprise attack."[17] If neither superpower has strategic nuclear forces reliably capable of surviving a first strike, then each will be motivated to strike first in a period of acute crisis lest it be disarmed. This would be a case of rival military postures effectively going off for reason of the dynamic grammar of their narrow military relationship and not because of any policy logic. This is the core of the reasoning that defines the theory of strategic stability and which launched the modern arms control movement in the late 1950s. The fact that people and states do not behave as the theory predicts continues to escape widespread notice.

Sixth, it is no criticism of arms controllers to notice that they are unable to predict the future with confidence. The same can be said for defense planners. On balance, however, it is prudent to provide democratic polities with as few excuses for not addressing strategic questions strategically as the political traffic will bear. Arms limitation regimes do require some military-technological prediction and, for democracies, tend to function more restrictively vis-à-vis solutions than they do toward problems. It is implausible to maintain that arms control negotiators can shape a future military-technological environment more friendly for the goals of arms control than could or would be shaped by unrestricted competition. In principle, arms control regimes can be abandoned or renegotiated, but in practice, that is rarely politically feasible. This sixth point claims that, far from promoting a useful predictability in strategic relations, arms control regimes

---

[17] Thomas C. Schelling, *The Strategy of Conflict* (Cambridge: Harvard University Press, 1960), chap. 9. Marc Trachtenberg, "Strategic Thought in America, 1952–1966," in his *History and Strategy* (Princeton: Princeton University Press, 1991), pp. 3–46, helped clarify and strengthen my understanding of the connection between stability theory and the Rand-style analyses of strategic-force vulnerability in the 1950s. I am in his debt.

restrict the flexibility available to policymakers striving to adjust to a changing security context. Moreover, Western democracies find that the existence of formal restraints on arms generally bear down unhelpfully upon the terms of debate in the politics of defense preparation.

Seventh, as the 1990s are revealing yet again, arms control policies, let alone extant regimes, do not adjust readily to swiftly moving political circumstances. Even arms control–friendly circles are noticing that the very institutions of arms control, with START and CFE as leading examples, look more and more like dinosaurs. The security world is changing rapidly, but Russia and the United States remain locked in an arms control embrace that appears to address too many of yesterday's problems, notwithstanding the deep cuts of the amended START regime.

That particular critique of START and CFE is both popular and trivial. More to the point is recognition that the pace of political change has outrun policy making in the West and the East. Arms control always is subordinate to political designs, be they well- or ill-considered, but at present, the political terms of security over the next decade are unknown. Although the political climate has rarely been more permissive of arms control agreement, rarely has less reliable political guidance for arms control policy been available. If the United States and Russia are moving toward a lasting cooperative relationship, though not without some sources of irritation—by analogy, a reasonable description of Anglo-American relations in the interwar years—what sense can there be in those great powers disarming each other? If nontrivial political issues such as that are not resolved, the probability that an arms control process will effect more good than harm is rather modest.

Eighth and finally, the diplomatic logic of an arms control process generally functions in a manner, and has consequences, that are not constructive for the national security of democracies. This is not to suggest that negotiability invariably triumphs over strategic common sense. Such has not been so. However, an arms control process takes on a life of its own, and its supervising officials naturally assume a solicitous concern for the welfare of that process which exceeds strategic considerations of national security.

None of the twentieth-century's major exercises in negotiated arms limitation have been strategically praiseworthy as prudent measures supportive of foreign policy. The 1922 and 1930 naval arms limitation treaties, SALT I (1972) and SALT II (1979), the INF treaty (1987), CFE (1990), START I (1991), and START II (1992) are all defensible in terms of the logic of an arms control process, but they are not readily praiseworthy in the means-ends terms of national or alliance strategy.

I am aware of the grounds for argument over whether or not, or to what degree, the military detail of arms control negotiations really matters. Indeed, this book shares some of the skepticism that critics have expressed. The purpose here, however, is to warn that the logic of diplomacy is not the logic of defense planning. Furthermore, the logic of diplomacy is not always the logic of foreign policy. Arms control policy should not be driven rigorously only by considerations closest to the hearts of professional military planners, but the negotiated outcomes of arms control processes repeatedly have made little strategic sense. Often, this does not matter. But occasionally, the margin for successful deterrence or military advantage for the party of order is so narrow that a military posture misshaped by arms control could make the crucial difference.

THE ARMS CONTROL VIRUS

Some of the major elements of my argument already are quite widely accepted across the political and emotional spectrum of attitudes toward arms control. The arms control paradox is familiar in public debate. Assertion of the primacy of politics and policy over military hardware similarly is less than a revelation. The deeply unsatisfactory state of scholarship on all aspects of arms races and the causes of wars likewise is not exactly a major research finding that previously had passed unnoticed. The criticisms leveled here at the negotiators and maintainers of the arms limitation regimes of the interwar years and of the SALT-START era, again, are far from unique. I have sought to recognize a unity, make a coherent pattern for a mosaic, in consideration of the theory and practice of arms control. My purpose has been to explain why arms control reveals a pattern of failure and to develop a theory which makes sense of that pattern and which has predictive value.

Arms control may be thought of as a generally mild virus that has infected the body politic and has proved to be resistant to antimicrobial drugs. Particular symptoms can be treated, which is to say, individual policy positions can be thwarted, but the virus itself would appear to be beyond extirpation. Arms control cannot work to register useful achievements with regard to its principal objective, the reduction of the risk of war. Arms control can work, to pervert language, when victors or the great gang up to discipline the vanquished or the much less great. It is difficult, though, to see such exercises of grossly superior power as triumphs for arms control (e.g., 1919, or the disarmament terms dictated to a defeated Carthage by Scipio Africanus in 201 B.C.).[18]

By and large, this discussion has focused upon *structural* arms control, or arms limitation, between countries that might go to war with each other, rather than upon *operational* arms control. The poor performance of the former has driven some arms controllers to seek solace in hopes for the latter (confidence-building measures, generically). Operational arms control cannot work as advertised for the same reasons that its structural associate must fail; both were as flawed in the 1930s as they are in the 1990s. To make the thread of argument as clear as a complex historical reality permits, some small risk of overstatement has been accepted. A fair comment would be that the occasional emphasis upon uncertainty in this text has implications for the authority of the argument presented as well as for that of the people criticized. I claim not that assuredly I am correct but rather that my argument explains more of the historical record of arms control (failure) than rival arguments. The theory presented here passes the tests of internal coherence, plausibility, and explanatory power and is not contradicted by any body of historical evidence.

It is desirable to conclude a policy-relevant work on a positive

---

[18] Even the France of 1919 could have learned some lessons about how to leave a former foe effectively disarmed. See Brian Caven, *The Punic Wars* (London: Weidenfeld and Nicolson, 1980), pp. 245–55.

note, with confident recommendations for better policy performance in the future. That is impossible in this case, at least through
arms control, because my argument is that arms control is a blind
alley and that provision of ever-improved maps of the world beyond the alley are beside the point: that world cannot be attained
via the alley. The overriding problem with arms control theory
and attempted practice is, like the notion of a flat earth, that it is
fundamentally wrong. The allocation of millions of dollars to develop better and better descriptions of a flat earth will fuel a cot-
tage industry of misguided, but profitable, scholarship; it will not
advance the cause of geographical truth or effectiveness in geog-
raphy-dependent policy. The practical damage that the fallacious
ideas of arms control might wreak certainly can be limited by edu-
cation. But the generally non–life-threatening virus that is arms
control theory is probably beyond eradication.

Index

ABM systems, arms control debates and, 44, 50

ABM Treaty (1972), 33; purpose of, 125–26; supreme interests and withdrawal from, 131

Accidental war, 41–42; crisis stability and, 65–66; reduction of crisis instability and, as an argument for/against arms control, 185–87

Accidents Measures agreement (1971), 41

Adelman, Kenneth L., 23, 88, 109, 120, 148

American Civil War, 63

Anglo-French relations in eighteenth century, 33

Anglo-German Naval Agreement (AGNA) (1935), 55, 94–96, 101–2, 108–9

Arbatov, Alexei, 219

Arms control: complaints about, 3–4; control of arms and, 9–10; defining, 6–10; faith in, 220–23; future of, 16, 215–35; historical evidence of, 14–16, 89–119; innovation encouraged by, 85–86; negative points on, 43; reasons for states to participate in, 27–28, 47–57; reasons why arms control does not work, 226–33; role of debate participants and, 10–11; and role of Europe in new world order, 217–18; role of policymakers/experts, 223–26

Arms control, arguments for and against: control of dangerous weapon development, 202–4; control of predictability and uncertainty, 204–8; control of rogue behavior, 197–200; control of the growth of military threats, 182–84; defense planning reinforced, 194–97; importance as a political process, 190–94; lock-in window of diplomatic opportunity, 187–90; reduction of damage and costs, 208–11; reduction of misunderstanding, 200–202; reduction of vulnerability and crisis instability, 185–87; verification of Soviet forces, 213

Arms Control Association, 166

Arms control paradoxes: arms race paradox, 21–22; danger of war and benefits of cooperation, 19–20; motivation for potential enemies to cooperate, 27, 37–47; need for arms control to avoid unwanted war, 17–19; problems with formal policies, 20–21; reactions to new weapons, 21

Arms race(s): as a cause of war, 37, 43–47; instability of, 64–65; paradox, 21–22; qualitative versus quantitative, 45–46; stability of, 59

ASAT, crisis instability and, 67

Attacks, surprise, 60–61

Axis grand or military strategy, 107

Baker, James, 187

Balance of power issues, 72

Barnett, Correlli, 102–3

Baruch, Bernard, 13

Index